THE PRESIDENCY OF ULYSSES S. GRANT

THE
PRESIDENCY
OF
ULYSSES S. GRANT

PERSERVING THE CIVIL WAR'S LEGACY

PAUL KAHAN

WESTHOLME
Yardley

Westholme Publishing, LLC
904 Edgewood Road
Yardley, Pennsylvania 19067
Visit our Web site at www.westholmepublishing.com

ISBN: 978-1-59416-273-2
Also available as an eBook.

Printed in the United States of America.

CONTENTS

Contents

PREFACE

WITH THE RECENT OUTPOURING of books about Ulysses S. Grant, you are forgiven if you wonder whether we really need another one. After all, the past five years have seen a profusion of Grant biographies, including H. W. Brands's *The Man Who Saved the Union: Ulysses S. Grant in War and Peace* (2012), Michael Korda's *The Unlikely Hero* (2013), Ronald C. White's *American Ulysses: A Life of Ulysses S. Grant* (2016), and Ron Chernow's *Grant* (2017). All of these are outstanding books, ably tracing Grant's rise from humble origins to statesman of worldwide stature. However, each in its own way gives short shrift to Grant's presidency. Moreover, by taking a biographical approach, these authors miss the nuances of American politics in the decade following the Civil War. Grant's presidency is a critical moment in American history and worthy of its own study. This short volume focuses on the unique political, economic, and cultural forces unleashed by the Civil War and thrown into contention during Andrew Johnson's administration, and is designed to provide an overview of Grant's tumultuous terms as president of the United States.

For too long, Grant's presidency has been overshadowed by his wartime service, and the one hundred fiftieth anniversary of his election (coinciding, as it does, with renewed public interest in the Civil War's legacy and the complex history of race in the United States) seems the perfect time to explore the unprecedented challenges the general-turned-politician faced as the country's chief executive. Grant himself apologized—unnecessarily, in my view—for his presidency, and, until recently, scholars have portrayed him as among the country's worst chief executives. Though the scholarly consensus about Grant's presidency is changing, the general public knows little, if anything, about his two terms, other than their outsized reputation for corruption. While scandals are undoubtedly part of the story, there is more to Grant's presidency than corruption: as president, Grant faced the severest economic depression in US history and a showdown with one of the most powerful members of Congress, and he adeptly avoided war with Spain over Cuba while laying the groundwork for the "special relationship" between Great Britain and the United States. That being said, his efforts to ensure justice for African Americans and Native Americans were undercut by his own decisions and by the contradictory demands of the various constituencies that made up the Republican Party. *The Presidency of Ulysses S. Grant: Preserving the Civil War's Legacy* is an evaluation of the Grant administration's frequently overlooked successes and undeniable failures, as well as a portrait of Reconstruction-era politics.

INTRODUCTION

"Mistakes Have Been Made"

O N DECEMBER 5, 1876, President Ulysses S. Grant transmitted his eighth and final message to Congress. Shockingly, in reviewing his tenure as president, Grant proclaimed, "Mistakes have been made, as all can see and I admit," though he assured Congress, his administration's "failures have been errors of judgment, not of intent."[1] That there had been failures was undeniable; the country was mired in the longest-lasting depression in US history, the administration was buffeted by a series of scandals, and many of the president's signature policies were unraveling. James G. Blaine of Maine, who was Speaker of the House of Representatives during most of Grant's presidency, remarked to journalist John Russell Young of the *New York Herald* that "no administration can do more than one thing in its career, and happy is the administration that can do that wisely and well."[2] The Grant administration, by choice and by force of circumstances, tried to do many things, with mixed success. On the one hand, Grant was the first US president to appoint a black man to a diplomatic post and the first to host a prominent black officeholder at the White House. He also appointed the first Native American, Ely Parker, to lead a major executive branch department and created the Justice Department to protect blacks' civil rights. At the same time, Grant enthusiastically signed the first restrictive federal immigration law in US history and was the first president whose administration was investigated by a special prosecutor. William W. Belknap, Grant's secretary of war, was the first cabinet member impeached by Congress, and Grant himself was the first sitting president to testify for a defendant in a criminal case (on behalf of an aide accused of accepting bribes).

Grant's assessment of his presidency was too harsh. After all, he faced several unprecedented challenges, the most vexing of which was Reconstruction. In addition, as president, Grant had to work with an abnormally assertive legislative branch.[3] Despite his promises during the 1868 presidential campaign to defer to Congress (a body controlled, for most of his presidency, by fellow Republicans), Grant not only vetoed more pieces of legislation than any of his predecessors, he issued more vetoes than all seventeen of his predecessors combined. Congress, and in particular the Senate, exhibited during these years what historian Robert L. Beisner has called "a haughty institutional pride" based on the belief that the "President should obey and enforce the laws, leaving to the people the duty of correcting any errors committed by their representatives in Congress," ensuring conflict between the legislative and executive branches.[4] US senator Carl Schurz of Missouri, who became one of Grant's bitterest critics, remembered calling on the president one day. Finding Grant engrossed in writing, Schurz apologized, offering to wait until the president finished. Grant immediately put the paper aside, saying, "Never mind, I am only writing a message to the Senate."[5] Grant's disdain for Congress is visible in his frequent trips away from Washington. As early as 1870, Grant remarked to his friend, US minister to France Elihu Washburne, "my peace is when Congress is not in session," and that same year the president shared with US representative Rutherford B. Hayes of Ohio his hope that the temperature in the Senate chamber would rise so high that that body would end its session for the day.[6] By 1873, he took to calling Congress his "natural enemy."[7]

A related problem was that in the late 1860s, the Republican Party was highly factionalized, so Grant as often quarreled with members of his own party as with Democrats. Secretary of State Hamilton Fish noted in June 1870 that the Republican Party was far from united and that, in part, Grant's attempt to annex Santo Domingo offered a chance "to concentrate and consolidate the party, to exhibit a policy. . . [that had] the capacity of rallying the party. This in truth has been the great want of the party; the presentation of some issue on which [Republican congressmen] should be required as party men, to say 'yea' or 'nay' distinctly upon some issue presented by the Administration; we have not done it before. Each man has been allowed to follow his own peculiar views."[8] Senator John Sherman of Ohio, writing to his brother, General William T. Sherman, shortly after Grant's election in 1868, put the matter even more bluntly: "our party has no policy."[9] One key to keeping this heterogeneous and unruly party together was the spoils system—in which politicians marshaled political support by doling out the spoils of office, such as government jobs and contracts—and corruption was the cost. As president, any action Grant took would likely end up alienating one or another faction of the party. Ironically, Grant owed his nomination to this factionalism; the most popular man in American at the war's end, he was nominated for president in 1868 because he was (more or less) inoffensive to the party's various factions.

With all these challenges, it is perhaps unsurprising that Grant called the day he left the presidency the happiest of his life.[10] After leaving the White House, Grant claimed, "I certainly never had either ambition or taste for a political life; yet I was twice President of the United States," as if the office had fallen, unsought and unexpected, into his lap.[11] That was, of course, not the case; he twice ran for and won the presidency and even sought a third term in 1880. Historian Brooks D. Simpson notes, "The crusade to save the Union . . . [gave Grant's life] meaning that transcended the personal. As savior of the Union, his reputation was inexorably tied to the fate of the nation," and that crusade continued after the war ended.[12] Grant's military service became the prism through which he understood the issues facing the nation after the Civil War. By 1868, Grant believed that his wartime sacrifices were being squandered and lost by politicians, and he saw himself as the only man who could save the peace. Grant came into office believing that he was responding to a higher calling—preserving the outcome of the Civil War—that transcended mere partisan politics, and that he could govern without the politicians. Writing to Adam Badeau in 1871, Grant noted that he wished to be out of politics but that he had "a deep interest in the Republican party keeping control of affairs until the results of the war are acquiesced in by all political parties."[13] Yet governing proved harder than he had imagined, and he soon found it necessary to ally with spoilsmen and make compromises in order to achieve tangible results.

Grant's presidency has much to teach us about nineteenth century American political history. The factionalism, political infighting, score settling, and manipulation of policy through leaking information to the press that characterized the 1860s and 1870s will strike the reader as eerily reminiscent of contemporary politics. On the one hand, the history of a presidency must, of necessity, focus on the actions of a president and his administration. On the other hand, it is ahistorical and incorrect to view the events chronicled in this book as driven solely by Grant. It is naïve and overly simplistic to believe that the buck stops at the president's desk, because policy is the sum total of decisions made by various individuals at all levels of government. Grant's presidency shows that presidential appointees, civil servants, Congress, the Supreme Court, and the military all play roles not only in formulating policy but also implementing it. Moreover, Grant's administration was surprisingly progressive; as president, Grant supported women's suffrage and created the first national park, the surgeon general's office, and the predecessor of the National Weather Service, in addition to trying to ensure just treatment for African Americans and Native Americans.

As an organizational device, this book tends to deal with these issues as if they were discrete, thereby creating the impression that they existed in a vacuum from one another. In part, this creates a cleaner, more coherent narrative and thereby avoids the trap of chronicling history as "one damn thing after another," to use Arnold Toynbee's memorable phrase. Chapter 1 describes Grant's life through the end of the Civil War, discussing his political development and the impact his military service played in shaping his identity. Chapter 2 explores the dramatic conflict between President Andrew Johnson and Congress over Reconstruction and the role it played propelling Grant into the presidency. Chapter 3 chronicles two early challenges facing the administration—the struggle for control of patronage and the New York Gold Conspiracy—while chapter 4 examines the administration's policies toward blacks and Native Americans, surely the thorniest issues Grant faced as president. Chapter 5 explores the conflict between the president and Congress for control of the administration's foreign policy, and chapter 6 describes the peculiar 1872 presidential contest, the catastrophic Panic of 1873, and the scandals that consumed Grant's second term. Finally, chapter 7 explores the collapse of Reconstruction and the "peace policy." The picture that emerges is of an administration neither as corrupt and feckless as its critics believed nor as virtuous and effective as it might have been.

One

"There Are but Two Parties Now, Traitors and Patriots"

HIRAM ULYSSES GRANT WAS BORN to Jesse Root Grant and his wife, Hannah, on April 27, 1822, in Point Pleasant, Ohio.[1] Largely self-educated, Jesse often compensated for his lack of formal schooling by adopting an aggressive, flamboyant persona that found expression in local debating societies. Jesse was a former Jacksonian Democrat who defected to the Whigs over the Bank War, or President Andrew Jackson's veto of the bill rechartering the Second Bank of the United States.[2] The Democrats were a strategic alliance of Southern farmers and the members of the North's emerging urban working class. As a party, the Democrats promoted expanded suffrage (for white men), territorial expansion, strict construction of the Constitution, and laissez-faire economics (with a particular revulsion toward federally chartered banks). By contrast, the Whigs were a diverse coalition of individuals opposed to Jackson's allegedly monarchical actions as president; they advocated a central bank and internal improvements, and generally believed that the president should defer to Congress. Generally speaking, Whigs were more nationalistic in outlook and sought to promote industrialization and economic growth through publicly funded education and internal improvements (roads, canals, etc.), all of which were reflected in Ulysses S. Grant's policies as president.

In 1839, Jesse Grant asked Ohio senator Thomas Morris to use his influence to find a position for Ulysses at the US Military Academy at West Point. Morris turned the letter over to Grant's congressman (and Jesse's former friend), Thomas L. Hamer. Though Hamer was a Jacksonian Democrat no longer on speaking terms with Jesse, he secured for Ulysses an opportunity to test for admission to West Point.[3] It was Hamer who was responsible for Hiram Ulysses Grant becoming Ulysses S. Grant: the congressman wrote what he (wrongly) assumed to be the boy's name on the nomination, and once Grant entered West Point, he was U.S. Grant for the rest of his life. Grant did not enjoy life at West Point, recalling years later that the day he left was the second happiest day of his life (the happiest being the day he left the presidency).[4] Despite Grant's unhappiness, and though he was unaware of it at the time, his college years reinforced the essentially nationalistic outlook that played an important role in his actions as president because West Point's educational curriculum was unabashedly national in scope and intent; the school brought together cadets from all over the country, encouraging them to abandon sectional or regional ties.

In June 1843, Grant graduated from West Point. He arrived for duty at Jefferson Barracks outside St. Louis on September 30, 1843. Over that winter he was a frequent visitor to the home of his West Point roommate, Fred Dent, who was the second of seven children in a prosperous St. Louis family. Fred's father, "Colonel" Frederick Fayette Dent, was a merchant and planter who owned numerous slaves and was a partisan Democrat. Despite the fact that Grant came from a vehemently antislave Whig background, he was welcomed into the Dent household and almost immediately became enamored of Fred's younger sister, Julia. Four years younger than Grant, Julia was hardly considered a beauty, but her family's social position and wealth made her a belle. Grant stayed with the Dents for only a week, but that was long enough: before departing, Grant, "declared his love [for her] and told [her] that without [her] life would be insupportable."[5] Grant's bliss at having proposed to Julia was leavened by the fact that war with Mexico was on the horizon. Spaniards under the command of Francisco Hernández de Córdoba reached the eastern coast of Mexico in 1517 and pushed west, eventually encountering the Aztecs in 1519. After a two-year struggle, the Spanish conquered the Aztecs, inaugurating a three-hundred-year period of colonial control. Now called New Spain, Mexico provided the mineral wealth and slave labor that made Spain a dominant European power. However, the American War of Independence and the French Revolution inspired anti-Spanish forces in Mexico. In 1821, Mexico declared itself independent of Spain and actively encouraged Americans to settle the country's northern territory. Americans immigrated in much larger numbers than the Mexican government anticipated or desired, and by 1829, the Mexicans were actively discouraging further American immigration. In 1832, General Antonio López de Santa Anna overthrew the Mexican national government, and over the next few years, he consolidated his control and centralized power in Mexico City, disbanding regional legislatures and weakening or eliminating local militias. By the end of 1835, English-speaking settlers in Texas were in armed revolt against Santa Anna's government. In April 1836, Texans under Sam Houston defeated Mexican troops under Santa Anna's command at the Battle of San Jacinto and took Santa Anna prisoner. In exchange for his freedom, Santa Anna signed the Treaties of Velasco—one public and one private—that obligated Mexico to (among other things) remove all its troops from north of the Rio Grande. The Mexican government repudiated these agreements, saying that Santa Anna had been coerced into signing them and had no authority to negotiate on the country's behalf. However, for the time being, Texas was an independent republic.

Though the United States was officially neutral in the conflict between Texas and Mexico, Americans served in the Texan army. Consequently, Mexico blamed the United States for Texas's independence and admonished Washington not to annex the territory, but that warning fell on deaf ears. John Tyler, who became president in 1841 following William Henry Harrison's death, actively worked to annex Texas in the hope of using the issue to secure reelection. In 1844, Tyler purged the federal government of opponents to annexation, but the president failed to win either party's nomination. Instead, Democrat James K. Polk won the presidential election that November, garnering 49.5 percent of the popular vote to Whig candidate Henry Clay's 48.1 percent.

One of the Democratic Party's core tenets was Manifest Destiny, or the belief that the United States should expand to fill the entire North American continent. The term *Manifest Destiny* originated in an 1845 article written by journalist (and ardent Jacksonian Democrat) John L. O'Sullivan in which he claimed "the right of our manifest destiny to overspread and to possess the whole of the continent which Providence has given us for the development of the great experiment of liberty and federated self-government entrusted to us."[6] Shortly before leaving office, lame-duck president Tyler signed a congressional resolution authorizing annexation of Texas. In July 1845, Texas accepted America's offer of annexation; by December, Texas became the twenty-ninth US state. However, the United States and Mexico differed on Texas's southern boundary, with Mexico claiming it extended no farther than the Nueces River and the United States claiming all of the territory to the Rio Grande. In January 1846, President Polk ordered US Army forces under the command of General Zachary Taylor (including Second Lieutenant Ulysses S. Grant) into the disputed territory. Ignoring Mexican demands that he withdraw, Taylor instead constructed a primitive fortification known as Fort Mexico on the Rio Grande's north bank. In response to this provocation, on April 23, Mexico declared war on the United States, and two days later, Mexican troops engaged a small American reconnaissance force; the shooting war had begun. On May 13, at Polk's urging, Congress declared war on Mexico.

Zachary "Old Rough and Ready" Taylor was a career military officer in his early sixties who had seen action during the War of 1812, the Black Hawk War, and the Seminole War. President Polk gave Taylor command of US forces as a result of politics, choosing him over Commanding General of the Army Winfield Scott. The president, a partisan Democrat, had no interest in making Scott, a Whig, into a war hero and chose a general allegedly without ambition.[7] As Grant biographer William S. McFeely noted, at the start of the war, "calculating Democrats, dreading a Whig war hero, no doubt sought comfort in Taylor's obscurity."[8] Grant clearly idolized Taylor and aspired to emulate him, even adopting the older man's casual deportment.[9] Taylor's battlefield victories, coupled with the war's transformation into a partisan political issue, set off speculation that the general might seek the presidency in 1848. According to Grant, Taylor did not entertain any political ambitions at the war's start, "but after the fall of Monterey, his third battle and third complete victory, the Whig papers at home began to speak of him as candidate for their party for the Presidency."[10] Concerned about Taylor's growing political stature, in late 1846, Polk began favoring General Winfield Scott, another Whig who had earlier been sidelined over concerns that he might run for president in 1848. The president approved Scott's plan to invade central Mexico and even transferred some of Taylor's troops—including those of Grant's regiment—to Scott's command. Though Grant respected Scott's military skill, he unfavorably compared "Old Fuss and Feathers" to "Old Rough and Ready," noting "General Taylor never made any great show or parade, either of retinue or uniform . . . but he was known to every soldier in his army and respected by all." By contrast, Scott "was precise in language, cultivated a style peculiarly his own; was proud of his rhetoric; not averse to speaking of himself, often in the third person, and he could bestow praise upon the person he was talking about without the least embarrassment." Yet despite this critique, it is worth noting that the men who had the most enduring impact on Grant's formative life—Jesse Grant, Winfield Scott, and Zachary Taylor—were all Whigs. Years later, Grant described himself as "a Whig by education" and noted that during the late 1850s, "most of my neighbors had known me as an officer of the army with Whig proclivities." Though much has been made of the fact that in the single prewar presidential election in which he voted, Grant cast his ballot for Democrat James Buchanan, this was only because the Whig Party had ceased to exist. Grant was far from the only former Whig who eventually migrated into the Republican Party, and his Whiggish impulses played an important role in his presidency.

In February 1848, the United States and Mexico signed the Treaty of Guadalupe Hidalgo, ending the war. Under the treaty's terms, Mexico ceded a vast swath of land to the United States. In return, the United States paid Mexico $15 million and assumed responsibility for $3.25 million that Mexico's government owed to American citizens. Peace allowed Grant to make good on his marriage proposal to Julia. The couple was married August 22, 1848, at the Dents' house in St. Louis in what Julia recalled more than half a century later as "a sweet, old-fashioned wedding."[11] Unfortunately, the couple's bliss was short lived because over the next six years, Grant bounced around a number of duty stations: Detroit; Sackets Harbor, New York; and Columbia Barracks, Oregon. His family grew: son Frederick Dent Grant was born May 30, 1850, followed by Ulysses S. Grant Jr. (July 22, 1852), and Ellen Grant (July 4, 1855). On August 5, 1853, the army promoted Grant to captain but assigned him to California's Fort Humboldt. Grant found the posting tedious and lonely because his family did not accompany him. Writing to Julia, he confessed to feeling "forsaken here" and complained, "I do nothing here but set in my room and read and occasionally take a short ride on one of the public horses."[12] Adding to his misery was the fact that he lost a considerable amount of money investing in a series of wild schemes that all ended in failure.[13] It was at Fort Humboldt that Grant's exaggerated reputation for alcoholism was born. Out of a combination of depression, loneliness, and boredom, many of Humboldt's officers and enlisted men turned to alcohol; Grant was no exception. Exacerbating the problem was Grant's low tolerance for drink, which became the basis for claims that he was an alcoholic. A fellow officer recalled that, "One glass would show on him, and two or three would make him stupid."[14] One day, while discharging his duties as paymaster, Grant was slightly intoxicated, which offended the fort's commander, Colonel Robert Buchanan. The colonel gave Grant an ultimatum: resign or face charges. On April 11, 1854, Grant resigned from the army.

Grant's decision to resign inaugurated a prolonged period of failure. Shortly after he submitted his resignation, his father wrote to Secretary of War Jefferson Davis and presciently noted that his son "will be poorly qualified for the pursuits of private life."[15] Crushingly, Jesse made a similar comment directly to Grant, telling him "West Point spoiled my son for business." His visibly wounded son could only meekly respond, "I guess that's about so."[16] In summer 1856, Grant and his family moved into a primitive house he built on a piece of land gifted by his father-in-law to Julia. In her memoirs, Julia called the house "so crude and homely . . . that we facetiously decided to call it Hardscrabble."[17] Undoubtedly a hard worker, Grant nonetheless seemed incapable of financial success. In 1857, he took over managing Colonel Dent's farm, which entailed overseeing the family's slaves. Grant had grown up in an antislavery household. His father had worked and lived with Owen Brown's family in Ohio; one of the Brown's sons, John, murdered proslave Kansans in the 1850s and then led the ill-fated 1859 attempt to seize the federal arsenal at Harpers Ferry and thereby foment a slave uprising. Grant recalled that though Jesse thought John Brown a "fanatic and an extremist," the elder Grant nonetheless regarded Brown as "a man of great purity of character."[18] Furthermore, Jesse was intolerant of those who did not share his abhorrence to slavery; he once quit a job rather than live in a state that allowed slavery, and he later disparaged Ulysses's in-laws as "a tribe of slave owners."[19] Though Grant was more tolerant than his father, he nonetheless strongly opposed slavery. Though his father-in-law and his wife owned slaves, and he even briefly owned a slave at one point, "he never got over the queasiness he felt from the ownership of another human." One friend recalled that Grant was too good-natured to succeed as a slave owner and, as a result, "he was not a slavery man."[20] Grant worked in the fields alongside the slaves, debasing him in the eyes of Missouri's elites. One of Julia Grant's slaves recalled many years later, "I have seen many farmers, but I never saw one that worked harder than Mr. Grant." According to Grant's cousin Louisa Boggs, "It was a hard situation for him. He was a Northern man married to a Southern, slave-owning family. Colonel Dent openly despised him. All the family said 'poor Julia' when they spoke of [her] . . . [and] everyone thought Captain Grant a poor match for Miss Dent."[21] In part, this was a function of the fact that despite all of his effort, Grant failed to achieve sustained success. In late December 1857, he was broke and was forced to pawn his watch in order to buy Christmas gifts for his children.[22]

Failure imbued Grant with a great deal of sympathy for other white men who struggled as he did. One incident is telling: a local day laborer's mule was repeatedly seized to satisfy a court judgment and, despite his own poverty, Grant purchased the animal three times and returned it to its owner. Grant eventually advised the mule's owner to move to another county to prevent the animal from being seized a fourth time, but regardless of what the laborer did, the future president declared his intention to prevent the animal's seizure "even if I have to buy it once a week all summer!"[23] Laudable as it was, Grant's generosity demonstrated a propensity for bad financial decision-making that contributed to his reputation for being a bit of a sucker when it came to money. Julia Grant recalled in her memoirs an instance after the Mexican-American War when a blacksmith called on Grant and presented the captain with a bill. Though Grant protested that he had already paid the bill, he nonetheless paid it again. Sometime later, the blacksmith reappeared and presented Grant with the same bill, and, again, Grant protested that he had paid the bill (twice) but grudgingly handed over the money. When the blacksmith appeared a third time, Grant lost his patience, exclaiming, "I have once paid this bill and twice I have given you the money because I thought you needed it, but this is impertinence. Now be off with you and do not let me see you again."[24]

In summer 1859, Grant (with Colonel Dent's help) managed to secure a partnership in a local real estate office, but that position lasted less than a year. At about this time, Grant sought appointment as superintendent of roads for St. Louis County. As a cadet, Grant had studied surveying at West Point, and he managed to secure nearly three-dozen local notables' signatures on a testimonial recommending him for the position. Unfortunately for Grant, he lost the appointment to another man, in part because three of the five members of the board making the appointment were Free-Soilers, or members of a short-lived political party opposed to slavery; though opposed to slavery, Grant was not a Free Soiler. Writing to his father afterward, Grant explained, "The Free Soil party felt themselves bound to provide for one of their own party."[25] A quarter century later, Grant was still angered by the fact that he was not appointed to this position, which he (erroneously) attributed to the fact that the successful candidate was an immigrant. According to Grant, "My opponent had the advantage of birth over me (he was a citizen by adoption) and carried off the prize."[26] In reality, the appointment went to a man named Edward Gray who was apparently a native-born American. Nevertheless, Grant's anger at having lost this position seems to have pushed him to briefly join the Know-Nothings, a party that burst on the political scene in the mid-1850s. Grant's flirtation with nativism was likely about more than just sour grapes at having lost out on a patronage appointment. Though primarily associated with opposition to Catholic immigration to the United States, the Know-Nothings also served as a vehicle for mobilizing antislave Northerners fleeing the Democratic and Whig Parties.

Grant was not the only antislavery Northerner who briefly jumped on the Know-Nothing bandwagon; Simon Cameron, a prominent

Pennsylvania Democrat and later Lincoln's first secretary of war, joined the party in the mid-1850s, and future secretary of the Treasury Salmon Chase enjoyed Know-Nothing support in his 1855 campaign for Ohio governor.[27] That is not to say, however, that Grant did not share some of the Know-Nothing Party's prejudices; throughout his life, he had a complex relationship with religious minorities. Perhaps the best-known example is his General Order No. 11, which he promulgated in 1862 and which ordered the expulsion of all Jews from the military district then under his command (discussed in greater detail later in this chapter). In his memoir, Grant wrote that he had "no apologies to make for having been one week a member of the [Know-Nothing] party" because he still thought "native-born citizens of the United States should have as much protection, as many privileges in their native country, as those who voluntarily select it for a home." While Grant claimed that no political party could "exist when one of its cornerstones is opposition to freedom of thought and the right to worship God," he nonetheless balanced that assertion by noting "if a sect sets up its laws as binding above the State laws, wherever the two come into conflict this claim must be resisted and suppressed at whatever cost." As president, Grant not only supported the Blaine Amendment (which aimed to prevent state money from being used to support Catholic schools), he aggressively enforced the Morrill Act in Utah, which criminalized polygamy. Writing about Mormons and polygamy in his memoirs, Grant condescendingly noted, "We forgive [Mormons] for entertaining such notions [polygamy], but forbid their practice."[28] In short, there is much to suggest that Grant's brief migration into the Know-Nothing Party was more complicated than simple nativism or religious bigotry, though there was certainly an element of both at work.

Yet Grant feared the breakup of the Union more than he opposed the expansion of slavery or feared Catholicism. The Mexican-American War, which had proven such a turning point in Grant's life, had also exacerbated the debate over slavery. Many Southerners supported the Mexican-American War in the belief that it would open vast new territories for slavery, which it did. When gold was discovered in northern California in 1848, the territory's population exploded in just a few months, and by the following year pressure mounted to bring the territory into the Union. The problem was that California bisected the line established by the Missouri Compromise demarcating slave and free territory. Eventually, Congress enacted a series of bills collectively known as the Compromise of 1850. These bills repealed the Missouri Compromise, substituting instead "popular sovereignty," leaving it up to a territory's voters to decide whether to enter the Union as a free or slave state. While this seemed an elegant and democratic solution to the problem, by the mid-1850s it led to bloody conflicts as pro- and anti-slave forces colonized Western territories in an attempt to influence the outcome of votes about entering the Union. Worse, one concession that Southerners had exacted for their support of the compromise was a new Fugitive Slave Law, which essentially forced Northern state officials to assist in the capture and repatriation of escaped slaves. Thus, by the mid-1850s, slavery had become the dominant political issue in the United States. Grant followed the debate closely; Julia recalled, "My dear husband Ulys read aloud to me every speech for and against secession," while one of Grant's friends claimed decades later that the future president avidly followed the debate over slavery and "no man was better informed than he on every phase."[29]

Grant was appalled by talk of secession; at the time he claimed that hearing his friends voice such sentiments "made my blood run cold."[30] In 1856, Grant voted (for the first time in his life) for James Buchanan, a Pennsylvania Democrat and perennial presidential candidate. Though not a slave owner, Buchanan was a "doughface"—a Northerner sympathetic to the South—and Grant hoped he might find a way to defuse the political dynamite threatening to blow the country apart. He recalled, "I wanted to leave the country if disunion was accomplished."[31] In fact, in a letter to his father, Grant justified his vote by saying he had cast a ballot not for Buchanan but against the Republican nominee, John C. Fremont.[32] In his memoirs, Grant noted, "It was evident to my mind that the election of a Republican President in 1856 meant the secession of all the Slave States, and rebellion. Under these circumstances I preferred the success of a candidate whose election would prevent or postpone secession, to seeing the country plunged into a war the end of which no man could foretell."[33]

Buchanan failed to quell the sectional tension (Grant called him a "granny of an executive"), which only got worse in the lead-up to the 1860 presidential election.[34] Nevertheless, Grant still loathed the Republicans, who he feared would provoke Southern states into seceding. "I still had hopes that the four years which had elapsed since the first nomination of a presidential candidate by a party distinctly opposed to slavery extension, had given time for the extreme pro-slavery sentiment to cool down; for the Southerners to think well before they took the awful leap which they had so vehemently threatened."[35] Thus, in 1860, Grant supported Senator Stephen Douglas, one of four Democratic candidates for president, but because the future general had not lived in Illinois for long (he had only recently moved to Galena to work at his father's leather goods store), he could not vote in the presidential election. The number of Democratic candidates split the party's vote and made Republican Abraham Lincoln, who received less than four in ten votes cast, president-elect of the United States. Lincoln's vote total was not the only alarming factor in the election: "Honest Abe" received no electoral votes from the South. In other words, not only did Lincoln become president by a plurality of votes, the country had chosen its president along sectional lines.

Though Lincoln ran on a conservative platform promising "the maintenance inviolate of the rights of the states . . . [to] control [their] own domestic institutions according to [their] own judgment[s] exclusively," the Republicans' assertion that "the normal condition of all the territory of the United States is that of freedom" suggested to Southerners that slavery was imperiled.[36] Consequently, within weeks of Lincoln's election, states across the South began leaving the Union. On December 20, South Carolina seceded, and ten days later the state seized the federal arsenal in Charleston. Over the next month, Mississippi, Florida, Alabama, Georgia, Louisiana, and Texas followed South Carolina's lead and seceded. Worse, South Carolinians fired on a supply ship, *The Star of the West*, as it made its way to Fort Sumter to deliver supplies. President Buchanan, paralyzed by the crisis, refused to take military action to put down the rebellion, effectively leaving the crisis to his successor. In his inaugural address, Lincoln promised not to interfere with slavery where it existed, but he unequivocally stated his belief that secession was illegal and that he meant to enforce federal law. Over the succeeding three weeks, Lincoln faced a wrenching decision: forcibly resupply Sumter, thereby in all likelihood provoking a violent confrontation with the South, or do nothing, implicitly conceding the right of states to secede. Fulfilling his pledge to maintain control of US property and territory, on March 29, Lincoln decided to resupply Fort Sumter. In an attempt to defuse hostilities, Lincoln made it known that he would only send provisions, not additional men or weapons, to Fort Sumter. In response, on April 11, the Confederates demanded that Fort Sumter's commander, Major Robert Anderson, surrender the fort. When Anderson refused, the Confederates undertook a thirty-four-hour bombardment of the largely defenseless fort. Eventually, Anderson was forced to surrender the fort, which was evacuated April 14. The following day, Lincoln issued a call to the states for seventy-five thousand militiamen to protect federal property and suppress the rebellion. The American Civil War had begun.

The outbreak of war led to many unexpected developments. Certainly one of the most dramatic was setting an undistinguished former military officer named Ulysses S. Grant on the road to international renown, military glory, and the presidency of the United States. The day after Lincoln issued his call for volunteers, Grant attended a patriotic rally in Galena, during which he decided to offer his services to defend the Union. In a letter to his father dated April 21, Grant spelled out the principles that would guide not only his military service during the war but his policies as president. According to Grant, "Whatever may have been my political opinions before, I have but one sentiment now. That is, we have a Government and laws and a flag, and they must all be sustained. There are but two parties now, Traitors and Patriots, and I want hereafter to be ranked with the latter."[37] On April 18, Grant orchestrated a recruitment rally, and a week later he accompanied the Jo Daviess Guards (named for the county) to Springfield. Two days after Grant's thirty-ninth birthday, Illinois governor Richard Yates placed the would-be soldier in charge of training the state's recruits. Here Grant shone: in the space of little more than a week, he mustered three regiments into state service. Responding to Grant's desire for a field command, Yates appointed him a colonel and gave him command of the 21st Illinois Infantry. Grant assumed command June 17, accompanying the regiment to Mexico, Missouri, where he guarded the Hannibal and Joseph Railroad.

Meanwhile, Grant's friend and patron, Republican congressman Elihu Washburne, successfully worked to secure for Grant a promotion: on July 31, at Washburne's behest, Lincoln nominated Grant to be a brigadier general in the US Army and the Senate approved the nomination on August 5. On September 1, 1861, Major General John C. Fremont, the 1856 Republican presidential nominee and Western Department commander, placed Grant in command of the District of Southeast Missouri. Four days later, Grant seized Paducah, Kentucky, earning a reputation for willingness to engage the enemy. In early February 1862, Grant scored major victories when he captured Forts Henry and Donelson, giving the Union control of the Tennessee and Cumberland Rivers and paving the way for the Union capture of Clarksville and Nashville (the first state capital to fall). These victories catapulted Grant to national fame and earned him a new nickname: "Unconditional Surrender" Grant, a nod to his note to Confederate general Simon B. Buckner during the Battle of Fort Donelson that he would accept "No terms except unconditional and immediate surrender."[38]

Grant discovered that popularity was a fickle thing: his immediate superior, Major General Henry W. Halleck, tried to blunt Grant's fame by resuscitating gossip about the his drinking. Halleck's campaign against Grant got so bad that President Lincoln intervened, ordering the general to formally investigate the rumors he was spreading or let the matter drop.[39] Halleck backed down, but Grant's reputation was still tarnished. Worse, the Battle of Shiloh, which was the costliest battle in American history up to that point, resulted in calls for Grant's removal (leading Lincoln to famously remark that he could not spare "this man; he fights").[40] At Shiloh, Confederate forces caught Grant's men by surprise, driving back the Union army. Only luck—General Albert S. Johnston was killed in the fighting and his successor, Pierre G.T. Beauregard, did not push the Confederate advantage—prevented an embarrassing rout. Though Grant, strengthened by units from the Army of the Ohio, managed to force Beauregard's army from the field the following day, the very fact that he was recapturing territory that he had lost dampened any sense of victory. Moreover, the cost of dislodging Beauregard—over thirteen thousand killed, captured, or wounded—was high and, coupled with inflammatory and exaggerated stories told by the battle's survivors, made Grant look incompetent. Union state governors and congressmen voiced their dissatisfaction with Grant's leadership, and in the midst of the controversy, Halleck assumed personal command of the Army of the Tennessee, a move

Grant interpreted as a censure.[41] It was only when Halleck was promoted to general in chief of all Union armies a few months after Shiloh that Grant returned to command of the Army of the Tennessee.

For all of its high costs, the Battle of Shiloh had one important consequence: it forced Grant to grapple with the nature of the fight ahead of him. According to Grant, "Up to the battle of Shiloh, I, as well as thousands of other citizens, believed that the rebellion against the Government would collapse suddenly and soon, if a decisive victory could be gained over any of [the Confederacy's] armies. . . . [After the battle, however] I gave up all idea of saving the union except by complete conquest."[42] With that insight in mind, in December 1862, Grant initiated a campaign to take Vicksburg, which surrendered July 4, 1863. Vicksburg was a major turning point for the war and for Grant. Coupled with the Union victory at Gettysburg a day earlier, the Confederacy was clearly on the defensive. Grant recalled that with the fall of Vicksburg, "New hopes for the final success of the cause of the Union were inspired."[43] Because of the victory, Lincoln promoted Grant to the permanent rank of major general.

However, in another sense, Vicksburg haunted Grant for years to come. Offended by the swarm of speculators and traders who profited from the war, Grant issued his infamous General Order No. 11, which included three points, the first of which commanded: "The Jews, as a class violating every regulation of trade established by the Treasury Department and also department orders, are hereby expelled from the Department [of the Tennessee] within twenty-four hours from the receipt of this order."

Meanwhile, in a letter Grant sent to the War Department the same day, he claimed:

> I have long since believed that in spite of all the vigilance that can be infused into Post Commanders, that the Specie regulations of the Treasury Dept. have been violated, and that mostly by Jews and other unprincipled traders. So well satisfied of this have I been at this that I instructed the Commdg Officer at Columbus [Kentucky] to refuse all permits to Jews to come south, and frequently have had them expelled from the Dept. [of the Tennessee]. But they come in with their Carpet sacks in spite of all that can be done to prevent it. The Jews seem to be

a privileged class that can travel any where. They will land at any wood yard or landing on the river and make their way through the country. If not permitted to buy Cotton themselves they will act as agents for someone else who will be at a Military post, with a Treasury permit to receive Cotton and pay for it in Treasury notes which the Jew will buy up at an agreed rate, paying gold.[44]

General Order No. 11 sparked immediate controversy, and years later Grant conceded that it was a blunder, writing, "It would never have been issued if it had not been telegraphed the moment it were penned, and without reflection."[45] Almost immediately, Lincoln ordered Grant's superior, Henry Halleck, to countermand General Order 11, and the president told newspapers that the government made no distinctions between Jews and Christians.[46] Fortunately for Grant, his success in the battlefield and his reputation for taking the fight to the enemy made him indispensible to the Lincoln administration, so he was not disciplined for this order. The controversy soon cooled, though his political enemies raised the issue during the presidential election of 1868, and it has proven an enduring part of Grant's legacy.

In September 1863, Confederate forces under General Braxton Bragg defeated Major General William S. Rosecrans at the Battle of Chickamauga. Braxton then besieged the Army of the Cumberland in Chattanooga. Lincoln ordered Grant to break the siege, placing him in command of the newly created Military Division of the Mississippi, which comprised the Departments of the Ohio, the Cumberland, and the Tennessee. Effectively, this made Grant commander of all of the Union's western armies, and he immediately went to Chattanooga to take command there, relieving Rosecrans of command. In late November, Grant broke Bragg's siege of the city, eliminating the last vestige of rebel control of Tennessee and laying the groundwork for a Union invasion of the Deep South. Grant's success in Chattanooga earned him a promotion to general in chief of the army. Initially, Lincoln was reluctant to promote Grant, fearing that doing so might create a powerful rival in the 1864 presidential election. This was a valid concern: in fact, in late 1863, prominent so-called War Democrats (those who demanded an aggressive prosecution of the war but nonetheless opposed the Lincoln administration on other issues) reached out to Grant to see if he might accept the Democrats' presidential nomination. Grant rebuffed these requests, claiming "I am not a politician, never was and hope never to be. . . . I scarcely know the inducement that could be held out to me to accept office, and unhesitatingly say that I infinitely prefer my present position to that of any civil office within the gift of the people."[47] In response to a query from US representative Francis P. Blair of Missouri, Grant wrote, "Everyone who knows me knows that I have no political aspirations either now or for the future." Blair's brother, Montgomery, was then serving as postmaster general and almost certainly shared Grant's letter with Lincoln.[48] Once it became clear that Grant had no interest in running for president in 1864, Lincoln authorized the promotion.

Now a lieutenant general and the army's general in chief, Grant relocated his headquarters to Washington, DC, and placed Major General William T. Sherman in command of the Union's Western armies. Arriving in Washington, Grant conferred with the president and developed a plan for total war designed not only to break the Confederacy's military power but also to destroy the rebels' willingness to keep fighting. Grant brought a new ruthlessness and uncompromising attitude demonstrated in his orders to General George Meade in April 1864. Grant told Meade, "Lee's Army will be your objective point. Wherever Lee goes, there you will go also."[49] This strategy of constant engagement had a downside: though the war had entered its final year, the Confederates demonstrated that they would not go gentle into that good night. Worse, like a wounded beast, the Confederates lashed out: On April 12, Major General Nathan B. Forrest captured Fort Pillow in Tennessee and ruthlessly slaughtered black Union troops instead of taking them prisoner. According to Grant, Forrest did this to "demonstrate to the Northern people that negro soldiers cannot cope with Southerners."[50] Enraged by Forrest's actions, Grant refused to exchange any more Confederate prisoners until the Confederacy released thirty thousand Union prisoners "owed" to the North and agreed to treat black and white soldiers equally.[51] The Confederates refused these conditions, which suited Grant just fine: every Confederate prisoner he released was one more that his own soldiers would face at some future battle.

The following month, Grant initiated the first in a series of battles in Virginia that came to be known as the Overland Campaign. The first engagement, the Battle of the Wilderness, took place May 5 and

6, and led to almost unimaginable casualties, even by the standards of this ghastly war: two days of fighting left nearly thirty thousand Union and Confederate casualties. Unlike previous Union commanders, however, Grant did not lick his wounds. Recognizing that the Union's main advantage over the Confederacy was its superior ability to replace men and material destroyed in battle, Grant pushed forward, confronting Lee's army May 14 at Spotsylvania Court House. Rainy weather fouled both sides' firearms, leading to fierce hand-to-hand fighting at a place called "bloody angle." Again, the battle resulted in shocking casualties: Grant lost 18,000 men to Lee's 12,867, but Grant (demonstrating the resolve that differentiated him from previous Union commanders) grimly promised to "fight it on this line if it takes all summer."[52] Grant was applying the lessons of Shiloh, but at terrifying cost.

Following a series of minor and inconsequential battles in the days after Spotsylvania, Grant's and Lee's armies confronted each other at Cold Harbor. Raging over twelve days, the fighting at Cold Harbor was bloody even by the Civil War's atrocious standards. Grant's casualties were nearly five times greater than Lee's, and Northern public opinion briefly soured on Grant, who was attacked as a "butcher." For his part, Grant was determined to keep fighting, which the president supported, though the general made every effort to keep casualties as low as possible in recognition of the upcoming presidential election. General George B. McClellan secured the Democratic presidential nomination in late August 1864, and the party's platform demanded "immediate efforts be made for a cessation of hostilities, with a view of an ultimate convention of the States, or other peaceable means, to the end that, at the earliest practicable moment, peace may be restored on the basis of the Federal Union of the States."[53] Lincoln believed he would lose the election, telling his cabinet on August 23 that "it seems exceedingly probable that this Administration will not be reelected. Then it will be my duty to cooperate with the President elect as to save the Union between the election and the inauguration; as he will have secured his election on such ground as he could not possibly save it afterwards."[54]

The stakes could not be higher, so Grant decided to gamble by marching deep into Virginia, thereby leaving Washington, DC, largely undefended. Grant saw an opportunity to take Petersburg, which was the Confederacy's main supply center. Petersburg was a convergence point for five railroads, and its capture would irreparably weaken the Confederacy and pave the way for the capture of its capital, Richmond. In mid-June 1864, Petersburg was only lightly defended because the unremitting losses caused by the Overland Campaign had forced Lee to strip the city of most of its defenders. Union forces under the command of Brigadier General William F. "Baldy" Smith attacked Petersburg's outer defenses June 15, but failed to push their advantage until the next day, which gave Confederate general Beauregard time to reinforce the city. From June 16 to 18, Union forces tried to take the city, giving Lee enough time to get to Petersburg and reinforce Beauregard's forces. Consequently, Grant decided to besiege the city, and Lee responded by sending a force under General Jubal Early to threaten Washington. Lee apparently hoped this would force Grant to dispatch forces to defend the capital, perhaps creating an opportunity for the Confederates to break the siege of Petersburg. As Lee anticipated, Grant dispatched troops to defend Washington, and though Early failed to take the capital, the presence of Confederate troops so near the city embarrassed the beleaguered Lincoln administration. Worse was the humiliation caused in late July 1864 by the Battle of the Crater. Following weeks of intensive preparation that involved tunneling underground more than five hundred feet between Union and Confederate lines and then seventy-five feet underneath the Confederates, Union forces exploded approximately eight thousand pounds of gunpowder, blasting a crater approximately 170 by 120 feet and at least 30 feet deep. The explosion killed nearly three hundred Confederates, and Union forces clearly had the advantage, but delay and poor planning, as well as the federal troops' decision to enter the crater (rather than walk around it) created an embarrassing reversal; by the end of the battle, Northern casualties were more than double Lee's. Grant was forced to concede, "It was the saddest affair I have witnessed in this war."[55] Congress agreed and investigated the event, focusing on the role played by Generals George Meade and Ambrose Burnside, the men most responsible for developing the battle plan; neither man's reputation recovered.

On the other hand, despite the fact that the Battle of the Crater was clearly a Confederate victory, even such an egregious loss could not turn the war's tide in Lee's favor. As historian Bruce Catton noted, though "every battle looked very much like a Union defeat," Grant's army continued pushing South, creating a tide "that would sweep the Confederacy out of existence no matter what skill or valor tried to stay it."[56] Despite the Union's setback at the Battle of the Crater, Lee remained unable to break Grant's siege of Petersburg and was therefore unable to move south to help repel Sherman's advance into Georgia. On September 2, Sherman took Atlanta, and six weeks later General Philip Sheridan defeated Confederate forces under the command of Jubal Early, allowing Union forces to seriously degrade the South's economic infrastructure in Georgia and the Carolinas. The quick succession of Union victories helped Lincoln trounce George B. McClellan in the presidential election, 55 to 45 percent. In the Electoral College, the result was even more lopsided: Lincoln won a commanding 10-to-1 victory over McClellan, resoundingly defeating the former general.

A little more than three weeks after Lincoln's second inauguration, Grant met with the president, General Sherman, and Rear Admiral David Dixon Porter aboard the steamship *River Queen*. The March 28 meeting, later immortalized in George P.A. Healy's classic painting *The Peacemakers*, was the only time that Grant, Sherman, and Porter simultaneously met with President Lincoln. At this meeting, Grant and Sherman pressed for another campaign. Lincoln was skeptical and expressed his desire to avoid any unnecessary bloodshed; according to Porter's recollection, the president wanted the Confederates "to return to their allegiance to the Union and submit to the laws," though he was clear he did not want army officers making any political settlements on behalf of the federal government, which suited Grant just fine: his mandate was to win the war, not negotiate the peace.[57] On March 25, Confederate forces tried to break the Union's siege of Petersburg at the battle of Fort Stedman. The battle was a Confederate rout—Lee's casualties were nearly four times Grant's—making Lee's capitulation inevitable. On March 29, Grant initiated the Appomattox Campaign, which, over the next twelve days, brought the war to a close. On April 9, 1865, Grant met with Lee; the latter surrendered his army to the former. Despite his tough reputation, "Unconditional Surrender" Grant offered Lee generous terms. Though this was not the end of Civil War bloodshed—minor skirmishing continued into the summer—Lee's surrender to Grant at Appomattox Courthouse was widely perceived (then and now) as bringing the Civil War to an end.

Lee's surrender made Grant one of, if not the, most popular men in America, but war's end left a number of unanswered questions: What did the war mean? On what terms would the seceded states be allowed to return to the Union? Now that slavery was abolished, what role (if any) would blacks play in American political, economic, and social life? These were not academic questions, for the answers dictated policy decisions and set the terms of the debate for Grant's two terms as president. As historian Joan Waugh sagely noted, "In Grant's mind, reconciliation and the 'Union Cause' had to be founded on southern acceptance of the victor's terms."[58] This placed him squarely at loggerheads with Lincoln's successor, Andrew Johnson, and convinced the reticent Grant to run for president in 1868.

Two

"Whatever May Be the Orders of My Superiors, and Law, I Will Execute"

ON APRIL 14, 1865, Grant attended a seven-hour cabinet session that began at 11:00 a.m. Before the meeting, the president asked Grant to accompany the first family to Ford's Theater that evening. After checking with his wife later in the day, the general declined Lincoln's invitation and that afternoon left for Philadelphia. This was a fateful decision: Lincoln dragooned Major Henry Rathbone and his fiancée, Clara Harris (daughter of Ira Harris, US senator from New York) into joining the first couple. During the play, John Wilkes Booth snuck into the president's box and shot Lincoln, who died several hours later. About ninety minutes after Booth shot Lincoln, a telegram containing the shocking news arrived for Grant at the general's hotel in Philadelphia. He and Julia immediately returned to Washington, though he did not attend Andrew Johnson's impromptu swearing in that morning. In her memoirs, Julia Grant claimed that her husband responded to news of Johnson's ascension to the presidency by saying, "for some reason, I dread the change."[1]

Lincoln's death occurred at a politically delicate moment. Though the war was over, the outlines of Reconstruction were far from clear. Even before Lincoln's death, there were signs of tension between the White House and Congress over Reconstruction. On December 8, 1863, Lincoln issued a proclamation of amnesty and reconstruction that laid out the terms for Confederates to rejoin the Union. Lincoln proclaimed "to all persons who have, directly or by implication, participated in the existing rebellion, except as hereinafter excepted, that a full pardon is hereby granted to them and each of them, with restoration of all rights of property, except as to slaves and in property cases where rights of third parties shall have intervened, and upon the condition that every such person shall take and subscribe an oath, and thenceforward keep and maintain said oath inviolate, and which oath shall be registered for permanent preservation." Lincoln's proclamation

> exempted from the benefits of the foregoing provisions . . . all who are, or shall have been, civil or diplomatic officers or agents of the so-called Confederate Government: all who have left judicial stations under the United States to aid the rebellion; all who are or shall have been military or naval officers of said so-called Confederate Government above the rank of colonel in the army or lieutenant in the navy; all who have left seats in the United States Congress to aid the rebellion; all who resigned commissions in the army or navy of the United States and afterward aided the rebellion; and all who have engaged in any way in treating colored persons, or white persons in charge of such, otherwise than lawfully as prisoners of war, and which persons may have been found in the United States service as soldiers, seamen, or in any capacity.

Once 10 percent of a state's voters took the prescribed oath, the state could reestablish a government "'which shall be republican,' and . . . shall be recognized as the true government of the State, and the State shall receive there under the benefits of the constitutional provision which declares that 'the United States shall guarantee to every state in this Union a republican form of government, and shall protect each of them against invasion; and, on the application of the legislature, or the executive (when the legislature cannot be convened) against domestic violence.'"[2] As historian Kenneth M. Stampp noted, this plan "was designed to restore the southern states to the Union with maximum speed and with a minimum of federal intervention in their internal affairs."[3]

Alarmingly, voters would be selected based on the state election laws in place in 1860; naturally, this would ensure that no freed slaves participated in creating the new governments, damaging Republicans' electoral prospects in this region and imperiling their control of Congress. As a result, congressional Republicans pushed back against the president, offering their own Reconstruction plan in July 1864. Passed with strong Republican support in both the Senate and the House, the Wade-Davis bill (named for its authors, Senator Benjamin F. Wade of Ohio and Representative Henry Winter Davis of Maryland), demanded that 50 percent of a state's white men take the oath of loyalty, that the state abolish slavery, and that former Confederate government officials and military officers be excluded from the constitutional process. Lincoln, believing the bill's terms too harsh, opposed it. It was passed on the last day of the congressional session, and Lincoln took no action; under the terms of Article 1, Section 7 of the Constitution, this meant that the bill did not become law, a course of action known as a pocket veto. The administration and Congress made little headway finding a compromise in the succeeding months.

Thus, when Johnson assumed the presidency on April 15, 1865, Republicans were far from united, and the new president was hardly the man to unify the party. Born into poverty (literally in a log cabin) in North Carolina, Johnson apprenticed as a tailor but later fled to Tennessee to escape his master. Succeeding as a tailor, Johnson invested in real estate and, at age twenty-seven, parlayed his wealth into a successful bid for the Tennessee House of Representatives as a Democrat. Interestingly, Johnson lost his bid for reelection in 1837 but tried to regain his seat in 1839, this time as a Whig. When another Whig ran for the seat in the same election, Johnson reverted to being a Democrat and was elected. Two years later, Johnson was elected to the Tennessee Senate, and in 1843 he began a ten-year stint in the House. Johnson did not fit easily into the mold of the two-party system, and his relations with Democratic president James K. Polk, who was also from Tennessee, were strained. Writing in 1849, Polk noted of Johnson, "Professing to be a Democrat, he has been politically, if not personally hostile to me during my whole term. He is very vindictive and perverse in his temper and conduct. If he had the manliness and independence to declare his opposition openly, he knows he could not be elected by his constituents."[4]

Though he won reelection to the House in autumn 1852, his political supporters maneuvered to get him elected governor of Tennessee the following summer. Tennessee's governor was relatively weak; serving only a two-year term, governors could propose but not veto legislation. Johnson was narrowly reelected governor in 1855, but in 1857, he decided to run for the US Senate. Johnson won the seat, and when Tennessee seceded from the Union in June 1861, he remained in the Senate, the only Southern senator to do so. This made him the most famous Southern Unionist in the United States, but this decision was not without personal cost; Johnson had to flee Tennessee in fear of his safety. These sacrifices endeared him to Northern Unionists. Simon Cameron, Lincoln's first secretary of war and an ardent Unionist, cheered the Tennessean as "lion-hearted Johnson."[5] Because of Johnson's staunch Unionism and popularity with Republicans, Lincoln appointed him military governor of Tennessee in March 1862; the Senate went further, confirming Johnson's nomination and conferring on him the rank of brigadier general. In response, Confederate troops seized Johnson's land and slaves and converted his home into a war hospital. Johnson took a hard line as military governor, demanding loyalty oaths and shuttering newspapers sympathetic to the Confederacy. He even went so far as to support the enlistment of African Americans into the Union armies, albeit reluctantly. All of these facts reinforced his popularity among members of the Republican Party.

Thus, when Lincoln's desire to avoid the appearance that the Civil War was a partisan affair made selection of a Democrat to be the Republican Party's vice presidential nominee imperative, Johnson looked like an outstanding choice: he was a Southern, slave-owning, Democratic Unionist popular with congressional Republicans. Though Lincoln's reelection was surely due, at least in some small part, to Johnson's presence on the ticket, the new vice president was quickly sidelined; he met only once with the president, on April 14. As a result, he did not know the president's plans for Reconstruction, and, in any case, he had his own agenda: bring the Southern states back into the Union, redistribute political power in those states from the planter elite to lower-class farmers, and secure election in his own right in 1868.

Though Johnson had been a successful politician prior to the war, rising from humble origins to the pinnacle of Tennessee's political establishment, he was temperamentally unsuited to the challenges that faced him in the aftermath of America's Civil War. For one thing, Johnson was a solitary man who had few friends and preferred his own counsel, isolating himself from his cabinet and Congress.[6] In addition, as a former Jacksonian Democrat, Johnson was viscerally opposed to "consolidation or the centralization of power in the hands of the few," a fact that made him hostile toward the expansion of federal authority necessitated by the war and Reconstruction.[7] Moreover, the Tennessean had an enormous chip on his shoulder as a result of having had to bootstrap his way up the social ladder. Ironically, this brought him into conflict with the freed slaves for two reasons: he saw them as the agents of their former slave owners, and he believed that emancipation retarded poor whites' social mobility. During a meeting with Frederick Douglass, Johnson shocked the former slave by claiming, "The poor white man . . . was opposed to the slave and his master; for the colored man and his master, combined, kept [poor whites] in slavery, by depriving [poor whites] of a fair participation in the labor and productions of the rich land of the country."[8] Though a committed Unionist, Johnson's prejudices boded ill for newly freed slaves. A former slave owner, Johnson, as president, seemed obsessed by the possibility that political equality for African Americans could lead to "race mixing" (i.e., miscegenation).[9]

Alarmingly for newly freed slaves, in spring 1865, Johnson was free to set his own course on Reconstruction: Congress was out of session until December 4. Johnson seems to have thought he could complete Reconstruction in the seven and a half months between his inauguration and December, when Congress came back into session, thereby sidestepping the need to negotiate with the legislative branch. Johnson anticipated conflict with Congress and sought to aggravate intraparty tension to his political benefit. When it first emerged in the mid-1850s, the Republican Party was composed of people who were all antislavery, but along a spectrum, and by 1865, the party was split into three factions: Radicals, moderates, and conservatives. The most vocal faction was the Radicals, or those who advocated black suffrage. At the other end of the spectrum were the conservatives, a small group that historian Kenneth M. Stampp described as "feeble."[10] The largest faction, by far, were the moderates, who set a much lower bar for Confederate readmission to the Union, focusing mostly on the protection of freedmen's liberty. More conservative than their Radical counterparts, the Moderates did not see Reconstruction as a social revolution and advocated the quick readmission of the former Confederate states into the Union, albeit with protections against the reenslavement of African Americans.[11] As Stampp noted, the Moderates "held the balance of power; whichever group they gravitated toward would ultimately win control of Congress."[12]

The president's tough line on secession led some Republicans to conclude that he would go even further than Lincoln had, a fact that initially endeared him to the Radicals (though not for long).[13] On May 29, with the support of his cabinet, Johnson issued two proclamations. One provided amnesty for all rebels who held less than $20,000 worth of property, though it excluded the Confederacy's political and military leaders. The other recognized North Carolina's provisional government and appointed former newspaper editor William Holden governor, charging him with creating a "republican form of government" using the voting qualifications that were in place when the state seceded. While the vast majority of those elected to write the Southern states' new constitutions were not members of the region's prewar economic elite (i.e., the men Johnson despised), most had served the Confederacy in one capacity or another. As a result, the new state governments were conservative ones designed to preserve as much of the prewar social and political order as possible, which included efforts to frustrate the enfranchisement of freed slaves. According to historian Eric Foner, "If the architects of secession had been repudiated, the South's affairs would still be directed by men who, while Unionist in 1860, formed part of the antebellum political establishment. Their actions would go a long way toward determining the fate of Johnson's Reconstruction experiment."[14]

Because Reconstruction was an extension of the war effort, the army naturally played a key role in implementing (and therefore interpreting) Johnson's policies. That spring, Grant attended cabinet meetings, though he spoke infrequently and only when his opinion was solicited.[15] Events were moving quickly: on April 18, General

William T. Sherman signed a convention in North Carolina with Confederate general Joseph E. Johnston. Though the document closed by noting, "Not being fully empowered by our respective principals to fulfill these terms, we individually and officially pledge ourselves to promptly obtain the necessary authority, and to carry out the above programme," it called for "a general amnesty, so far as the Executive of the United States can command, on condition of the disbandment of the Confederate armies, the distribution of the arms, and the resumption of peaceful pursuits by the officers and men hitherto composing said armies."[16] Under the terms of the Sherman-Johnston compact, Confederate armies would lay down their arms and the existing Confederate state governments could continue in existence (provided they adhered to federal government authority); in other words, "everything would . . . be restored essentially to the status quo antebellum."[17] Instead of embracing these relatively generous terms, Johnson abolished the existing Confederate state governments, appointed provisional governors, and required elections to create entirely new state governments. These would be required to ratify the Thirteenth Amendment, which abolished slavery; repudiate their war debts; and void their ordinances of secession. Moreover, he directed Grant to travel to North Carolina to resume hostilities. It was only Sherman's renegotiation of the compact to bring it in line with the agreement signed by Grant and Lee at Appomattox that prevented the resumption of fighting.

Thus, by midsummer 1865, Johnson's policies had come into focus: "amazing lenience" for former Confederates and no black suffrage, an arrangement that was "not so much reconstruction as reunion."[18] Johnson's Reconstruction policies had the unintended effect of making him popular in the South. Recognizing that as an accidental president, a Southerner, and (until recently) a Democrat, he had little chance of being nominated by the Republicans in 1868, Johnson increasingly became, in the words of one historian, "the prisoner of southern voters."[19] As a result, Johnson increasingly made common cause even with the former plantation-owning Southern elite in its attempt to limit and, if possible, roll back African Americans' political rights. Within a few months, that is exactly what happened: South Carolina and Mississippi (the first two states that seceded) passed the first of what came to be known as Black Codes, which essentially forced freedmen to reenslave themselves by mandating that they have jobs or face imprisonment for "vagrancy." Furthermore, the codes banned blacks from testifying against whites, owning firearms, or purchasing liquor. South Carolina even went so far as to forbid blacks from pursuing any occupation other than farming unless they paid an exorbitant tax.[20] In sum, the "purpose of the Black Codes was to keep the Negro, as long as possible, exactly what he was: a propertyless rural laborer under strict controls, without political rights, and with inferior legal rights."[21]

More disturbing was the fact that in August, Johnson instructed Oliver O. Howard, head of the Freedmen's Bureau (a federal agency charged with helping former slaves adjust to freedom), to return all property confiscated from former Confederates who had received presidential pardons, which Johnson issued indiscriminately.[22] Meanwhile, violence against the freedmen surged, with riots breaking out in Memphis and New Orleans during the summer. Johnson's moves enraged Republicans of all stripes, who saw him as squandering the war's gains. At Johnson's behest, former newspaperman and US minister to Spain Carl Schurz toured the South and reported on conditions there. In particular, Schurz found a "spirit of persecution" against former slaves "so strong as to make the protection of the freedmen by the military arm of the government in many localities a necessity."[23] Schurz's report was a damning indictment of Johnson's Reconstruction policies, so when US senator Charles Sumner of Massachusetts called on Johnson and demanded that the president share it with the Senate, Johnson requested that Grant undertake a two-week tour of the south Atlantic coast and describe conditions there. Grant's report was far more positive than Schurz's (one biographer has called it worthless "except as propaganda"), so Johnson paired it with Schurz's in order to blunt the latter's political impact.[24]

When Congress reconvened in December 1865, Republicans were appalled at the results of the elections in the former Confederate states. On a nearly party-line vote, the Thirty-Ninth Congress voted to exclude the newly elected representatives of the former Confederate states, going so far as to deny Southern congressmen's claims for living expenses.[25] In addition, Congress established the Joint Committee of Fifteen on Reconstruction whose role was to investigate the former Confederate states to determine which, if any, were entitled to representation in Congress. Clearly, congressional Republicans were dissatisfied with Johnson's handling of Reconstruction, and the president added fuel to the fire in his annual message. While Johnson claimed that, "'The sovereignty of the States' is the language of the Confederacy, and not the language of the Constitution," he nevertheless also noted that "the Government of the United States is a limited government," implying that the executive would do little on behalf of the South's blacks. Moreover, he asserted, "Slavery was essentially a monopoly of labor, and as such locked the States where it prevailed against the incoming of free industry. Where labor was the property of the capitalist, the white man was excluded from employment, or had but the second best chance of finding it." Of the former slaves, Johnson said, "The career of free industry must be fairly opened to them, and then their future prosperity and condition must, after all, rest mainly on themselves. If they fail, and so perish away, let us be careful that the failure shall not be attributable to any denial of justice."[26] As historian Kenneth M. Stampp noted, Johnson's message was clear: "there would be no social or political revolution in the South after all. Southern Unionists and others who had hoped to bar the prewar politicians from positions of power in the New South now turned against the President; his former enemies, who had despised him in earlier years, now came to his defense."[27] Less than a year after Lincoln's death, Johnson found he had more in common with the Democrats than with congressional Republicans, going so far as to accuse abolitionists of being willing to "break up the Government to destroy slavery."[28]

Johnson went beyond rhetoric when he vetoed two key pieces of legislation: a bill extending the life of the Freedmen's Bureau and a civil rights bill. The Freedmen's Bureau was established in March 1865 to help former slaves adjust to emancipation by teaching them to support themselves and by establishing public schools. Though it was intended to operate for only a year, most Republicans agreed that the challenges facing newly emancipated slaves were so large that the organization needed to continue beyond its original mandate. The bill extended the bureau's life indefinitely and expanded its authority, giving the president the authority to reserve 3 million acres of unoccupied public land to be rented to former slaves.[29] Johnson opposed the bureau on principle and because of racism, believing that the federal government ought not to use tax money to support former slaves, especially when (in his mind) doing so harmed poor whites. Three days after vetoing the bills, Johnson delivered a speech in which he claimed that US representative Thaddeus Stevens of Pennsylvania and Senator Sumner were "laboring to pervert or destroy" the United States.[30]

This was heady stuff at this moment in American history, when the veto was infrequently used; the first six presidents had resorted to the veto only ten times, and in the entire history of the republic up to that point, Congress had overridden only six vetoes. Though congressional Republicans failed to override Johnson's veto of the Freedmen's Bureau bill, they did succeed with the civil rights bill. It was the first time in US history that Congress overrode a presidential veto of a major piece of legislation and a clear threat (from the president's perspective) to executive prerogatives. It also augured an increasingly confrontational relationship between the executive and the legislative branches that, at least temporarily, led to the empowerment of the latter at the expense of the former. In an attempt to seize control of Reconstruction, congressional Republicans began framing the Fourteenth Amendment, which would establish the terms of the Confederate states' readmittance to the Union. Under its terms, anyone born in the United States was a citizen regardless of color, and states were expressly prohibited from making or enforcing any law that abridged "the privileges or immunities of citizens of the United States; nor shall any state deprive any person of life, liberty, or property, without due process of law; nor deny to any person within its jurisdiction the equal protection of the laws." Any state that restricted the voting rights of males over age twenty-one would have its congressional representation "reduced in the proportion which the number of such male citizens shall bear to the whole number of male citizens twenty-one years of age in such state." In addition, former Confederate government officials and military officers were barred from becoming US representatives or senators unless two-thirds of both houses voted to remove the disability. Finally, the amendment repudiated Confederate war debts, expressly prohibiting either states or the federal government from repaying "any debt or obligation incurred in aid of insurrection or rebellion against the United States, or any claim for the loss or emancipation of any slave."[31]

All of this took place in the lead-up to the midterm elections of 1866, which were the voters' first chance to register their opinions about Johnson's policies. The Fourteenth Amendment was, in the words of historian Martin E. Mantell, "the perfect platform upon which the Republican Party could unite in the approaching Congressional elections," and Johnson's veto melded the party's various factions into a more coherent whole by giving them something to oppose—namely, the president.[32] Meanwhile, the Democrats ran on a single issue: opposition to the Republicans' Reconstruction plan. Thus, Republicans and Democrats sought to make the 1866 midterm elections a referendum on presidential Reconstruction by providing two different visions for the future of the newly reunited United States.

Seeing he had no future as a Republican, Johnson tried to create a new party from the disparate strands of conservative Republicans, Southerners, and Democrats. This was not as crazy as it sounds: party identity in the mid-1860s was far more fluid than it would become. Johnson's political allies called for a "National Union" convention to meet in Philadelphia in June 1866. It attracted nearly seven thousand spectators, but the president's dream of a new party foundered; the convention only called for the election of congressional candidates committed to Johnson's Reconstruction agenda. In mid-August 1866, the president embarked on a tour of Northern and Western states that came to be called the "swing around the circle"; reluctantly, and only because Johnson personally asked him to, Grant accompanied him. During the eighteen-day tour, Johnson spoke in front of thousands of people, usually in favor of Democratic candidates, and he compared himself to Jesus Christ. Grant resisted being used as a prop for Johnson's purposes. When Secretary of State Seward implied that Grant's presence indicated that the general approved of Johnson's policies, the latter angrily countered, "No one has the right or authority to commit me on that or any other political question."[33] By summer 1866, Grant believed that the president was jeopardizing the Union's victory in the war, and he complained, "A year ago, [Southerners] were willing to do anything; now they regard themselves as masters of the situation."[34] By alienating Grant, Johnson had created a powerful enemy who could seriously hamper the president's efforts to reassert control over Reconstruction policy, a fact that the Tennessean belatedly recognized.

The midterms were disastrous for Johnson, as the voters elected veto-proof Republican majorities to both houses of Congress. The results were such a setback for Johnson that Wendell Phillips, a well-known abolitionist, joked, "Let us pray to God that the president may continue to make mistakes."[35] The outgoing Thirty-Ninth Congress even called the Fortieth Congress into special session immediately (as opposed to waiting to convene until December 1867), thereby preventing Johnson from asserting control of Reconstruction during the recess. Perhaps most important, on March 2, the Thirty-Ninth Congress passed (over Johnson's veto) two key pieces of legislation that limited the president's control over Reconstruction: the Tenure of Office Act, which essentially prevented Johnson from removing any of his cabinet members without Senate approval, and "An Act to Provide for the More Efficient Government of the Rebel States." The second bill's preamble proclaimed that "no legal State governments or adequate protection for life or property now exists in the rebel States of Virginia, North Carolina, South Carolina, Georgia, Mississippi, Alabama, Louisiana, Florida, Texas and Arkansas; and . . . it is necessary that peace and good order should be enforced in said States until loyal and republican State governments can be legally established," and the law itself divided the South into five military districts overseen by "an officer of the army, not below the rank of brigadier-general."[36] Though the law's provisions empowered Johnson to appoint the generals in command of the military districts, it was clear that the War Department, rather than the White House, would be setting policy in these states.[37]

Because the law made the army the main implementer of Reconstruction policy, Grant, then the army's commanding general, became the defender of the Radicals' agenda, though his relationship with their most prominent leaders was complicated. The inquiry into the debacle at the Battle of the Crater, which had been driven by Radicals like Senator Sumner, left a sour taste in Grant's mouth, and he had aroused Radical suspicions by advocating amnesty for Robert E. Lee. Grant was concerned that harsh terms might alienate the South and imperil reunification; he wanted to end the war and bring the seceded states back into the Union quickly. Moreover, Grant requested that the units of black troops raised in the North be mustered out of the service. His goal seems to have been to deal with the growing chorus of complaints about black soldiers quickly, without investigating them. Though regiments of Southern blacks continued to serve (which allowed the federal government to control their behavior), Grant demonstrated that he was trying to strike a balance between quickly reunifying the nation and creating wide-reaching social change.[38] That being said, throughout 1866, Grant had shown a willingness to use the army to protect Southern blacks. For instance, in mid-January, he issued General Order No. 3, directing commanders to ensure that local officials were not disproportionately prosecuting blacks for crimes. That summer, Grant went even further, ordering local commanders to arrest and hold individuals charged with violent acts when civil authorities failed to prosecute such cases. In October that year, Grant resisted Johnson's pressure to send troops to Baltimore to buttress the city's Democratic administration against Maryland's Republican government; in doing so, Grant sent a subtle but unmistakable message that he was not the president's man. By summer 1867, the general was thoroughly alienated from the president. Though in 1862, Grant had declared to a friend, "So long as I hold a commission in the Army I have no views of my own to carry out. Whatever may be the orders of my superiors, and law, I will execute," now the general claimed that "Congress's will ought to be heeded."[39]

A festering crisis in Mexico provided Johnson with a possible way to elbow Grant aside and thereby reestablish White House control over Reconstruction. One consequence of the Mexican-American War was that it forced Mexico's political leaders to recognize that the country's disunity had essentially made it ripe for military conquest. As a result, during the 1850s, Mexico embraced a period of liberal reforms known as *la reforma*. The goal was to modernize the country by educating rural peasants and thereby foster the sort of industrial progress that would prevent a repeat of the Mexican-American War. In 1855, reformers overthrew Santa Anna in the Revolution of Ayutla, but within two years the country was mired in a civil war that pitted Liberals against Conservatives. Initially, the Conservatives seemed poised to win the war, but the Liberals turned the tide in late 1860, forcing their opponents to surrender in December that year. In March 1861, Benito Juárez, a staunch Liberal and president of Mexico's Supreme Court of Justice, was elected president. However, he faced daunting challenges: conservative guerillas continued fighting in the countryside, and the civil war had devastated Mexico's economy and infrastructure. Seeing no other option, on July 17, Juárez suspended interest payments on Mexico's debt, enraging Spain, Great Britain, and France. The three European powers signed a treaty in London on October 31, 1861, agreeing to coordinate their efforts to force Mexico to resume interest payments on its state debt. Within weeks, a fleet of British, Spanish, and French ships arrived off Mexico's coast, and before year's end European armies had seized various Mexican cities, including, Veracruz.

The United States, then mired in the Civil War, considered all but Great Britain's claims to be unjust but was hardly in a position to enforce the Monroe Doctrine's terms (which the Europeans never recognized in any event). Seeing the potential threat of having European countries intervening in Mexican affairs while its own country was distracted and weakened by the Civil War, the Lincoln administration offered to pay the arrearages on Mexico's debt. The European powers refused, and though the United States remained officially neutral in the events that followed, there were some minor skirmishes between British ships dispatched to the Gulf of Mexico and American ships enforcing the blockade of the Confederacy. Over the next eighteen months, European and Mexican forces fought for control of Mexico. Veracruz changed hands in 1862 and 1863. In spring 1863, Juárez and his cabinet fled to Chihuahua, where they were a government in exile until 1867. In the meantime, French emperor Napoleon III arranged for Maximilian, the younger brother of Austrian emperor Francis Joseph, to become emperor of Mexico, though he was widely considered to be a French puppet. One of Maximilian's biggest problems was the United States, which, though officially neutral in the conflict, nevertheless made it clear that it viewed the imposition of a puppet monarchy on Mexico by European powers as a threat to its own interests. Despite the Civil War, Secretary of State Seward made it clear that the United States took a dim view of the French-backed government in Mexico, and in 1864, the House unanimously demanded that the French withdraw from Mexico. A combination of US pressure and mounting troubles at home convinced Napoleon to comply, and in spring 1866, France announced its forces would leave Mexico shortly.[40]

Grant strongly opposed Maximilian's regime and believed that the United States should intervene on behalf of Juárez's government in exile. Don Matias Romero, Mexico's minister to the United States, recalled meeting Grant in 1864 and the general's insistence "that the attempt to set up a monarchy in Mexico with foreign bayonets was a step intended to co-operate in the downfall of republican institutions on this continent."[41] Like many Americans, Grant believed that reestablishing republican government in Mexico using an army composed of former Confederates and Union soldiers would help reunite the United States by creating a common enemy that all Americans—North and South—could fight.[42] Furthermore, Napoleon III had agreed to American demands that the French cut off aid to Maximilian's regime, all but ensuring a relatively easy fight.

Johnson named his old friend Lewis A. Campbell minister to Mexico, and hit upon the idea of ordering Grant to accompany Campbell to Mexico, thereby removing the troublesome general from Washington. Johnson hoped that with Grant out of the way, General Sherman would implement the president's policies. On October 17, Johnson suggested that Grant accompany Campbell to Mexico, and the general, unaware of Johnson's ulterior motives, agreed. However, over the next four days, Grant pieced together Johnson's plan, and on October 21, he told the president that he would not go to Mexico, citing the fact that he was "not fitted either by education or taste" for a diplomatic mission.[43] Johnson was determined not to take no for an answer, and during a cabinet meeting on October 23, he inquired of Seward whether the State Department had prepared Grant's instructions for the mission to Mexico. Grant was startled by Johnson's inquiry and reminded the president that he did not wish to go to Mexico. Furious, Johnson turned to Attorney General Henry Stanbery and asked if there was any legal basis for Grant to refuse an order from the president. Before Stanbery could fully answer, Grant interjected that he was subject to the president's orders only in military matters, and the mission in question was diplomatic. Furthermore, Grant declared, "No power on earth can compel me to do it." Chastened, Johnson let the matter drop, but later in the day Grant complained to some of his subordinates of the president's "scheme to get him out of the way in case of trouble here between Congress and [Johnson]."[44]

Meanwhile, things got worse for Johnson. On January 7, 1867, the House voted overwhelmingly to authorize its Judiciary Committee to investigate the president's conduct in discharging executive duties. Despite an intensive and grueling investigation, the committee voted 5 to 4 on June 3 not to recommend impeachment. But it was a close vote and represented a veiled threat to Johnson that he chose to ignore. On June 20, 1867, less than three weeks after the Judiciary Committee vote, Johnson curtailed the powers of the commanders of the South's five military districts, and on August 5, he requested Secretary of War Stanton's resignation. Johnson had made it known days earlier to Grant that he was thinking of firing Stanton, and the general pushed back; in a letter to the president, Grant noted that the Tenure of Office Act protected Stanton.[45] Grant's response belied his personal dislike of Stanton; Julia Grant recalled her husband saying at the time, "Stanton would have gone, and on a double-quick, long ago if I had been President."[46] Despite Grant's advice, Johnson pushed ahead with his plan to oust Stanton from the War Department and thereby reassert control of Reconstruction. When Stanton refused to resign, Johnson suspended him on August 12 and then appointed Grant as interim secretary of war, perhaps in the hope of blunting Radical opposition to Stanton's removal. Grant took the position in part because he believed it necessary to consolidate the gains from the war.[47]

It did not take Grant long to prove himself a thorn in Johnson's side. Almost immediately, the two men clashed over how to interpret the Third Reconstruction Act. Grant believed that the act gave him, as interim secretary of war, supervisory powers over the district commanders. This interpretation ensured that the War Department, rather than the White House, would continue to control the implementation of Reconstruction policy. Ultimately, Johnson forced Grant to accept his interpretation of the act—namely, that the act made district commanders independent of all control—which was a Pyrrhic victory: while Grant did not directly control district commanders, neither did the president. The net effect was to magnify, rather than diminish, Grant's control over Reconstruction because it remained a fundamentally military operation and the district commanders answered to Grant in his role as general in chief of the army.[48]

Under the terms of the Tenure of Office Act, Johnson had to explain his removal of Stanton to Congress once it reconvened. In his third annual message to Congress, in December 1867, Johnson boldly declared:

> On this momentous question [Reconstruction] and some of the
> measures growing out of it I have had the misfortune to differ
> from Congress, and have expressed my convictions without re-
> serve, though with becoming deference to the opinion of the leg-
> islative department. Those convictions are not only unchanged,
> but strengthened by subsequent events.[49]

A few days later, the Judiciary Committee reversed itself, voting 5 to
4 for impeachment. The House rejected the Judiciary Committee's recommendation by 57 to 108, but the fight was far from over.

On January 11, 1868, Grant met with Johnson and informed him
that if the Senate rejected Johnson's reasons for removing Stanton, the
general could not remain as secretary of war *ad interim*; doing so
could expose Grant to fines or even imprisonment.[50] Two days later,
the Senate refused to accede to Stanton's removal, and the following
morning Grant locked the secretary's office and gave the keys to Assistant Adjutant General Edward Townsend, who in turn gave them
to Stanton. Johnson accused Grant of having deceived the president
of his intentions. This precipitated a bitter series of charges and coun-
tercharges that did nothing to improve relations between the two men,
especially after Grant refused Johnson's directive to ignore all orders
emanating from the War Department unless he knew they had the
president's sanction. Not content to suffer Stanton to be his secretary
of war for the year left in his term, on February 21, Johnson appointed
General Lorenzo Thomas to the position *ad interim* and notified Stanton of his dismissal. Johnson ordered Thomas to physically remove
Stanton from the War Department. This initiated a comical situation
in which Stanton refused to vacate his position, remaining barricaded
in the office day and night.

Johnson's actions were the final straw, convincing many congressional Republicans he had to go. On February 24, the House voted
126 to 47 to impeach the president of the United States, the first time
in the nation's history this had happened. A week later, the House formally adopted eleven articles of impeachment against Johnson, and
on March 5, the president's trial began in the Senate. Johnson managed to keep his office by a single vote, a fact that had more to do
with many senators' uneasiness about his replacement—Senate President Pro Tempore Benjamin F. Wade—than it did with Johnson's

guilt.[51] Recognizing that her husband would likely be the next president, Julia Grant was relieved that the Senate did not remove Johnson from office, fearing potential repercussions for Grant's presidency.[52] Ominously, however, former Confederates, who only three years earlier worried about the harsh terms they expected Johnson to exact on the South, celebrated the president's acquittal with fireworks and celebratory gunfire.[53] The lame duck president repaid their support with a pair of amnesty proclamations that restored suffrage to most former Confederates.[54]

All of this took place against the backdrop of the upcoming presidential election. The Republican Party was hopelessly fractured on most issues; with slavery abolished, the party struggled to redefine itself. As early as summer 1867, party insiders began a "Grant for President" campaign, seeing the popular general as the only potential candidate who had a chance of uniting the party. On May 21, 1868, the delegates to the Republican National Convention unanimously nominated Grant on the first ballot. To do otherwise would have forced the country to "fight all our old political issues all over again," noted Senator John Sherman. Later, Sherman called the election of Grant the Republicans' "only salvation from serious trouble," a reflection of the threat the party's deep factionalism posed to its electoral success.[55] On the fifth ballot, the delegates selected Speaker of the House Schuyler Colfax for vice president. Colfax was the Radicals' candidate, and his selection for the second slot on the ticket was designed to stoke their enthusiasm.[56] Once news of his nomination reached him, Grant made only a short public statement. Saying he was "unaccustomed to public speaking," the Republican nominee claimed "it is impossible for me to find appropriate language to thank you."[57] However, in what was clearly a jab at Johnson, Grant promised that he "shall have no policy of my own to interfere against the will of the people," a very Whig position.[58] Over the next eight years, Grant's tense relations with Congress tested that promise more than once.

In becoming a candidate for president, Grant believed he was saving the gains of the war from the politicians, at one point writing to General Sherman that he "could not back down, as it seems to me, leaving the contest for power for the next four years between mere trading politicians, the elevation of whom, no matter which party won, would lose to us, largely, the results of the costly war which we have gone through."[59] General Philip Sheridan wrote to Grant and refused to congratulate the nominee because "I believe you are sacrificing personal interests and comforts to give the Country a civil victory."[60] Grant endorsed the Republican Party's 1868 platform (which mostly congratulated the Republicans for winning the war, called for Congress to repay the national debt, and committed the United States to an open immigration policy). Beyond that, he refused to commit himself on specific issues lest doing so limit his freedom of action as president.[61] He also did not campaign for the presidency, instead taking several weeks to tour forts in the West. Grant believed that his nomination would force the Democrats "to adopt a good platform and put upon it a reliable man who, if elected, will disappoint the Copperhead element of their party."[62] Contrary to Grant's prediction, on July 4, the Democrats nominated former New York governor Horatio Seymour for president and former US representative and senator Francis Preston Blair Jr. for vice president. During the war, Seymour had been a vociferous critic of the Lincoln administration, while Blair (whose brother was Lincoln's postmaster general, Montgomery Blair) opposed congressional Reconstruction. Historian Brooks D. Simpson described the 1868 presidential campaign as "a refighting of the war" designed to "obscure those issues that might divide [Republican] party regulars."[63] Grant's campaign slogan was simple and evocative, promising a program all Republicans could embrace: "Let us have peace."

During the campaign, General Order No. 11, by which Grant had tried to expel Jews from his military district in 1862, came back to haunt him. Democrats appealed to Jews, reminding them of the order, and letters from Jews deluged Grant's campaign across the United States asking about it. Grant eventually drafted a letter to a friend, Isaac Morris, in which he claimed to have "no prejudice against sect or race" but to want "each individual to be judged by his own merit."[64] The letter, which was designed for public consumption, seemed to allay many Jews' concerns about Grant, and despite the controversy, all signs pointed to his winning the presidency. Grant spent election night at Elihu Washburne's home in Galena, quietly absorbing election returns as they came in on a specially installed telegraph line. He won 52.7 percent of the popular vote to Seymour's 47.3 percent. In the Electoral College, Grant's total was commanding: he won 214 votes (including those of South Carolina, North Carolina, Florida, Tennessee, Alabama, and Arkansas) to Seymour's 80. Arriving home the next morning, he told Julia, "I'm afraid I'm elected."[65]

Alarmingly, however, a majority of white males voted for Seymour, and Grant's popularity among voters was greater than that of the Republican Party's other candidates, suggesting the voters supported him but not the party's platform.[66] This was not unexpected; one of the reasons Republicans selected Grant was that he was the most popular man in America in 1868 and all but ensured the party would win the White House. Nevertheless, translating Grant's personal popularity into sustained support for the Republican legislative agenda (to the degree that such a thing existed) was one of the main challenges facing the new administration and one reason for the failures Grant cited in his eighth annual message to Congress.

Three

"A Great Soldier Might Be a Baby Politician"

NEWLY ELECTED REPUBLICAN representative George Frisbie Hoar of Massachusetts (brother of Grant's first attorney general, Ebenezer Rockwood Hoar) recalled that following the 1868 presidential election, "the feeling everywhere among the Republicans in Washington and throughout the North was of exultant and confident courage."[1] Representative James G. Blaine, soon to become speaker of the House, recalled that Grant took the oath of office "amid a great display of popular enthusiasm."[2]

In his inaugural address, Grant laid out his four priorities as president. First, he pointed to the ongoing process of Reconstruction, a challenge "preceding Administrations have never had to deal with." In confronting the smoldering resentment caused by the war, Grant promised to act "calmly, without prejudice, hate, or sectional pride; remembering that the greatest good for the greatest number is the object to be attained." Second, Grant mentioned the federal debt that had been contracted to pay for the war and promised "payment of this principle and interest, as well as a return to a specie basis, as soon as it can be accomplished without material detriment to the debtor class, or to the country at large." Third, with regard to foreign affairs, Grant said little, other than to promise, "I would protect the rights of all nations demanding equal respect for our own; but if others depart from this rule, in their dealings with us, we may be compelled to follow their precedent." Fourth, and of greatest consequence, Grant discussed the enfranchisement of African Americans. Calling this the issue most "likely to agitate the public," he asserted, "I entertain the hope and express the desire" the Fifteenth Amendment would be ratified and that it would settle the issue permanently.[3]

Grant ran for the presidency believing he had to do so to save Reconstruction from the politicians, not to advance the Republican Party's interests. Having won the election and being clearly more popular than Republicans generally, Grant believed he owed party leaders no deference. He was widely reported to have said in February 1869, "I am not the representative of a political party, though a party voted for me."[4] While this was a noble sentiment, it was naïve to believe he could effectively govern without placating the Republican Party's various factions. Even before Grant was inaugurated, members of the party's various factions began jockeying for position and influence with the new administration. Less than a month into his presidency, Grant complained to his sister, "Office-seeking in this country, I regret to say, is getting to be one of the industries of the age. It gives me no peace."[5]

Congress reconvened March 4, and the following day Grant submitted his cabinet nominees. Though all were solidly Republican, historian William B. Hesseltine pointed out that none "would have been chosen by the politicians," a clear sign that Grant intended to govern independently of congressional Republicans.[6] Recalling this period years later, William H. Crook (who was Lincoln's bodyguard and worked at the White House into Woodrow Wilson's administration) noted, "The President's determination not to be ruled by party considerations or by outside advice led to an apparent haste and secrecy which really made a great deal of trouble."[7] Grant's failure to consult with party leaders offended many important Republicans; as George F. Hoar noted, "during the controversy with Andrew Johnson, the members of the two Houses of Congress had come to think that they were entitled to control all the appointments of civil officers in their own States and Districts and they were ready with scarce an exception to stand by each other in this demand," which did not bode well for harmonious relations between the executive and legislative branches.[8]

Grant's cabinet choices worried men like Senator Sherman, a former Whig who saw them as clear evidence of the president's militaristic impulses and ignorance of American political traditions. Sherman recalled, "The impression prevailed that the President regarded these heads of departments, invested by law with specific and independent duties, as mere subordinates, whose functions he might assume. . . . The President has no more right to control or exercise the powers conferred by law upon [cabinet secretaries] than they have to control him in the discharge of his duties."[9] This was more or less the argument that the Radicals had made in framing the Tenure of Office Act, and it ensured that the battles of the Johnson era were far from over. In fact, the controversy over Grant's cabinet illustrates some important elements of political life in the capital following the Civil War. The war had necessitated a massive expansion in federal power, most of which accrued to the executive, and the showdown between Johnson and the Radicals in Congress can be understood in part as an attempt to rebalance that dynamic. Many congressional Republicans were former Whigs who believed that the executive branch should defer to the legislative. In his speech accepting the Republican nomination and in his inaugural address, Grant seemed to concede this, referring in the former to the president as a "purely administrative officer" and promising in the latter to "on all subjects, have a policy to recommend, but none to enforce against the will of the people."[10] These were exactly the sentiments that anti-Johnson Republicans wanted to hear from the new president. But by selecting cabinet members without consulting prominent Republicans, Grant appeared to violate his promises to defer to Congress.

These political missteps led historian Henry Adams (great grandson and grandson of former presidents) to complain "a great soldier might be a baby politician."[11] Undoubtedly, some of the controversy had to do with frustrated ambition, not abstract arguments about the proper deference the executive owed to the legislative branch. For instance, Senator Charles Sumner expected to be appointed secretary of state. On its face, this was reasonable: Sumner was one of the most prominent Senate Radicals and a man who had literally bled for the cause (Congressman Preston Brooks of South Carolina had caned Sumner unconscious on the Senate floor in May 1856, and it took nearly three years for him to recover sufficiently to return to work). Since 1861, Sumner had been chairman of the Committee on Foreign Relations, giving him the best claim to the State Department. From his perch on the committee, Sumner exercised what one contemporary called "a domineering power in this branch of public service."[12] What doomed Sumner's chances was his style, which often shaded in the pompous, a fact captured by a remark that Grant allegedly made about him. When told that Sumner did not believe in the Bible, Grant is supposed to have replied, "Well, he didn't write it."[13] Grant soon came to loathe Sumner, who he claimed "has abused me in a way I have never suffered from any other man living!"[14]

Instead of Sumner, Grant appointed his old friend and patron, Representative Elihu Washburne, secretary of state, though only temporarily; both men understood that the appointment was designed to enhance Washburne's prestige so he could more effectively function as US minister to France.[15] Washburne served only eleven days as secretary of state—still the shortest tenure in US history—and during that time the president sought a replacement. Grant's friend and staffer Adam Badeau suggested a former US minister to the Austrian Empire, John Lothrop Motley. In that position, Motley had acquitted himself well, working successfully with other US diplomats to prevent European recognition of the Confederacy. Moreover, Motley actively campaigned for Grant during the 1868 election, which certainly recommended him for the position. Despite Motley's obvious competence and the diplomat's support of Grant's presidential bid, he was passed over, for two reasons. The first was stylistic: after meeting Motley in person, Grant complained to Badeau that the diplomat "parts his hair in the middle, and carries a single eyeglass," a statement Badeau interpreted as meaning that Motley was too "foreign" for Grant's taste.[16] The second consideration was political: Motley was widely perceived as politically allied with Charles Sumner. In fact, when Grant nominated Motley to be minister to Great Britain, the president let it be known that he did so "as a compliment" to Sumner, a move that had the perverse effect of antagonizing the senator.[17]

To succeed Washburne, Grant turned to former New York governor Hamilton Fish. Sixty years old at the time of his appointment, Fish had represented New York in the US House and the Senate, and during the war he had vigorously supported the Union cause in a variety of voluntary capacities. In his early years, Fish was a Whig, and he migrated to the Republican Party in the mid-1850s, though he "never embraced the slavery issue as the main concern of American politics."[18] Now out of politics for more than a decade, Fish was astonished when he learned that Grant had nominated him to head the State Department. From Grant's perspective, Fish was the ideal candidate because he was not beholden to any political faction and did not plan to use his position as a stepping-stone to the presidency.[19] Yet Fish was reluctant to take the position; the New Yorker telegraphed the president and told him he would not accept the nomination. Grant begged Fish to reconsider, adding, "should you not like the position, you can withdraw after the adjournment of Congress."[20] This seemed to quiet Fish's concerns, and he quickly became one Grant's most trusted advisors, serving until the end of his second term.[21]

For Treasury secretary, Grant selected Alexander T. Stewart, owner of New York's largest department store, A.T. Stewart & Co. The Irish-born Stewart immigrated to the United States in 1818 and, using several thousand dollars he inherited, opened his first dry-goods store in 1823. By 1869, Stewart was the most successful merchant in the United States, which gave Grant the "utmost confidence in [his] ability to manage the affairs of the Treasury Dept."[22] Unfortunately for Stewart and for Grant, the 1789 law that established the Treasury Department contained a section mandating that "no person appointed to any office instituted by the Act, shall directly or indirectly be concerned or interested in carrying on the business of trade or commerce."[23] Grant claimed that he selected Stewart because of the latter's business success, saying, "I wanted the Treasury conducted on strict business principles," and the president tried in vain to get the Senate to exempt Stewart from the law, but Sumner worked to frustrate a compromise that might have allowed Stewart to serve as Treasury secretary.[24] Adding insult to injury, Sumner was rather smug about the whole episode, writing to a friend that he hoped "General Grant will make no more mistakes."[25] The fiasco—and Sumner's condescending attitude—did nothing to improve Grant's relationship with him.

There was another element to Stewart's nomination that in retrospect became an important issue in Grant's choice of subordinates: Grant had an uncomfortably close relationship with the country's titans of industry, often accepting gifts or special treatment from them. For instance, shortly before moving into the White House, Grant sold the house on I Street that he had bought in 1865. Initially, Grant had agreed to sell it to Washington's mayor, Sayles J. Bowen, for $40,000. Bowen made an initial payment to Grant of $1,000, but when Stewart, representing a group of prominent New York Republicans and business leaders, approached Grant about selling the house to them for $65,000, the president-elect decided to take the higher price. Once the sale was final, Grant returned the $1,000 to Bowen, and Stewart gifted the house to William T. Sherman. The entire transaction looked like influence peddling, especially given the fact that Stewart had handed Grant the $65,000 check in late February and less than a month later, the newly inaugurated president appointed him Treasury secretary. Though Grant steadfastly asserted that these transactions in no way influenced his judgment, the appearance of corruption (what today we would call "the optics") created a narrative that came to dominate his presidency. Following the debacle over Stewart, Grant nominated former Massachusetts governor George S. Boutwell for Treasury secretary. Though Boutwell had shown little previous interest in fiscal matters, he had strong Republican credentials that made him a good choice for the cabinet: earlier in the decade, he had doggedly supported freedmen's rights, and as James G. Blaine noted in his memoirs, Boutwell "made one of the strongest and most pointed arguments delivered in Congress for the adoption of the Fifteenth Amendment."[26] Boutwell was also an early champion of impeaching Andrew Johnson, even serving as one of the managers of the president's trial in the Senate.[27]

Initially, Grant gave the War Department to his closest friend, John A. Rawlins. Only thirty-eight at the time of his nomination, Rawlins was born in Galena and became acquainted with Grant when assigned to the latter's headquarters early in the war. He eventually became Grant's chief of staff, though in 1863 he developed tuberculosis (the ailment that had killed his wife). Not wanting to leave Grant's side, Rawlins ignored his doctors' requests that he go to Arizona, instead remaining secretary of war until his death in September 1869. Six weeks later, Grant appointed William W. Belknap, a Union Army general and Iowa's former collector of internal revenue. Belknap served for nearly the rest of Grant's presidency, though he left under a cloud of scandal, becoming the first cabinet secretary in US history to be impeached (a fact that further added to the general impression that Grant's administration was particularly corrupt).

For attorney general, Grant nominated Ebenezer Rockwood Hoar, then serving as an associate justice of the Massachusetts Supreme Judicial Court. Hoar was an antislavery Whig who migrated to the Republican Party in the mid-1850s, and he had served a few years in the Massachusetts Senate before becoming a judge of common pleas in Boston in 1849. Though Hoar opposed Johnson's impeachment, his antislavery bona fides were unquestionable, and his appointment appears to have been a sop to Massachusetts's Republicans. Representative George Hoar recalled his brother's appointment this way: "[I]t seemed quite important that General Grant, who had no experience whatever in political life, should have some person among his counselors who had the full confidence of the leaders of Congress."[28] Hoar's first task in his new position was delivering to Grant the decidedly unhappy news that Stewart's appointment to the Treasury Department was illegal. Things did not improve from there: many of Hoar's cabinet colleagues disliked him (Fish thought him "supercilious"), and that December Grant tried to rid himself of Hoar by nominating him to be an associate justice of the Supreme Court. Unfortunately for the president, Hoar by then had made powerful enemies in the Senate, and the nomination was permanently tabled.

Because Pennsylvania was a critical state (it was the second-largest electoral bloc in the United States and had delivered the largest single bloc of electoral votes to Grant in 1868), its Republicans expected the new president to reward them by taking a Pennsylvanian into the cabinet. Shortly before the inauguration, Grant promised a delegation of Pennsylvanian Republicans that the Keystone State would be rewarded with a cabinet post. Making good on that pledge, Grant nominated Philadelphia businessman Adolph E. Borie to be secretary of the navy. A former Whig, Borie became a Republican in the late 1850s and had supported Lincoln's 1860 bid for the presidency. Once the war broke out, Borie was a committed Unionist who served as the Philadelphia Union League's vice president. Beyond being Grant's close personal friend, Borie's sole qualification seems to have been that he was not allied with the Republican political machine controlled by Pennsylvania's senior senator, Simon Cameron. Blaine disparaged the appointment in his memoirs, describing Borie as lacking "aptitude or desire for public affairs."[29] Borie's term of office was brief; he delegated most of his responsibilities to Vice Admiral David Porter. Even with Porter doing most of the day-to-day work of the department, Borie found the job too stressful and resigned June 25, 1869; his only notable accomplishment was desegregating the Washington Navy Yard. Grant then appointed George M. Robeson to succeed Borie at the Navy Department. A former public prosecutor and brigadier general, Robeson was then New Jersey's attorney general. Robeson and Fish were the only two members of Grant's cabinet to serve throughout the president's two terms.

For the Interior Department, Grant chose former Ohio governor and state senator Jacob D. Cox, who had been a brigadier general during the war and was widely known for his strong abolitionism. The Interior Department was an incredibly important appointment given Grant's interest in improving US-Native American relations. Yet Cox was controversial: as postwar governor of Ohio, he had opposed enfranchising African Americans and even went so far as to advocate racial segregation. Not surprisingly, Cox and Grant soon found themselves at cross-purposes, with the interior secretary opposing one of the administration's signature policies, the doomed attempt to annex Santo Domingo. After leaving the presidency, Grant reflected, "the trouble was that General Cox thought the Interior Department was the whole government, and that Cox was the Interior Department. I had to point out to him in very plain language that there were three controlling branches of the government and that I was the head of one of these, and would like to be so considered by the Secretary of the Interior."[30] Finally, Grant appointed John A.J. Creswell postmaster general. A former US senator and representative from Maryland, Creswell had been a Whig and a Democrat before becoming a Republican. He distinguished himself during the war as a passionate and vocal Unionist. During the nineteenth century, the post office was the richest source of patronage of all cabinet departments, and Creswell, who was a Radical, appointed more African Americans than any of his predecessors. Moreover, he improved the speed of mail service, reduced the cost of international shipping, and improved the post office's efficiency.[31]

These were far from the only nominations the incoming president made, and in the days following Grant's inauguration, the White House was deluged by brooms—many emblazoned with the legend "make a clean sweep"—that testified to Republicans' desires to replace Johnson's appointees with their own.[32] Only a few months into the new administration, Henry Adams described Grant as "penned up in the White House . . . surrounded by a hungry army of political adventurers whose trade was an object of popular odium or contempt."[33] During the war, Grant had given his subordinates wide latitude, and he continued this practice as president; the lack of oversight contributed to the scandals that plagued his administration during the second term. However, from the beginning, the president's nominations of his family members, political supporters, and personal friends to government office aggravated reformers who had hoped Grant would leverage his popularity to end the tradition of appointing political supporters to government office. Adams noted that Grant's appointments "made Congress madder than the Devil."[34] Eventually, Pennsylvania's Republicans extracted a compromise from Grant: though the president had set his own course on the cabinet appointments, he promised to consult with them on most of the appointments made in their state. Later the same day, he told another congressional delegation that he would follow Lincoln's policy of soliciting recommendations from senators and representatives before making appointments, though a few days later he made it known that he wanted all applications to come through cabinet secretaries rather than directly to him.[35]

That control of appointments was to be a major issue in Grant's presidency was reinforced by the continuing fight over the Tenure of Office Act. Grant saw the law, which Congress had enacted to solidify its control of Reconstruction, as an injudicious curtailment of presidential power. A long as it remained on the books, Grant promised to appoint people only to vacant offices. Congress thus came under enormous pressure to repeal or modify the act from a wide variety of individuals, including Democrats, who saw repeal of the act as vindication of Johnson, and Republicans, who were eager to use patronage to strengthen the party. In an effort to ingratiate himself with Grant, Representative Benjamin F. Butler of Massachusetts (nicknamed "Beast" for his allegedly harsh treatment of New Orleans civilians while he served as military governor during the war) tried to engineer the repeal of the Tenure of Office Act before inauguration day. While Butler succeeded in getting the House to vote 121 to 47 to repeal the law, the Senate rejected the measure, and the law remained when Grant became president. Yet the effort to repeal it continued, and after a week of debate, the Senate offered to "suspend" the law temporarily, allowing Grant to fire Johnson's appointees without conceding the principle of legislative supremacy. When this proved unsatisfactory to the new president, the Senate offered another compromise: an amendment to the law that gave Grant full authority to remove members of his cabinet. This, too, was unsatisfactory to Grant, but fortunately for the president, the House defeated the bill, protecting him from being in the awkward position of having to veto it. The Senate and the House then formed a conference committee to develop a bill that suited both chambers and the president. Ultimately, the bill Congress sent to the White House was vague and therefore subject to conflicting interpretations, and Grant's supporters urged the president to veto it. Grant looked at the situation differently, however, as historian William B. Hesseltine noted, "Practically, [the president] had gained a modification which removed most of his objections, and with the realism which characterized all his acts he ignored the theoretical fact that the law was not repealed. His explanation was that he did not want to 'seem captious' about the matter."[36] In doing so, Grant signaled that he would not allow the perfect to become the enemy of the "good enough," though this attitude infuriated more idealistic Republicans, who believed Grant was violating his campaign promises.

Grant quickly settled into a routine in the White House: the cabinet typically met on Tuesday afternoons. Grant worked in "fits and starts" and (as had been his practice in the army) delegated responsibilities; the White House employed four personal secretaries: Grant's brother-in-law, Frederick Dent; Horace Porter; Orville Babcock; and (for a time) Robert Douglas, son of the famous late senator from Illinois, Stephen A. Douglas.[37] Visitors to the White House met with Dent, who decided which callers would be admitted to see the president and which would be referred to one of Grant's secretaries (or simply sent away).[38] Though Grant complained frequently of being busy, the presidency was then essentially a seasonal job, and the president completely separated "his business life from his social life."[39] Due to the job's seasonal nature and the president's dislike of Congress, the

Grants usually summered in Long Branch, New Jersey (in a house purchased for them by several prominent businessmen), often for six to eight weeks.[40] His frequent absences from the capital reflected the fact that Grant did not enjoy the presidency; he generally preferred to be called "General Grant," even while in office. Even after his death, Julia referred to him by his military rank and never as "President Grant."[41] Grant ended his memoirs in 1865, despite writing them in 1885, and complained to Julia in 1876 that he wished his presidency "was over," saying that once he left the White House he "never want[ed] to see it again."[42] Late in his presidency, Democrats in the House tried to create a scandal by demanding information regarding "where Executive acts have, within the last seven years, been performed," a tacit rebuke of his frequent absences from Washington. Grant shot back a caustic reply in which he refused to comply with the request and lectured the House on the long history of presidents taking vacations during their times in office.[43]

By contrast, Julia loved living in the White House and reveled in being first lady of the United States. When the Grants moved into the White House, Julia initiated a series of sweeping changes; according to her memoirs, she found the mansion dilapidated and its staff uncouth. Julia undertook a program to improve the White House by adding two large and expensive chandeliers to the East Room and a grand stairway at the end of the west corridor, as well as tapestries, clocks, and a painting of Lincoln.[44] She also insisted that the mansion's staff dress formally and banned them from smoking while on duty (ironic, given her husband's well-known affinity for cigars). Yet Julia Grant cared about the mansion's staff; Grant's executive clerk, William H. Crook, recalled that she "was particularly anxious that servants should be thrifty and saving. She urged them to begin to buy homes, that they might be more independent and self-respecting. One of the footmen owes the fact that he owns the home he now lives in to her advice."[45] Fearing for her husband's safety in the wake of Lincoln's assassination, and desirous of some privacy for her family, Julia ordered the mansion's grounds closed in order to prevent locals from wandering onto the White House's lawn, though Grant dismissed the bodyguards who had been hired following Lincoln's assassination.[46] The first family remained "very popular with the people," doorman Thomas F. Pendel recalled, noting "the number of people who called on them, socially, in the evening, was simply wonderful."[47] In many ways, this was due to Julia, who transformed the capital's social life, hosting two weekly receptions—one in the afternoon and another in the evening—where she and the various cabinet secretaries' wives greeted people. After leaving the White House, Julia described her eight years there as "like a bright and beautiful dream."[48]

Over his two terms, Grant appointed four justices to the Supreme Court, more than all but three of his predecessors (George Washington, Andrew Jackson, and Abraham Lincoln). Three of those nominations came during Grant's first term. The large number of appointments resulted from the Judiciary Act of 1869, which increased the number of seats on the Supreme Court and ended the practice of having justices ride circuit by creating permanent judgeships for all federal courts. Shortly after Grant's election, Justice Robert C. Grier, who was extremely frail, came under enormous pressure to retire. Grier finally decided to do so at the end of the year, and Grant nominated former secretary of war Edwin Stanton, largely because of Republican pressure and to repay Stanton for campaigning for Grant the previous year. However, Stanton died shortly after being confirmed without ever taking his seat. Thus, a few days after Grier actually stepped down from the court at the end of January 1870, Grant nominated former Pennsylvania Supreme Court justice William Strong. An abolitionist Democrat who joined the Republican Party in the late 1850s, Strong was sworn in March 14, 1870. To fill a newly created seat on the court, Grant nominated New Jersey lawyer Joseph P. Bradley, who had earned a national reputation as a commercial litigator; he was sworn in a week after Strong. Shortly after the 1872 presidential election, Associate Justice Samuel Nelson stepped down from the court. To replace him, Grant nominated chief justice of the New York Court of Appeals Ward Hunt, who was closely associated with the Empire State's political boss, Roscoe Conkling.

The change in the court's composition had a demonstrable impact on several administration policies. For instance, in 1870, the Supreme Court ruled in *Hepburn v. Griswold* that aspects of the 1862 Legal Tender Acts, which had authorized the creation of paper currency (greenbacks) not backed by specie, were unconstitutional. Crucially, the federal government had mandated that creditors had to accept these notes, even for debts incurred before the act's passage, which naturally made the bill controversial. The court was split on this decision, 5 to 3 (there were only eight members when the court heard the case), and Chief Justice Salmon P. Chase, who as Lincoln's Treasury secretary had been instrumental in coordinating the federal government's efforts to finance the war (including devising the Legal Tender Act), joined the majority in ruling the law unconstitutional. Chase even wrote the majority opinion, asserting that the Legal Tender Act's requirement that creditors accept greenbacks violated the Fifth Amendment because it deprived creditors of their property without due process of law. Following Bradley and Strong's confirmations, the court revisited the constitutionality of greenbacks in two cases: *Knox v. Lee* and *Parker v. Davis*, both decided in 1871. These cases affirmed the constitutionality of the Legal Tender Act as a justifiable response to the emergency of the Civil War. Chase again voted against the constitutionality of the greenbacks, but this time he was in the minority, because Bradley and Strong joined the majority, which ruled 5 to 4 in favor of the Legal Tender Act. In short, Grant's appointees to the court provided the margin of victory in these cases and, as a result, played a key role in shaping American monetary policy in the last half of the nineteenth century. This should not be underestimated; monetary policy was a key issue facing the new administration, and it exposed several fault lines in the Republican Party. Some historians have even argued that the president selected justices he knew would sustain the Legal Tender Act, a demonstration of the incredibly important role monetary policy played in Grant's administration.[49]

Next to Reconstruction, the "currency question," as it was called, "is what most interest[ed] the mind of the American people" in the late 1860s.[50] To fund the war, the federal government had circulated $500 million in greenbacks and lacked the gold to redeem all of this paper. Beginning almost with the cessation of hostilities, the Johnson administration began withdrawing greenbacks from circulation, destroying $72 million between October 1865 and summer 1868.[51] Following the end of the war, the federal government cut back on its purchases of war materials, slowing the economy. Doing so seriously weakened the economy by reducing the supply of money in circulation, thereby causing prices to decline (a process known as deflation). In addition, Congress had lowered or eliminated tariffs and taxes on incomes, thereby seriously reducing the federal government's revenue.

On March 18, 1869, Grant signed the Public Credit Act, which committed the United States to redeem the bonds used to finance the war with gold. Within weeks, the Treasury Department was purchasing approximately $2.5 million in greenbacks per month.[52] Though the Republicans had no coherent platform on monetary policy, Grant committed himself to continuing Johnson's contractionist policies, which laid the groundwork for the administration's first major crisis, the New York Gold Conspiracy.

The two main players in the scandal were James Fisk and Jay Gould. Fisk was a pudgy and flamboyant thirty-four-year-old who made a fortune in government contracts during the war. Described by Henry Adams as "coarse, noisy, boastful, ignorant," Fisk had worked for Daniel Drew in the latter's successful attempt to win control of the Erie Railroad.[53] Drew rewarded Fisk by making him a member of the railroad's board of directors. It was in this position that Fisk met Jay Gould, a Pennsylvanian railroad speculator. Gould's biographer asserts that Gould "made a bad impression and he did not much care. He labored in a pit where the devil took the hindmost."[54] Together, Fisk and Gould successfully conspired to wrest control of the railroad from Drew, and they soon became notorious for their ruthlessness and greed. Initially, their interest in gold was a means to an end—improving their railroad's finances. From September 1868 to March 1869, the price of gold tumbled from $145 an ounce to $130.25, its lowest price in three years.[55] The falling price of gold added to farmers' woes because the international price for crops was fixed in gold, but they were paid in currency; thus, as the price of gold sank, so too did the number of dollars farmers could expect for their crops, depressing railroad earnings.[56] Raising the price of gold would increase the price of grain and other crops relative to paper currency and make American crops more attractive to European consumers. This would give farmers an incentive to export their crops, which would necessitate shipping them east on the Erie Railroad, increasing the railroad's profits. Gould and Fisk convinced themselves that Grant, always eager to help average Americans (one of his first acts as president was to cut federal employees' hours to eight per day but not cut their pay) would tacitly sanction their scheme to corner the gold market (or at least do nothing to stop it).[57] On a certain level, this was a sound conclusion; after all, Treasury Secretary Boutwell recalled that in mid-1869, the president thought "it was undesirable to force down the price of gold. . . . His idea was that if gold should fall the West would suffer and the movement of the crops would be retarded. The impression made upon my mind . . . was that he had a rather strong opinion to that effect, but at the same time . . . he had no desire to control my purpose in regard to the management of the Treasury."[58]

Meanwhile, on May 13, 1869, Grant's thirty-seven-year-old sister, Virginia, married sixty-one-year-old Abel R. Corbin, former editor of St. Louis's Democratic newspaper, the *Missouri Argus*. Corbin, who had moved to New York in 1863, was a Grant family friend who had been involved in some moderately successful speculations and had offered the general financial advice. Following the gold controversy, Grant lamented, "I always felt great respect for Corbin and thought he took much pleasure in the supposition that he was rendering great assistance to the administration by his valuable advice. I blame myself now for not checking this (as I thought) innocent vanity."[59] The Corbins were the key to connecting the president to Fisk and Gould: in June 1869, Grant visited his sister and brother-in-law in New York while en route to Boston. During the evening, Jay Gould (who was a friend of Corbin's and attended the dinner) advised the president to expand the money supply in an attempt to stimulate the economy. Seeking to ingratiate himself to the president, Fisk allowed Grant the use of his steamboat from New York to Boston. Over the next three months, Corbin ensured that Fisk and Gould repeatedly "bumped-into" the president, though Grant disliked Fisk, who he felt was "always trying to get something out of me."[60]

Meanwhile, Fisk and Gould tried to influence people close to Grant: they ordered $500,000 in gold for the president's secretary, Horace Porter, and purchased $1.5 million in gold on Corbin's behalf, thereby tying Grant's brother-in-law to the scheme.[61] To his credit, Porter disavowed the transaction once he became aware of it, but Fisk and Gould's machinations did not stop there: Gould, Fisk, and Corbin left nothing to chance, even going so far as to try to engineer the appointment of Robert B. Catherwood as assistant treasurer of the United States. Catherwood was son-in-law to Corbin's first wife, and he was expected to send Gould and Fisk coded messages alerting them if the Treasury planned to sell gold. To his credit, Catherwood refused to pursue the appointment under such circumstances, so they next turned to Civil War general Daniel A. Butterfield, who accepted $10,000 from Gould (which he later claimed was an "unsecured real estate loan"). Acting on Corbin's recommendation, Grant appointed Butterfield to the Treasury Department, but that was not all: rumor had it that the three men had created speculative accounts for various members of the Grant inner circle, including Julia.

By the end of summer, there were clear signs that something was afoot in the gold market. In mid-September, Treasury Secretary Boutwell was scheduled to speak at New York's Union League, and it was rumored that the speech was arranged by "parties short of gold, who expected to use the occasion to influence the Secretary in favor of increasing his sales of gold, and breaking up the supposed clique."[62] Grant too recognized that something was happening in the gold markets and wrote to Boutwell on September 12, noting that "a desperate struggle is now taking place [between contractionists and expansionists], and each party wants the government to help them out. . . . I think, from the lights before me, I would move on, without change, until the present struggle is over."[63] Gould, alarmed by the signals coming from the White House and Treasury Department, pressured Corbin to write Grant a letter that exhorted the president not to sell government gold. Corbin entrusted the letter to W. O. Chapin, one of Fisk's employees, who delivered it to Grant in Washington, Pennsylvania, where the president was vacationing with Julia's relatives. Upon reading the letter, Grant said "all right" and that he had no answer. Chapin then went to a nearby telegraph office and relayed the following message to Gould: "Delivered. All right."[64] This message later became a focal point of the congressional investigation into Gould, Fisk, and Corbin's actions. From the telegram Chapin sent, Gould could reasonably conclude that his message had been delivered and that the president had acquiesced to Corbin's request by saying "all right." Chapin later testified that he only meant that Grant "had received the letters and read them; that they had been delivered all right." Shortly after receiving Gould's message, Grant dictated to Julia a message he wished sent to Virginia Corbin: "If you have any influence with your husband, tell him to have nothing whatever to do with Jay Gould and Jim Fisk. If he does, he will be ruined, for come what may [the president] will do his duty to the country and the trusts he is keeping."[65]

Aware now of the details of the plan, Grant had made clear he would not allow it to succeed.

Unfortunately for the conspirators, they misinterpreted the president's attitude. On September 22, Fisk and Gould met with Corbin and his wife and discussed the telegram that seemed to indicate that Grant would not interfere with their scheme. The Corbins' confidence was dampened the following day by the receipt of Julia's letter; Abel Corbin later testified, "I never did have a more unhappy day than I had when witnessing the distress that letter inflicted on my wife."[66] That evening, Gould called on Corbin at the latter's request and learned of Julia Grant's letter.[67] Corbin, panicking, begged Gould to buy his share of the gold so he could truthfully report to Grant that he was not speculating in the market. Gould could not allow Corbin to sell; doing so would dump gold on the market, the very thing Gould was trying to prevent Grant from doing. Instead, Gould offered Corbin $100,000 more or less to suppress news of the letter and to indemnify him against any losses that he would suffer if Grant chose to sell government gold. Apparently, Corbin refused the offer and Gould left, but the financier returned the following morning (Friday, September 24) and again offered his unhappy partner $100,000 to remain in the gold market. Corbin refused, so Gould immediately went to Wall Street, where he forced the price of gold even higher by arguing that the fact that Corbin remained in the gold market represented a tacit promise from the president not to sell the Treasury's gold. At the same time, Gould recognized that sooner or later the Treasury would intervene in the gold market, and he began anonymously unloading his own gold holdings. Gould did not tell his erstwhile partner Fisk what he had learned, and the latter kept buying, pushing the price of gold ever higher.

At roughly the same time as Gould and Corbin's meeting on Thursday, September 23, Grant and Boutwell met at the White House and agreed that if the price of gold began climbing the next day, the Treasury would intervene by selling $4 million in gold. Thus, the following morning, when the price of gold began climbing, Boutwell sent the order to sell. The Treasury's order reached Wall Street at about lunchtime, just after the price of gold had reached $160 per ounce, though by that time it had begun dropping (likely due to Gould's sales of his own holdings). The Treasury secretary's directive sent the price into free fall. Shortly after noon, the price was down to $140, and it eventually tumbled to $135.[68] The entire market seized under the massive injection of gold; according to the House Banking and Currency Committee's report, the gold clearinghouse "was suffocated under the crushing weight of its transactions, and its doors were closed."[69] Aggregated stock prices dropped by one-fifth, and trading volume dropped sharply. Worse, the price of crops dropped markedly; according to Grant biographer Jean Edward Smith, "Battered by tight money and dwindling markets, American agriculture went into a steep decline from which it did not recover for years."[70] On the other hand, an even greater monetary crisis had been averted, for now.

In retrospect, it is clear that Grant moved decisively to thwart Gould and Fisk's machinations, a fact that biographer Smith called "A watershed in the history of the American economy."[71] The inevitable congressional investigation agreed. Representative James A. Garfield of Ohio chaired the committee that investigated the panic. Garfield was no fan of Grant's; during the war he had opposed giving the general his third star. However, the Banking and Currency Committee's report exonerated Grant, concluding "that the wicked and cunningly devious attempts of the conspirators to compromise the President of the United States or his family utterly failed. . . . [T]he testimony has not elicited a word of an act of the President inconsistent with that patriotism and integrity which befit the Chief Executive of the nation."[72] But Grant did not emerge unscathed; rumors about his and his associates' role in the debacle spread quickly (aided by baseless statements made by Fisk and Gould implying the president's guilt), and it was nearly impossible to squelch them. Writing to a friend, Grant asserted, "I will say that I had no more to do with the late gold excitement in New-York City than yourself, or any other innocent party, except that I ordered the sale of gold to break the ring engaged, as I thought, in a most disreputable transaction. If the speculators had been successful you would never have heard of any one connected with the Administration as being connected with the transaction."[73] This did not quiet rumors, even among some Republicans, that Julia Grant had profited from Fisk and Gould's speculations. The two bankers started a whispering campaign that they had given her a $100,000 bribe to influence Grant.[74] Though untrue, the rumor proved remarkably difficult to dispel. Worse, Gould and Fisk escaped punishment for their actions, and Gould eventually realized a profit of $11 million from the abortive scheme. Even among those who believed that the president had not profited from the crisis, and despite Grant's best efforts, as historian Joan Waugh noted, Black Friday (as September 24, 1869, soon came to be known) "cast doubt . . . on his gullible nature and questionable associations," creating a narrative about the president that became a crucial part of his legacy.[75]

Four

"When I Said 'Let Us Have Peace,' I Meant It"

THOUGH THE NEW YORK GOLD CONSPIRACY was a dramatic test of presidential leadership, the thorniest issues facing the new administration concerned Reconstruction. The Republican Party was founded in the mid-1850s by a diverse coalition of former Whigs, Know-Nothings, and even some Democrats. What held them together was antipathy toward slavery, which ranged from opposition to the peculiar institution's spread into territories to outright calls for slavery's immediate and total abolition. Now, given that slavery had been abolished, Republicans needed to decide whether abolition was the end, or just the beginning, of what the country owed former slaves. "Reconstruction" implied a thoroughgoing economic, political, and social transformation of the South, turning it from a slave economy to a modern industrialized one; agreeing on the specifics of such an expansive program of reform was bound to exacerbate factional tension within the party and between the executive and legislative branches.

There were several challenges to developing and implementing a consistent Reconstruction policy. For instance, there were the competing priorities of quickly reunifying the country and successfully integrating African Americans into the nation's political, economic, and social life. On the one hand, the future of America's blacks was incredibly important to Grant, who was an engaged and effective executive concerned about African Americans' rights. Before the inauguration, he met with a committee from the National Convention of Colored Men, telling them, "I hope sincerely that the colored people of the nation may receive every protection which the laws give them."[1] A month after becoming president, Grant made history by hosting at the White House the first elected black lieutenant governor in US history, Louisiana's Oscar J. Dunn. Grant also appointed the first black diplomat in American history when he made Ebenezer Don Carlos Bassett minister resident to Haiti. Moreover, his efforts extended beyond the symbolic: within days of taking office, Grant signed a bill granting blacks equal rights in the District of Columbia, and in 1870, he signed into law the Naturalization Act, which made Africans and those of African descent eligible for naturalization to the United States. In December of his first year in office, Grant boasted to a delegation from the National Labor Convention, a mostly black organization, "I have done all I could to advance the interests of the citizens of our country, without regard to color, and I shall endeavor to do in the future what I have done in the past."[2] These efforts bore real fruit: during Grant's two terms, fourteen blacks were elected to Congress and dozens of others served in state-level offices.

On the other hand, Grant also fervently desired to put the war behind the country. During his inaugural ball, the Treasury Department was adorned with lights that spelled out "peace."[3] Moreover, Grant's impulses were toward leniency, particularly for former Confederate officers, many of whom he knew personally. The president signed a bill in February 1871 easing restrictions against former Confederates holding office, which angered Radicals in Congress. Worse, Grant had to placate the desires of a Northern public that was weary of war and had largely concluded that the work of Reconstruction was over.[4] The importance of this cannot be overemphasized: Reconstruction's success depended entirely on "popular support and partisan interest in the North"; should these ebb, the administration would soon find itself incapable of effecting the sweeping (and costly) transformation of the South's political, economic, and social structure implied by the word *reconstruction*.[5] Ultimately, this played a key role in hobbling the administration's efforts, particularly in Grant's second term.

The first step in achieving true reconstruction was ratifying the Fifteenth Amendment, which prohibited states from abridging citizens' rights to vote "on account of race, color, or previous condition of servitude" and empowered Congress to protect suffrage rights "by appropriate legislation."[6] To get the amendment ratified, Republicans needed four former Confederate states to adopt it. Achieving ratification involved some horse-trading that Grant's critics viewed as corrupt and duplicitous. For instance, in Virginia, Republicans were forced to hold a separate referendum for the state constitution, which protected black suffrage and accepted the terms of the Fifteenth Amendment, and for a provision in the constitution disenfranchising former Confederates; the state's voters approved the former but not the latter, so Virginia returned to the Union with its former Confederates fully enfranchised. As a result, a coalition of conservative Republicans and Democrats took office in Virginia, thereby ensuring that Reconstruction in the Old Dominion would be limited at best. Worse, this formula became the template for the readmission of Texas and Mississippi. Georgia had been readmitted to the Union in 1868 only to be placed back under military rule by Congress after its state legislature expelled its black members. In January 1870, the army forced the legislature to reseat blacks legally elected, creating a Republican majority. Soon thereafter, Georgia's state legislature approved the Fifteenth Amendment, and in July 1871, the Peach State was readmitted (for the second time) to the Union, proving what strong and decisive federal action could achieve.

Grant was pleased by the Fifteenth Amendment's ratification, waxing that it "completes the greatest civil change and constitutes the most important event that has occurred since the nation came to life."[7] Writing to Elihu Washburne, who was then US minister to France, Grant rejoiced that the amendment's ratification had taken "this question out of politics."[8] The army celebrated the occasion with a one-hundred-gun salute, and thousands of Washingtonians—black and white—paraded down Pennsylvania Avenue to the White House, where Grant addressed them.[9] The entire event seemed to fulfill the promise of the war and augur a smooth, and quick, transition to peace.

Curiously, many Southerners were happy to see the Fifteenth Amendment ratified because it forced Northerners to also allow African Americans to vote, potentially creating a white backlash that might sweep the Republicans from power. In fact, many Republicans had seen this, adopting a platform in 1868 that, while demanding black suffrage in the South, was more equivocal about black suffrage in the North.[10] These concerns seemed prescient: several states that never left the Union—Delaware, Maryland, Kentucky, Oregon, and California—failed to ratify the Fifteenth Amendment. It took New Jersey two tries (1869 and 1870), and New York State tried to rescind its ratification. In the congressional elections of 1870, Republicans lost thirty-two House seats while Democrats gained thirty-seven (the additional five were previously held by the Conservative Party of Virginia). In the Senate, Republicans lost four seats and the Democrats gained three (the other seat went to a Liberal Republican). The writing was on the wall: many white Northerners were hardly invested in protecting blacks' voting rights and would punish Republicans if they pursued civil rights too aggressively.

Furthermore, the paradox of the Fifteenth Amendment was that it counted freed slaves as people for apportioning congressional representation; because, under the Constitution, each slave had been counted as only three-fifths of a person, the amendment actually raised Southern states' representation in the House, making it essential to aggressively enfranchise Southern blacks and ensure they voted Republican. Perhaps Representative William D. Kelley of Pennsylvania summarized the situation best when he asserted that "party expediency and exact justice coincide for once."[11] What he did not say was that when justice and the party's needs diverged, the Republicans would have to make a painful choice.

Moreover, ratifying the Fifteenth Amendment was one thing; as Grant soon discovered, enforcing it was another. Southern whites viewed the Republican governments in the South as illegitimate, and as a result, state officials "could command neither respect nor obedience."[12] In his magisterial *Reconstruction: America's Unfinished Revolution, 1863–1877*, Eric Foner described the challenges facing Reconstruction governments this way: "Bequeathed few accomplishments and nearly empty treasuries by their predecessors [the Confederate governments], [Reconstruction governments] faced the mammoth problems of a society devastated by warfare, new public responsibilities entailed by emancipation, and the task of consolidating infant political organizations."[13] Believing in the democratic process (even when its outcome was not to his liking), the president did little to sustain the Republican government in Georgia. As a result, the state House went Democratic in 1870, followed by the governorship the following year. Georgia's new Democratic government instituted poll taxes and increased residency requirements, and even went so far as to jail state Senator Tunis Campbell, the highest-ranking African American official in Georgia, on trumped-up charges.

More concerning was the fact that several organizations formed to violently oppose the amendment's enforcement, the most notable of which was the Ku Klux Klan, or KKK. The KKK was formed in Pulaski, Tennessee, between December 1865 and June the following year, and by the time Grant was elected president, it was a "vigilante army" unleashing what historian Wyn Craig Wade called a "reign of terror" designed to intimidate black voters.[14] The KKK became so bold that on August 28 1868, Grand Wizard Nathan Bedford Forrest (a former Confederate lieutenant general) described the organization in an interview with the *Cincinnati Commercial* as a "protective, political, military organization . . . giving its support, of course, to the Democratic Party."[15] Though decentralized, the Klan and similar organizations (like the White Brotherhood and the Knights of the White Camellia) were "deeply entrenched in nearly every Southern state" and posed a real threat to those states' Reconstruction governments.[16]

To effectively combat these organizations, the states needed help from the federal government, and Congress obliged by passing a series of enforcement acts designed to neutralize white Southerners' attempts to intimidate black voters and oppose Reconstruction governments. On May 31, 1870, Congress passed the first Enforcement Act, which declared that citizens qualified to vote were entitled to do so, regardless of race, and it penalized officials who sought to bar blacks from voting. In addition, it took direct aim at the Ku Klux Klan by prohibiting individuals or groups from using "force, bribery, threats, intimidation, or other unlawful means" to "hinder, delay, prevent, obstruct, any citizen from doing any act required to be done to qualify him to vote or from voting at any election."[17] Because of these laws, the Klan became "an object of special concern" to the US Army, which functioned in a law-enforcement capacity in the South.[18] Despite the increased power granted to federal authorities under the law, in fall 1870, the former Confederacy "witnessed an unprecedented wave of Klan violence in portions of the South."[19] Grant used the new powers to aggressively pursue the Klan, particularly in the Carolinas. For instance, in July 1870, Grant sent US troops to South Carolina and instructed army commanders to make whatever arrests were necessary to cripple the Klan.[20] Yet this was not enough, and as a result of largely successful efforts to suppress black voters and intimidate Republican officeholders, the South quickly repudiated Republican control. Following the party's losses in the 1870 midterm elections, congressional Republicans passed the Second Enforcement Act on February 28, 1871. The law aimed to regularize and standardize election procedure by mandating poll watchers from both parties in towns of twenty thousand or more, and it required that ballots in federal elections be printed to reduce election fraud. Some historians have argued that the Second Enforcement Act's target was actually urban Democratic machines in the North, asserting that congressional Republicans' concerns over Democratic gains in the midterm elections manifested a desire to end voting fraud in their own backyards.[21] Wade writes that the Second Enforcement Act "marks the first major peacetime absorption of the federal government of powers and protective functions formerly allotted to the states."[22] Soon thereafter, Congress passed the Third Enforcement Act. While the target of the second act's provisions is debatable, there is no ambiguity about the third: also called the Ku Klux Klan Act, the new law prohibited "any person, under color of any law . . . of any state [from] depriving another of any right . . . secured by the Constitution of the United States." Furthermore, it forbade "two or more persons within any State or Territory of the United States [from conspiring] to overthrow, or to put down, or to destroy by force the government of the United States . . . [or] by force, intimidation, or threat to prevent, hinder, or delay the execution of any law of the United States."[23]

The administration's war on the Klan led to an expansion in the size and scope of federal law enforcement. For instance, in 1870, Congress passed a bill creating the Department of Justice, overseen by the attorney general (which had previously been a part-time job that paid less than other cabinet positions). After pushing Hoar out of the cabinet in December 1869, Grant appointed Amos T. Akerman attorney general. Grant's decision to appoint Akerman, a Northerner who had served in the Confederate army and was a delegate to Georgia's 1868 constitutional convention, perfectly symbolized the president's desire for national reunification and aggressive federal action to protect the voting rights of (male) African Americans. Using the resources at his disposal, Akerman vigorously pursued the Klan, convicting 74 percent of defendants indicted for violations of the Enforcement Acts in 1870.[24] Though Akerman often receives most of the credit for the aggressive prosecution of the Klan and similar organizations, the attorney general himself credited Grant, telling a friend that no one was "stronger" when it came to enforcing federal law.[25]

Though Grant's use of federal authority against the Klan was undeniably effective—Foner notes that the federal government's use of "its legal and coercive authority . . . had broken the Klan's back" by 1872—it also represented the high-water mark of federal government activism to protect blacks and Republican officeholders.[26] As early as spring 1869, Akerman perceived among congressmen "a hesitation to exercise the powers [of the federal government] to redress wrongs in the states." Akerman was so focused on pursuing the Klan that Secretary of State Hamilton Fish complained to his diary that the attorney general had the KKK "on the brain" and it had become "a bore to listen twice a week to this thing."[27] Fish's statement is stunning considering the New Yorker's unimpeachable (if moderate) antislavery statements before the war and is a good indication of the degree to which many Republicans had simply moved on from the war's lingering racial tension to (what they considered) more important things. In fact, Grant asked Akerman to resign after only thirteen months because the attorney general had run afoul of the Union Pacific Railroad, bringing into conflict the administration's goals of internal improvements and racial justice.[28] Following Akerman's departure, the federal government's success rate in cases brought under the Enforcement Acts dropped precipitously, and by 1874, the Justice Department secured convictions in only about 10 percent of cases.[29] According to historian Foner, the anti-Klan legislation Congress passed in 1871 "pushed Republicans to the outer limits of constitutional change," and there were some in the party who thought it went too far.[30]

The US Army bore much of the brunt of combating the Klan. Frequently, federal courts issued warrants empowering US marshals to arrest suspected Klan members; the marshals in turn requested assistance from the local army post commander in the form of escorts.[31] Federal troops engaged in 200 anti-Klan missions in 1870 and 160 in 1871 in the former Confederate states of South Carolina, Georgia, Florida, Alabama, Mississippi, and Tennessee. However, several issues hobbled the army's efforts. William T. Sherman, then commanding general of the US Army, opposed most of the president's Reconstruction policies and reluctantly enforced them, thereby limiting their efficacy and seriously damaging his friendship with Grant.[32] In fact, in 1874, Sherman moved his headquarters from Washington to St. Louis after clashing with Secretary of War Belknap, leading to rumors that he would resign.[33] Moreover, even if Sherman had been fully committed to executing the administration's Reconstruction policies, US expenditures on the military shrank as Republicans tried to pay down the country's wartime debt. From 1868 to 1876, the number of US troops stationed in the South dropped by more than 75 percent, from approximately twelve thousand to about three thousand. On a practical level, this meant there were simply not enough soldiers to properly enforce the law and to protect officeholders and black voters.

Finally, there was the problem of contradictory policy imperatives. While Grant was committed to protecting blacks' rights, he also wanted to extinguish the festering resentments caused by the war. As a step toward the latter goal, in summer 1872, Grant mulled pardoning some convicted Klan members. He addressed a letter on the subject to Gerrit Smith, a well-known abolitionist who nonetheless had (along with *New York Tribune* founder and editor Horace Greeley) contributed money toward Jefferson Davis's bail. Grant's letter expressed some of the president's contradictory impulses; on the one hand, he showed a "desire that all citizens, white or black, native or foreign born, may be left free, in all parts of our common country, to vote, speak & act, in obedience to the law, without intimidation or ostracism." That being said, Grant also assured Smith that once this was achieved, "there is no political offence that I would not advocate forgiveness and forgetfulness of." Nor were the pardons of Klan members an election-year stunt: Grant made clear he could issue no pardons before the election because they "would be misinterpreted," and he did not pardon the individuals until the following year.[34] Going further, in May 1872, he signed the Amnesty Act, which removed the limitations on most former Confederates' political rights established by the Fourteenth Amendment.

However, the problem of resistance to political equality for blacks was not limited to the states of the Confederacy or even the South. Delaware, which had been a slave state but had not seceded from the Union, witnessed efforts to keep blacks from voting. Here, whites tried to prevent blacks from paying county poll and property taxes, which were a prerequisite for voting. Worse, whites showed up at polling stations on Election Day and intimidated black voters with shouts of "down with the nigger." Naturally, this quickly degenerated into physical violence, and a riot broke out in Wilmington.[35] Many Northern cities had racial problems as well that required federal enforcement of voting rights. Various Northern states, including Massachusetts, Connecticut, Rhode Island, and Pennsylvania, placed restrictions on the franchise designed to limit black voting. In fact, Eric Foner observed, "the Northern states during Reconstruction actually abridged the right to vote more extensively than the South."[36] The Second Enforcement Act, passed by Congress in February 1871, provided for election supervisors in cities with populations in excess of twenty thousand; at the time, the United States had fewer than seventy such cities, and all but five were in states that remained loyal to the Union. Moreover, as historian William Gillette notes, most of the money that went into implementing the Second Enforcement Act flowed into Northern cities.[37] In short, the Second Enforcement Act demonstrated that intimidation of black voters was not merely a Southern problem, and it vindicated Republicans' fears that Northern support for sweeping social and political change was shallow and ephemeral.

While many whites, Northern and Southern, believed Reconstruction had gone too far and cost too much, many blacks pressed the state and federal governments to do more to promote political and social equality. Southern blacks convened "labor conventions" in Georgia and South Carolina in 1869, the purpose of which was to pressure state governments to regulate wages and rents to prevent white landowners from taking advantage of former slaves.[38] Such proposals ran counter to the Republicans' free-labor ideology, which asserted that workers and employers should be free to negotiate wage rates unconstrained by outside interference. Free labor was the opposite of "unfree labor"—that is, slavery—in that unfree laborers were unable to leave their employers (i.e., their masters) and seek better wages elsewhere. Add to that Southern whites' hostility to blacks and desire to reinstitutionalize as much of slavery as possible, and what was left was a situation where blacks had few actual opportunities for economic or social advancement. Shortly after being dislodged from his position as chairman of the Senate Foreign Relations Committee, Senator Sumner struck back at the administration, summing up much of the frustration of Radical Republicans when he asserted that if the Grant administration had put as much effort into protecting black voters as it had annexing Santo Domingo (discussed in the next chapter), "our Southern Ku Klux Klan would have existed in name only."[39] Undoubtedly, Sumner had an axe to grind with Grant, and surely the situation was more complicated than the senator admitted, but the criticism was certainly valid: the administration could have done more to protect Southern blacks, but only at the cost of competing priorities.

There was more to Reconstruction than improving conditions for African Americans; Republicans wanted to use the federal government to sweep away the South's prewar economic system and replace it with one based on free-labor ideology, which they believed would improve conditions for poor whites as well. The end goal was making the South a prosperous, capitalist, industrialized society like the North. To that end, Congress passed a variety of business-friendly laws, including using federal dollars to support infrastructure projects like railroad construction. Southern governments under Republican control gave railroads generous economic inducements to construct rail lines connecting the region, and over Grant's first term the South's total miles of track grew by 40 percent. Unfortunately, government aid for such projects often drained Southern states' treasuries and encouraged corruption. For instance, Louisiana Governor Henry C. Warmouth instituted a kickback scheme that made him a wealthy man but at the expense of the state's treasury. By 1871, the staggering costs and undeniable corruption of infrastructure projects fueled a backlash against not only economic and industrial modernization but against Reconstruction in general. Across the South, Democrats exploited the backlash by organizing so-called taxpayers' conventions, which could denounce Republican governments and Reconstruction in seemingly nonracialized ways.[40]

Factionalism within the Republican Party exacerbated these challenges, and Republicans' divergent opinions about how much social and political change was desirable, let alone achievable, made it difficult to create a coherent and sustained approach to Reconstruction.[41] For instance, in what Eric Foner called "the most byzantine factional struggles," Louisiana's Republican Party was split into the "statehouse" faction, allied with Governor Warmoth, and the "customhouse" faction, which included Grant's brother-in-law James E. Casey.[42] Grant had supported the customhouse faction by directing federal patronage its way, which alienated the statehouse faction. As a result, Warmoth drifted toward white Southerners, sacrificing black Republicans in his desire to remain in office. Warmoth was reelected and, owing his office to white Southerners, weakened efforts to protect black voters.[43] Nor was this a fluke; it represented a conscious effort on the Democrats' part to capitalize on Republican factionalism. Instead of running their own candidates, Southern Democrats frequently supported one Republican faction against another with the understanding that the cost of that support would be the restoration of former Confederates' voting rights.[44]

The administration also encountered resistance in implementing one of Grant's signature initiatives, his so-called peace policy with Native Americans. Following the war's end, there was a major flare-up of violence between white settlers and members of various plains tribes, including the Sioux, Cheyenne, and Arapaho. General Sherman noted in April 1868 that the "Indians are getting restless" and complained of the War Department's inability to "fulfill any of the promises we held out to them of ploughs, seed, cattle, etc., to begin their new life [sic] of peace."[45] Sherman ordered General Sheridan to take command of the Army of the Missouri and to conduct a harassment campaign during fall and winter to push the Native Americans back onto reservations. This is where things stood when Grant became president in March 1869. Shortly after inauguration, Grant and Secretary of the Interior Jacob Cox met with a delegation of prominent Pennsylvanians who had come to convince the president to appoint a commission to ensure that the terms of a recent treaty with the Sioux be implemented faithfully and fairly. The Pennsylvanians got more than they bargained for: in April, at the president's request, Congress created a ten-member Board of Indian Commissioners and charged Grant to appoint to it "men eminent for their intelligence and philanthropy, to serve without pecuniary compensation."[46]

The commission recommended several steps to improve relations between natives and whites, including concentrating Native Americans on reservations, ending the practice of making treaties with Indian nations, and removing most of the current Indian agents. Perhaps the most shocking recommendation was to confer citizenship on members of the Five Civilized Tribes (the Creek, Cherokee, Choctaw, Chickasaw, and Seminole). The report's suggestions became the basis of the Grant administration's approach to dealing with Native Americans. To implement the administration's policy toward Native Americans, Grant appointed Ely S. Parker commissioner of Indian affairs in 1869. Parker was a Seneca Indian born on a reservation in upstate New York in 1828. Though he prepared for a career in law, New York State would not admit him to the bar because Native Americans were not considered US citizens. As a result, Parker studied engineering at Rensselaer Polytechnic Institute, eventually becoming supervisor of government projects in Galena, Illinois, where he met Grant. When the war broke out, Parker tried repeatedly to join the army but was rebuffed because he was not a citizen. Grant, who needed an engineer, pulled strings to get Parker in uniform, and he quickly rose through the ranks. It was Parker who drafted the surrender terms for Lee at Appomattox, and after the Confederate general signed them, he is reputed to have turned to Parker and said, "I am glad to see one real American here." Parker shook Lee's hand but said, "We are all Americans."[47] Parker's appointment as commissioner of Indian affairs was groundbreaking; he was the first Native American named to head a major government bureau.

The key to implementing Grant's policy was effective Indian agents, or the federal employees who actually oversaw Native American education programs on the reservations. Grant biographer William S. McFeely described the agents as a "combination governor, teacher, supplier, and—in theory at least—representative of the interests of the Indian in transactions with those who, for whatever reason, wanted to have dealings with him."[48] Grant filled about half of the Western agencies with Quakers, who had a reputation for fair dealings with the Native Americans; the other half he filled with army officers on the premise that those actually fighting Native Americans would be less inclined to needlessly antagonize them. This was perhaps more optimistic than the situation warranted, given the fact that General Sheridan, then commander of the Department of the Missouri, allegedly believed that "the only good Indian is a dead Indian."[49] Many congressmen opposed Grant's moves because the Indian office was a rich source of patronage for their supporters, and in 1870 Congress barred army officers from filling civil offices. The president responded by replacing army officers with evangelical Protestants, Catholics, and even some religious Jews, all of whom he believed would treat the Native Americans more fairly than patronage appointees.[50] In his 1870 annual message to Congress, Grant boasted of the success of his peace policy, noting, "Reform of the management of Indian Affairs has received the special attention of the Administration," and expressing his hope that "the policy now pursued will, in a few years, bring all the Indians onto reservations, where they will live in houses, have school houses and churches, and will be pursuing peaceful and self sustaining avocations, and where they may be visited by the law abiding white man with the same impunity that he now visits the civilized White settlements."[51]

Obviously, Grant's hope—of natives adopting white culture and living on reservations almost like a zoo—is condescending and offensive. Grant himself described the policy as "conquest through kindness." Yet Grant's strategies paid dividends; according to historian H. W. Brands, conflict between the United States and Native Americans declined during Grant's first term, particularly with the plains tribes. Shortly after his reelection in 1872, Grant crowed about his administration's success in dealing with Native Americans, claiming he had "reduced the expense of [managing relations between the United States and Native Americans]; decreased [Native American] forays upon the white settlements; tended to give the largest opportunity for the extension of the great railways through the public domain and the pushing of settlements into more remote districts of the country; and at the same time improved the condition of the Indians."[52] As Grant himself proudly boasted in 1871, "When I said 'Let us have peace,' I meant it."[53]

However, that is not to say that all was well: On January 23, a cavalry detachment massacred 173 Piegan Indians, most of whom were women and children, which was widely reported and caused something of a scandal in Washington. In January 1871, Grant sent Congress a proposed constitution drafted by representatives from the Five Civilized Tribes. The president included a message approving the constitution, which highlighted some of his thoughts about his policies. According to Grant, it was desirable "that the civilized indians of the country should be encouraged in establishing for themselves forms of territorial government. . . . [It is] highly desirable that they become self sustaining self relying, Christianized and Civilized," and this constitution was the first step in that direction (with the understanding that Congress "should hold the power of approving or disapproving of all legislative action of the territory").[54] Congress refused to accept the constitution, in large part because various representatives and senators wanted to ensure that whites received the offices created by the Native Americans' new government. In addition, the railroads—always an important constituency for Republicans—opposed the constitution, fearing it would jeopardize the land grants Congress was in the process of giving them. As a result, the "effort to extend citizenship to the tribes in Indian territory went for naught."[55]

Moreover, despite the reduction in violence, there were approximately two hundred violent altercations between Native Americans and the army during Grant's eight years in office. Ironically, in at least one case, the violence was an indirect result of Grant's reforms. As the president's peace policy improved relations with Native Americans, some Apaches gathered at Arizona's Camp Grant for protection and food. Local whites, feeling the pinch of decreased government expenditures, blamed them for depredations real and imagined. On April 28, local whites massacred nearly 150 Apaches (including women and children), in a shocking outbreak of brutality. Despite Grant's threat to place Arizona under martial law unless the perpetrators were punished, in October 1871 a jury found those arrested not guilty. The result was a flare-up of violence between whites and Apaches that threatened US-Mexican relations because the Native Americans frequently fled across the border to elude the US Army. The conflict did not officially come to an end until 1886 when the army captured

Geronimo (and even then sporadic violence took place well into the twentieth century).

Furthermore, Indian policy was another instance where the administration's various priorities—in this case, better relations with Native Americans and fostering the development of American railroads— clashed. Under the terms of treaties negotiated in 1866 with various tribes and subsequent legislation, the three railroads in Kansas were authorized to build on land bordering Cherokee territory. When railroad workers violated the treaty by entering Cherokee territory as part of their work on the line, the Native Americans appealed to the federal government. As Interior Secretary Cox noted in a letter to Grant dated May 21, 1870, "The policy of preserving the Indian Territory as free as possible from intrusion by white settlers, under any form, has been hitherto regarded as firmly established in this country. . . . [W]e cannot honestly advise the scattered and small tribes, now within our organized states, to migrate to the Indian Country, except upon the honest assurance . . . [that they will be] protected from the temptations which have, heretofore, been so ruinous to them, [and] that they may work out the problem of their possible civilization and final incorporation into the nation."[56] As a result, for all the fanfare, the peace policy failed to live up to expectations, though in the short term it improved relations between the United States and Native Americans.

Ulysses S. Grant, the eighteenth president of the United States, March 4, 1869, to March 3, 1877.

Julia Boggs Dent Grant, First Lady of the United States. The Grants wed in 1848.

Ulysses S. Grant, center, delivering his first inaugural address, March 4, 1869.

Schuyler Colfax, vice president, March 4, 1869, to March 4, 1873.

Henry Wilson, vice president, March 4, 1873, to Nov. 22, 1875.

Elihu Washburne, secretary of state, March 5, 1869, to March 16, 1869.

Hamilton Fish, secretary of state, March 17, 1869, to March 12, 1877.

George S. Boutwell, secretary of the Treasury, March 12, 1869, to March 16, 1873.

William A. Richardson, secretary of the Treasury, March 17, 1873, to June 3, 1874.

Benjamin H. Bristow, secretary of the Treasury, June 4, 1874, to June 20, 1876.

Lot M. Morrill, secretary of the Treasury, June 20, 1876, to March 9, 1877.

John A. Rawlins, secretary of war,
March 13, 1869, to Sept. 6, 1869.

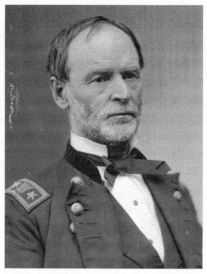

William T. Sherman, secretary of war
(interim), Sept. 6, 1869, to Oct. 25,
1869.

William W. Belknap, secretary of war,
Oct. 25, 1869, to March 2, 1876.

Alphonso Taft, secretary of war,
March 8, 1876, to May 22, 1876; at-
torney general of the United States,
May 22, 1876, to March 4, 1877.

J. Donald Cameron, secretary of war, May 22, 1876, to March 4, 1877.

Ebenezer R. Hoar, attorney general of the United States, March 5, 1869, to Nov. 22, 1870.

Amos T. Akerman, attorney general of the United States, Nov. 23, 1870, to Dec. 13, 1871.

George H. Williams, attorney general of the United States, Dec. 14, 1871, to April 25, 1875.

Edwards Pierrepont, attorney general
of the United States, April 26, 1875, to
May 21, 1876.

Adolph E. Borie, secretary of the navy,
March 9, 1869, to June 25, 1869.

 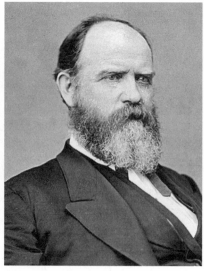

George M. Robeson, secretary of the
navy, June 25, 1869, to March 12,
1877.

John A. J. Cresswell, postmaster general, March 5, 1869, to June 22, 1874.

James W. Marshall, postmaster general, July 3, 1874, to August 24, 1874.

Marshall Jewell, postmaster general, August 24, 1874, to July 12, 1876.

James N. Tyner, postmaster general, July 12, 1876, to March 3, 1877.

Jacob D. Cox, secretary of the interior, March 5, 1869, to Oct. 31, 1870.

Columbus Delano, secretary of the interior, Nov. 1, 1870, to Sept. 30, 1875.

Zachariah Chandler, secretary of the interior, Oct. 19, 1875, to March 11, 1877.

A Currier & Ives cartoon published in 1872 parodying President Grant's reelection campaign slogan, "Let Us Have Peace," showing Grant supporters lobbying for civil service jobs.

Five

"The Man and the Fanatic"

THOUGH GRANT'S PRESIDENCY is typically regarded as one of the worst in US history, paradoxically, his secretary of state, Hamilton Fish, is generally rated among the country's best.[1] One reason is the record of diplomatic success the administration compiled during Grant's first term. However, the president also suffered his share of defeats and failures: for instance, his ongoing feud with Charles Sumner derailed one of Grant's dearest priorities, the annexation of Santo Domingo (today's Dominican Republic). The administration's foreign policy is the most vivid illustration of the conflict between the executive and legislative branches of government during Grant's two terms. Grant came to the presidency with several well-developed ideas about American foreign policy. The first was an expansionist impulse. Grant predicted, "to maintain peace in the future it is necessary to be prepared for war," asserting that there was little chance of another civil war but "growing as we are, in population, wealth, and military power, we may become the envy of the nations which led us in all these particulars only a few years ago; and unless we are prepared for it we may be in danger of a combined movement being some day made to crush us out." Despite his recommendation falling largely on deaf ears, Grant's words reflected an expansionist impulse that in the words of one diplomatic historian amounted to "grabbiness."[2] In fact, Representative Nathaniel P. Banks of Massachusetts, chairman of the House Foreign Affairs Committee, predicted in March 1869 that territorial expansion would be "the event of this administration."[3] In addition, Grant's worldview was heavily shaped by his experiences during the Mexican-American War and the Civil War. For instance, Grant noted, "The conduct of some of the European states during [the Civil War] shows the lack of conscience of communities where the responsibility does not come upon a single individual."[4] As a result, he strongly supported the Monroe Doctrine, which asserted American opposition to European powers interfering in, or trying to colonize, countries in South and Central America.[5]

There was also an idealistic side to Grant's thinking on foreign affairs that is worth considering. In 1870, Grant appointed Benjamin F. Peixotto, a Jewish lawyer, US consul to Bucharest, largely in response to Romanian persecution of Jews, an ironic turn of events given Grant's promulgation of the infamous General Order No. 11 during the war. Simon Wolf, who was present at a meeting between Grant and Peixotto shortly after the latter's appointment, recalled the president saying, "Respect for human rights is the first duty of those set as rulers over nations, and the humbler, poorer or more abject and miserable the people be, be they white or black, Jew or Christian, the greater should be the concern to extend protection, to rescue and redeem them and to raise up to an equality with the most enlightened."[6]

That being said, American foreign policy is not merely pure distillation of the president's will; all presidents rely on their subordinates to advise and implement their policies, and Grant was no exception. One key to understanding the Grant administration's foreign policy was the relationship between the president and Secretary Fish. Journalist John Russell Young noted that the president "leaned heavily upon [Fish] and believed in [him] as in no other man. To Grant, [Fish] was the nearest counselor in statesmanship, friend in personal relations, [and] choice for the Presidency in succession to himself."[7] Yet, initially Fish assumed his responsibilities more out of a sense of duty than affection or respect for Grant, writing in spring 1869, "I would very gladly be out [of the administration]. . . . I have been embarrassed by some of the things done before I came here; by some incautious commitments of the President which will make me responsible before the country for some things I would prefer should be very different from what they will be. But I am 'in for it' and must take the consequences."[8] A skilled bureaucratic infighter, Fish managed to assert greater control over US foreign policy during Grant's first term, particularly after Secretary of War John Rawlins died in fall 1869. By 1873, Fish was Grant's most trusted adviser in the cabinet.[9]

In addition, the mechanisms of foreign policy—the ministers abroad and the State Department staff at home—played a crucial role in the formulation, interpretation, and implementation of the administration's foreign policy. According to diplomatic historian Robert L. Beisner, for much of the nineteenth century, most US diplomats and diplomatic officials "were amateurish and maladroit in their diplomacy, ignorant of other societies and their affairs."[10] To some degree, this was a function of the longstanding practice of rewarding political supporters and friends with diplomatic posts. Moreover, it was also the logical outgrowth of the fact that few American diplomats received salaries, and even those who did were responsible for the costs of their offices, making the independently wealthy the only truly viable candidates for diplomatic office.[11] Fish was aware of these problems and tried hard to regularize and professionalize the State Department's operations, with some notable successes.[12]

Congress has a say in foreign policy as well, and in an era of unusually strong congressional action, Grant's range of choices was not unlimited. As was the case with Reconstruction, certain congressmen had priorities that conflicted with the president's, militating against a coherent approach to foreign affairs. For instance, Grant recommended that Congress abandon the policy of drawing down the US Army and mothballing the country's warships, calling instead for "a good navy" and putting "our sea-coast defences . . . in the finest possible condition."[13] On the other hand, military expansion conflicted with his administration's goals of financial retrenchment and debt reduction, and Congress paid little heed to Grant's recommendations. In an effort to reduce expenditures, Congress slashed the number of State Department clerks by more than a third in 1869, and some congressmen advocated shuttering most of the United States' embassies as a way of balancing the budget and paying down the debt.[14] Fortunately, that proposal went nowhere, but it serves as a reminder that policy decisions were (and are) made by balancing a series of competing, and sometimes contradictory, policy imperatives, a theme that runs throughout this book.[15] In 1869, the men in charge of the relevant congressional committees—Senator Charles Sumner and Representative Nathaniel P. Banks—disliked Grant personally and worked to wrest control of American foreign policy from the White House. The new president had tangled with Sumner before; in 1865, the senator had viciously attacked Grant's report on conditions in the South as a "whitewashing message," leading the Democratic *New York World* to assert, "Never were the MAN and the FANATIC more sharply brought face to face than here."[16] Understanding the interplay, and relative strength, of Congress and the president is crucial to accurately interpreting the administration's diplomatic triumphs and failures.

The settlement of the *Alabama* controversy (about damages caused to the Union by a British ship sold to the Confederacy during the war) is generally regarded as the Grant administration's greatest diplomatic achievement because it not only improved relations with Great Britain but also enshrined international arbitration as the key mechanism for adjudicating international disputes.[17] Though Great Britain was officially neutral during the Civil War, the British had leaned toward the Confederacy, particularly early on. In fact, during fall 1862, Prime Minister Lord Henry John Temple, Third Viscount Palmerston, and Foreign Secretary Lord John Russell discussed offering British assistance in mediating the conflict with an eye toward securing Confederate independence. Chancellor of the Exchequer William E Gladstone went even further, asserting in a speech:

> We know quite well that the people of the Northern States have not yet drunk of the cup—they are still trying to hold it far from their lips—which all the rest of the world see they nevertheless must drink of. We may have our own opinions about slavery; we may be for or against the South; but there is no doubt that Jefferson Davis and other leaders of the South have made an army; they are making, it appears, a navy, and they have made what is more than either, they have made a nation.[18]

Gladstone's speech was inflammatory and seemingly portended British recognition of the Confederacy. Worse, Britons were actively helping the Confederacy by building ships for the South. All told, British shipbuilding firms constructed five ships for the Confederacy—the *Florida*, the *Shenandoah*, the *Lark*, the *Tallahassee*, and the *Alabama*—but the focus of the conflict after the war was the *Alabama*. In 1862, the British shipbuilding firm John Laird Sons and Company secretly built a ship for a Confederate procurement agent named James Bulloch. Originally known as "hull # 290" and then the *Enrica*, the ship was sailed to the Azores where it was refitted for combat and rechristened the CSS *Alabama*. Over the next two years, the *Alabama*'s crew boarded nearly five hundred ships, captured or burned several dozen merchant vessels, and took approximately two thousand US sailors prisoner. The *Alabama* was eventually sunk by the USS *Kearsage* on June 11, 1864, but not before several of the ship's officers and sailors were rescued by a yacht owned by John Lancaster, a British member of Parliament, thus preventing them from being taken prisoner. Perhaps it's no surprise that during and immediately after the war, many Americans believed that but for British interference, the war would have ended much earlier.[19] American diplomatic policy toward Great Britain reflected the general sense of outrage at the latter's aid to the Confederacy, particularly after the war's outcome became clear. Most of America's retaliation focused on Canada: in 1864, the United States threatened to repudiate the Rush-Bagot Treaty of 1818 by dispatching armed units to the Great Lakes, and the following year Congress canceled a reciprocity treaty with Canada and made it more difficult for Canadian passport holders to enter the United States.

In an effort to settle these issues, President Johnson's minister to Great Britain, Reverdy Johnson (no relation to the president), negotiated an agreement with English secretary of state for foreign affairs George Villiers, Earl of Clarendon, that came to be called the Johnson-Clarendon Treaty. Under its terms, US citizens could press their claims for losses due to British actions during the war to a panel of four commissioners (two British and two American). If the commission could not agree, then the matter was referred to an arbiter chosen by the committeemen; if they could not agree even on a referee, then one would be chosen by lot. Worse, the Johnson-Clarendon Treaty dropped any national claims the United States might press against

Great Britain for damages caused by the latter's actions. In a speech on the Senate floor, Sumner called it, "A treaty which, instead of removing an existing grievance, leaves it for heartburning and rancor" and "nothing but a snare."[20] Consequently, the Foreign Relations Committee recommended that the full Senate reject the treaty. Committee chairman Sumner confided to James G. Blaine that "it was the first time since [Sumner] had entered the Senate that such a report had been made concerning any treaty."[21] On April 13, the Senate rejected the Johnson-Clarendon Treaty 54 to 1, only the seventh time in US history that the body refused to ratify a treaty.

Surely, it was a bad treaty, but there was a healthy dose of politics at work as well. Radicals despised Reverdy Johnson, who was personally and politically close to President Johnson (it was at Reverdy Johnson's house that President Johnson received senators during the impeachment trial and made the promises that allowed him to serve out his term). While in Great Britain, Reverdy Johnson embarrassed himself in the Radicals' eyes by displaying unbecoming obsequiousness; at one banquet he even shook hands with John Laird, who owned the company that built the CSS *Alabama*.[22] In addition, Charles Sumner's opposition to the Johnson-Clarendon Treaty was about more than just outrage at Great Britain; he also relished the idea of the United States annexing Canada. In a biographical essay about his friend and former Senate colleague, Carl Schurz asserted that Sumner believed "perpetual peace with England would be promoted by the disappearance of the British flag from the American continent," which is what led the senator from Massachusetts to seek the annexation of Canada.[23] Nor was Sumner alone; even his political enemy, Representative Benjamin Butler, supported the idea of annexing Canada, as did Nathaniel Banks, chairman of the House Foreign Affairs Committee. In part, this reflected the politics of the Northeast, where Americans and Canadians clashed over claims to cod-fishing grounds and where many Irish immigrants supported, and even participated in, raids against British installations in Canada from 1866 to 1871. Furthermore, Anglophobia was a key tactic to attract voters, and in general the Republicans were more aggressive in foreign policy than the Democrats.[24]

Grant supported the Senate's rejection of the treaty and even drew up a message to that effect to send to the Senate, though Fish counseled against sending it.[25] In his annual message in December 1869,

Grant criticized the Johnson-Clarendon Treaty and cited Great Britain's actions during the war as creating a "sense of unfriendliness." Calling the tension with Great Britain "the only grave question which the United States has with any foreign nation," Grant said, "I hope that the time may soon arrive when the two Governments can approach the solution of this momentous question with an appreciation of what is due to the rights, dignity, and honor of each, and with the determination not only to remove the causes of complaint in the past, but to lay the foundation of a broad principle of public law which will prevent future differences and tend to firm and continued peace and friendship."[26] Surveying the damage Reverdy Johnson's actions had done to the treaty's chances of passage, Fish rejected the idea of pursuing individual claims against the British government because most of those claims had been satisfied by insurance and were, in any case, beside the point; as historian Allan Nevins noted, the United States' "real claim against Great Britain was national."[27]

Almost immediately, Fish ran into trouble with Minister to Great Britain John Lothrop Motley, who took the same hard-line stance against the British as his friend and patron Sumner. Fish now faced a problem: Grant had appointed Motley minister as a fig leaf to the politically powerful (and easily antagonized) Sumner, so removing Motley at this moment was not an option. However, Fish fundamentally disagreed with Sumner by arguing that sovereign nations had an unimpeachable right to issue proclamations of neutrality when, in their view, a civil conflict in another country warranted such a proclamation.[28]

Consequently, Fish tried to limit Motley's freedom of action by issuing him a carefully worded set of instructions. Those instructions took a more measured tone than Sumner's rhetoric, noting that both countries shared "common origin[s], [a] common language, common literature, and common interests and objects." Motley was also instructed to tell the British that while American public opinion supported rejection of the Johnson-Clarendon Treaty (because it had not dealt with America's actual grievances), the Senate's actions in no way implied "discourtesy" toward Great Britain. Moreover, Motley was to convey to the British the administration's desire to resume negotiations as soon as possible. Crucially, Fish decided that the State Department in Washington would handle the negotiations rather than the minister in London, believing that "the atmosphere and surroundings on this side of the ocean are more favorable to proper solution of the question than the dinner-tables and the public banquets of England."

Sumner was outraged by the tone of Fish's instructions to Motley and upbraided Assistant Secretary of State Bancroft Davis, demanding to know if "the purpose of this Administration is to sacrifice me—me, a Senator from Massachusetts?" Later that day, Fish met with Sumner and cut off the latter's harangue by saying, "Sumner you roar like the bull of Basham." Yet even that was not the end of the matter; Sumner returned to the State Department the following day and claimed he would pressure Motley to resign. Fish responded coolly, saying that if Motley did resign, he would be replaced. At that point, Sumner took another tack, sending Fish a letter outlining the senator's ideas that vaguely threatened to cause trouble for the administration. Fish ultimately revised Motley's instructions, but the revision in no way changed administration policy. Interestingly, the new instructions contained a clause that offers insight into the Grant administration's approach to dealing with foreign powers. According to Fish, "The President recognizes the right of every Power when a civil conflict has arisen within another state, and attained a sufficient complexity, magnitude, and completeness, to define its citizens and subjects toward the parties to the conflict, so far as their right and interests are necessarily affected by the conflict." This statement was carefully crafted, and for good reason: Fish wanted to preserve the United States' independence of action in the case of the Cuban Revolution, discussed later in this chapter.

Motley's tenure in London got off to a rocky start: on his arrival, the US minister found the British government in ill temper about the Senate's rejection of the Johnson-Clarendon Treaty. After Motley met with Lord Clarendon on June 10, his report to Fish indicated he violated the secretary of state's careful instructions by misrepresenting the United States' position regarding declarations of neutrality in cases of insurgency.[29] When this came to light, Grant was furious and wanted to remove Motley immediately, but Fish counseled restraint and patience; instead the secretary simply removed negotiations from Motley's hands and, by that move, strengthened his own position in the administration. When Sumner fulminated that summer that the administration should take a harder line with the British, Fish ignored him. However, in August, Fish hosted Sumner at his home in Garrison, New York, and the two discussed the situation. When Fish asked Sumner to draw up a paper presenting America's position in the conflict, Sumner demurred but suggested having former attorney general Caleb Cushing do it, and Fish agreed. Cushing wrote the position paper, and though far more temperate than Sumner's rhetoric, it nonetheless reflected the senator's perspective and satisfied those in Congress who wanted the administration to take a hard line with the British. This paper allowed the administration to play a version of good cop/bad cop with the British by using Sumner's aggressiveness to paint itself as moderate and reasonable.

Working in Grant's favor was the fact that it was a particularly propitious moment to negotiate with Great Britain. Distracted by the growing tension between France and Prussia, and fearful that conflict with the United States would limit Britain's ability to respond to events on the Continent, the British were eager to reach a settlement.[30] In June 1869, Fish met with Sir Edward Thornton, British minister to the United States, sounding him out about the terms for settling the *Alabama* claims and the possibility of transferring Canada from Great Britain to the United States. Thornton was equivocal; on the one hand, he indicated that the British did not wish to keep Canada, but, on the other hand, any transfer would have to be approved by its population.[31] In March 1870, Fish suggested to Thornton that Great Britain might grant Canada independence as a first step to transferring it to the United States, and again the British hedged, desirous of a settlement but unwilling to make the first move. Canada's government did not take kindly to being reduced to a bargaining chip in these negotiations (nor to the prospect of being annexed by the United States). In mid-1870, Fish met with the Canadian minister of finance, John Rose, ostensibly to negotiate a trade reciprocity treaty between the United States and Canada. Rose was an old hand at negotiating with the Americans; in 1864, he had represented the British on a commission formed to settle disputes arising from the Oregon Treaty the United States and Great Britain had signed twenty years before. Their discussion quickly turned to the tension over the *Alabama* claims. During the meeting, Rose suggested that the British government might send an envoy to Washington to negotiate a new treaty, and Fish responded enthusiastically. As part of the deal, Fish agreed not to pursue Canadian annexation and to drop American demands that the British pay the massive "indirect" costs of prolonging the war. In addition, the British and the Americans would establish a commission to settle the other sources of friction—fishing rights, etc.—and to submit the issues directly related to the war to an international arbitration board.[32]

Meanwhile, Irish nationalists living in the United States tried to engage American help in their struggle against British rule of Ireland, threatening the emerging deal to settle the *Alabama* claims. Beginning in 1866, the Fenian Brotherhood, an organization of Irish Republicans based in the United States, began crossing into Canada to harass British soldiers and government installations. The Johnson administration responded by arresting Fenians. Shortly after Grant entered office, the Fenians undertook a wave of activities designed to undermine the Canadian government. Grant had to decide if he would continue the prior administration's policy of retarding the Fenians' efforts. From a political standpoint, changing policy could work to the Republicans' electoral advantage: the Irish typically voted Democratic, but if the administration supported, even tacitly, the Fenians, it might create a new bloc of Republican voters in crucial Northern states.

This was no small concern given that Republicans faced eroding white support in the North for the administration's Reconstruction policies, particularly among urban voters. Describing this process in summer 1869, Charles Francis Adams, who had been Lincoln's minister to Great Britain and was the son and grandson of US presidents, complained, "Fearful of the gradual disintegration of the [Republican Party] from its internal dissensions, they are for forming an alliance with the Fenians, on this basis, and cutting under the democrats."[33] In fact, Grant was under enormous pressure from members of his own party to help free Americans who had been captured by the British while aiding the Irish resistance; for instance, one correspondent described the "unparalleled horrors in the treatment of Americans—native and adopted—in British dungeons," and several months later US representative John A. Bingham of Ohio asked the president to "extend your good offices" to secure the release of William G. Halpin, a Civil War veteran convicted of treason against the British government in 1867.[34] Ultimately, the administration adopted a two-pronged approach to dealing with the Fenians. In May 1870, Grant issued a proclamation designed to discourage Americans from participating in raids into Canada by warning that citizens who did so "will forfeit all right to the protection of the Government or to its interference in their behalf to rescue them from the consequences of their own acts."[35] On the other hand, Grant ultimately decided to pardon the Fenians in August 1870 in the hope that the issue would just go away, though Fish counseled him to wait a few weeks because neither wanted to derail negotiations.

On January 26, 1871, Britain's Thornton formally proposed creating a commission to resolve the various disputes. The commission met for nine weeks before emerging with a treaty in early May 1871. The following month, largely due to pressure from both Grant and Queen Victoria on their countries' respective legislatures, the US Senate and Britain's Parliament ratified what came to be known as the Treaty of Washington, a document that had long-lasting effects in international law. In the short term, it paved the way for arbitration in Geneva that resulted in a British apology for the destruction caused by the *Alabama*. Shrewdly, Grant's allies asked Charles Francis Adams to represent the United States at the arbitration. Sharp-tongued and irascible, he would hardly have been Grant's first choice (the president once remarked "The Adams' do not possess one noble trait of character I ever heard of"), but sending him to Geneva prevented him from playing a part in the 1872 presidential campaign (in which he would likely have opposed Grant's reelection) and led to a tangible result: an accord signed in September 1872, just weeks before the election.[36]

Cleverly, the administration continued its good cop/bad cop approach to negotiating with Great Britain by presenting for arbitration the indirect claims that Sumner and his supporters sought. The British were surprised at this move, because Fish had communicated to Rose his belief that the senator from Massachusetts' claims were unreasonable, but there was method to the secretary of state's madness: he fully expected the arbiters to rule the claims inadmissible. As a result, by Election Day 1872, Grant not only had an agreement, but he had managed to embarrass one of his main political antagonists *and* create a plausible explanation for the administration's decision not to push these claims any further. Sweeter still, the following month, arbiters ruled in favor of America's claim that it owned the San Juan Islands, an archipelago in present-day Washington State. Long term, historian H. W. Brands noted, the Treaty of Washington resolved "decades of tension between the two great English-speaking nations and pav[ed] the way . . . for the most important and enduring alliance in modern world history."[37] Moreover, the treaty (which international law scholar John Bassett Moore called "the greatest treaty of actual and immediate arbitration the world has ever seen") enunciated concepts and values that decisively shaped organizations like the League of Nations and the United Nations.[38] Visiting Geneva during his European tour after leaving the presidency, Grant celebrated "the principle of international arbitration . . . which I hope will be resorted to by other nations and be the means of continuing peace to all mankind."[39] Grant's comments written in 1885 about Great Britain reflected the diminution of tension occasioned by the Treaty of Washington. The former president asserted, "England and the United States are natural allies, and should be the best of friends" because the two countries shared a common language and "are related by blood and other ties." He downplayed British support for the Confederacy during the war—calling it "not so much real as it was apparent"—a sign of the changed tone of relations between Great Britain and the United States and paving the way for the two countries' "special relationship."[40]

The *Alabama* claims were far from the only diplomatic issues left over from the Civil War. Though France evacuated Mexico in 1867, the country's actions in the United States' southern neighbor had left a bitter taste in Grant's mouth. Though Grant claimed to have believed "France is the traditional ally of the United States," as president he tacitly sided with the Germans during the Franco-Prussian War (1870–71).[41] Grant admired the Germans; in March 1871, the president congratulated the Prussians on German unification, asserting, "The states of this Union which severally bear a relationship to the others similar to that which Prussia bears to the other states of Germany, have recently made such sacrifices and efforts towards maintaining the integrity of their common country for general purposes in peace and war that they cannot fail to sympathize in similar proceedings for a like object elsewhere."[42] In July 1870, France declared war on Prussia as a way of halting German unification, which had been taking place since the end of the Austro-Prussian War in 1866. A unified Germany threatened the European balance of power established after the

Napoleonic Wars and posed a potential threat to France. Reflecting on the Franco-Prussian War almost fifteen years later, Grant cheered it as bringing about Napoleon III's ultimate downfall, though at the time the president declared the United States neutral.[43] Grant wanted to stay out of the war, and he told Congress on July 15, 1870, that it should authorize the enlargement of the merchant marine because "the vessels of this Country at the present time are insufficient to meet the demands which the existence of War in Europ[e] will impose upon the Commerce of the U.S."[44] Following the disastrous Battle of Sedan in September 1870, which ended with the Prussians capturing Napoleon III and the French army, France sought American help in negotiating an end to the war. The French minister to the United States begged Grant to issue a statement supporting France's territorial integrity, but the president refused. Meanwhile, he ordered the US minister to France, his friend Elihu B. Washburne, to remain in Paris even as that city descended into chaos. While other ministers fled, Washburne worked diligently to protect Americans caught in France, dispensing aid and even searching for Americans who had gone missing.[45] One consequence of the outbreak of violence in France and the unification of Germany was that England began casting about for other allies and became much more amenable to settling the *Alabama* claims.[46]

During the first term, the Grant administration also faced a minor conflict with Russia, one of the United States' most important European allies, over diplomatic personnel. Russia and the United States had been close since the 1850s, when the latter supported the former during the Crimean War. In 1869, this relationship was challenged when Russian czar Alexander II named Konstantin Catacazy his minister plenipotentiary to the United States. In his instructions to Catacazy, the czar reminded the minister to tread carefully because "the American people are our best friend." Catacazy managed to offend the Grant administration by trying to undermine the *Alabama* settlement, fearing that a rapprochement between the United States and Great Britain would imperil US-Russian relations. Worse, when confronted with evidence of his actions, Catacazy aggressively (and undiplomatically) criticized the administration and its allies in Congress.

As a result, in mid-June 1871, the president formally requested that the Russian government recall Catacazy. When the Russians stalled out of concerns that recalling Catacazy would mar the upcoming visit of the czar's third son, Grand Duke Alexei Alexandrovich, the administration renewed its request. The Russians asked the United States to tolerate Catacazy until after Alexei's visit, and the president agreed. As a result, Grant had to tolerate the indignity of Catacazy presenting Alexei at the White House. The meeting was short—approximately fifteen minutes—and the president did not host a formal dinner, a stunning slight for the representative of such a friendly government. On November 21, the Russians formally announced that Catacazy had been recalled. Though Grant excoriated Catacazy in his annual message, citing the former minister's "inexcusable course," which "rendered it necessary to ask his recall . . . [because it was] impossible with self-respect . . . to permit Mr. Catacazy to continue to hold intercourse with this Government," the president nonetheless asserted, "The intimate friendly relations which have so long existed between the United States and Russia continue undisturbed."[47] Catacazy did not see it that way; in 1872, he published the book *Diplomatic Incident,* in which he tried to justify his actions. Framed as a letter addressed to US chief justice Salmon P. Chase, the book provided Catacazy an opportunity to tell his side of the story, but the Grant administration ignored it, lauding in April 1872 the appointment of Heinrich von Baron d'Offenberg, whom the president and secretary of state found much more congenial.

In the Western Hemisphere, the Grant administration adopted the essentially bipartisan expansionism of the preceding several decades. Grant's interest in modernization and his commitment to the Monroe Doctrine converged in his desire to construct a canal across Central America. The president took for a given that the United States would build such a canal, and a driving force behind American expansionism in the Caribbean was getting territory to build bases to protect such a canal.[48] Importantly, Grant was far from the only Republican looking to build a canal across Central America; Speaker of the House James G. Blaine was also a strong supporter of a Caribbean canal. Inspired by the example of the Suez Canal, in fall 1869, Grant authorized US minister resident to Colombia Stephen A. Hurlbut to negotiate a treaty for the construction of a canal connecting the Atlantic and Pacific Oceans. In January 1870, Fish confided to his diary that the president was optimistic that such a treaty could be negotiated and that the canal itself could be built within five years, but the Senate rejected the treaty on the basis of a clause that would have required it to be open to all ships, even those at war with the United States.[49] As a consequence, the project was stalled, but the president, as was his wont, did not give up. Grant met with Colombia's new minister to the United States, Santiago Perez, in September 1870, and discussed the construction of an interoceanic canal. In March 1872, Grant had created a special Interoceanic Canal Commission to study the matter; this organization joined the several similar commissions and study groups operating under the aegis of the US Navy from 1870 to 1872. All came to the same conclusion: the only serious options were to build the canal across Panama or Nicaragua, and on February 7, 1876, the commission recommended the latter country. Fish and Grant worked diligently throughout the administration's final year to secure a treaty to build the canal, but little was achieved in these discussions, and it was nearly half a century before a Central American canal opened.[50]

Considerations about America's simmering racial tension also played a role in the administration's foreign policies, including its largest first-term defeat: the failure to annex Santo Domingo. This failure was doubly stinging for Grant because he saw the island as an easy fix to the country's racial problems. Grant noted, "I took it that the colored people would go down there in great numbers, so as to have independent states governed by their own race." Reflecting on these events nearly a decade after leaving the White House, Grant argued, "It is possible that the question of a conflict between the races may well come up in the future. . . . The condition of the colored man within our borders may become a source of anxiety, to say the least."[51] More than just a safety valve for America's black population, Santo Domingo represented an opportunity to decrease American trade with slave countries like Cuba and Brazil; as Grant noted at the time, on every pound of sugar or coffee Americans bought from those countries, "an export duty is charged to support slavery."[52]

American designs on Santo Domingo went back decades, and President Franklin Pierce's administration had unsuccessfully tried negotiating the establishment of a US naval base in Samana in 1854. The Johnson administration had made some preliminary steps toward official relations with Santo Domingo in January 1866, but the Senate refused to confirm the president's nomination of William L. Cazneau for US commissioner and consul general to the island. During the waning days of Johnson's administration, New England businessman Joseph W. Fabens approached Secretary of State Seward to sound out the government's interest in leasing or even purchasing Samana Bay, where the United States had long desired to establish a naval base. Fabens was a business partner of Cazneau's with a long history of dealings in Santo Domingo; he was hardly a disinterested party to the deal, representing a cabal of American businessmen whose schemes hinged on American annexation of Santo Domingo.[53]

In 1868, Fabens and Cazneau created the Santo Domingo Company and sought American investors who would profit from the annexation with the idea that these men would pressure Congress and the administration to annex the island. Given that Johnson was a lame duck, Fabens simultaneously tried to interest several congressmen in championing annexation, but a resolution to extend American protection over Santo Domingo failed in the House, 126 to 36. On February 1, the annexationists tried again when Representative Godlove Stein Orth of Indiana introduced a resolution calling for the annexation of "San Domingo" provided that its people consented, formed a republican government, and submitted a constitution to Congress for approval. This resolution also failed, though by a much narrower margin (110 to 63), a fact that heartened annexationists.[54]

When Grant took office in March 1869, Santo Domingo was governed by Ramón Buenaventura Báez Méndez, who was then serving his fourth nonconsecutive term as the nation's president. A skilled political operator, Báez had played a role in the rebellion against Haiti that established Santo Domingo as an independent nation in 1844. Over the next decade, he tried to persuade the French to establish a protectorate over Santo Domingo and, when that failed, worked to interest the United States in buying the country. Living in exile in Spain during the American Civil War, he persuaded his host nation to take over Santo Domingo. This proved temporary, however, with Spain leaving in 1865. Báez returned to Santo Domingo and became the country's president in December 1865, but his tenure was cut short by a coup the following spring. He eventually regained the presidency in 1868 and served his longest term of office (until 1874), during which he tried to rekindle US interest in annexing the island. Just a few weeks after Grant took office, Fabens met with Secretary Fish and made an astonishing proposal that, he claimed, came directly from Santo Domingo's government: that the United States annex the country. Though Fish told Fabens he was disinclined to pursue the scheme, the secretary of state nonetheless brought it up at a cabinet meeting the following day. Initially, the cabinet was cool to Fabens's proposal; Fish recorded in his diary he expressed the belief that action on Santo Domingo should originate in Congress and, due to the end of the current session, there was no time to take action and therefore no reason to discuss it.[55] Consequently, the cabinet moved on to other subjects, but annexation appealed to the president, and on May 17, he sent the USS *Nipsic*, a warship, to reconnoiter Santo Domingo and report back on conditions. Then, in summer 1869, Grant dispatched Orville Babcock, his former aide-de-camp, to Santo Domingo.

Fish's instructions to Babcock were clear, and rather limited: Babcock was to report on local conditions, but he was granted no diplomatic standing. Grant, by contrast, asked Babcock to sound out Baez's terms for the purchase of Santo Domingo. The US Navy also dispatched a ship, the *Seminole*, to provide Babcock with what historian Allan Nevins called "moral support of her guns" and to, if possible, capture a rebel gunboat that was harassing Baez's forces.[56] When Babcock returned to Washington in mid-September, he came with a proposal that was almost too good to be true: the United States could lease Samana Bay for $2 million or annex all of Santo Domingo by assuming its public debt of $1.5 million. To move forward, all Grant had to do was remit $100,000 in cash and $50,000 in arms (to be credited against the total purchase price). Fish, who opposed annexation and rightly saw Babcock's negotiations as far exceeding his instructions, was aghast; he complained to Interior Secretary Cox that Babcock had "no more diplomatic authority than any other casual visitor" to Santo Domingo."[57] Nevertheless, Grant ordered the secretary of state to work up treaties along the lines sketched in Babcock's agreement with Baez. On October 19, Fish presented the treaties to the cabinet, where various members made suggestions for minor changes. Fish believed the other cabinet members' feelings ranged from antipathy to lukewarm opposition to annexation, but Grant pushed ahead: in November, the president again dispatched Babcock to Santo Domingo carrying two treaties—one for the lease of Samana Bay and the other for outright annexation. By the end of the month, Báez had signed the treaties, and on December 4, he ceremoniously raised the US flag over Samana.

That was the easy part, as subsequent events showed. On December 21, Grant convened his cabinet and triumphantly showed the signed treaties. Sumner, having heard reports about the treaty-making process from Fabens and Cazneau's enemies, and disposed to oppose annexation anyway, called on the president December 31 to discuss the matter. During their conversation, Sumner proclaimed himself an "administration man" and promised, "whatever you do will always find in me a most careful and candid consideration," which Grant took to be a commitment to get the treaties ratified.[58] Despite what Grant took to be Sumner's promise to support the treaty, the senator was horrified by the terms Babcock negotiated: the United States was committed to assuming Santo Domingo's large national debt, would find itself at cross-purposes with Haiti and many European nations, and would be obligated to support Báez, whose hold on office was tenuous at best and accomplished through brutality and repression. Furthermore, Sumner resented the manner in which the treaty had been negotiated.[59] Sumner was also offended that he and the Senate had been sidelined in the negotiations and by what he considered the slights inflicted on him by the Grant administration. Fish, who was clearly aware of this dynamic, tried to manage the president by leaking information to Sumner, which likely emboldened him in opposing the administration.[60] Fish was pursuing his own agenda, somewhat at odds with the president's, by leaking information to one of the administration's most vociferous critics, and he was not the only one: Assistant Secretary of State Bancroft Davis routinely fed Sumner confidential information about the administration's foreign policy.[61] Without knowing any of this, and thinking he had Sumner's support, on January 10, 1870, the president sent the treaties to the Senate for its advice and consent.

Meanwhile, events in Santo Domingo swung against the annexationists. In January, Haitian president Sylvain Salnave was overthrown in a coup and killed. Salnave had supported US annexation of Santo Domingo, but his successor, Jean-Nicolas Nissage Saget, vehemently opposed it. As a consequence, Báez now faced a hostile neighboring power as well as an energized political opposition. In order to secure his hold on power, Báez asked the Grant administration for military assistance, which raised serious questions about the stability of his regime. Nevertheless, Grant obliged and dispatched warships, souring many legislators on the annexation treaty. Worse, the plebiscite that Báez organized for Dominicans to express their opinions on annexation was so lopsided—16,000 in favor and 11 opposed—it was clearly corrupt. Meanwhile, time was running out: the treaty expired if the US Senate failed to act by March 29, 1870, so in mid-March, Grant sent a message to the chamber strongly urging ratification. Two days later, the Senate Foreign Relations Committee reported negatively on the treaty. When Senate debate on the treaty opened March 24, Grant and the proannexationists were at a significant disadvantage.[62] As a result, the Senate allowed the treaty to expire March 29, 1870.

Not one to be deterred, Báez authorized Fabens to travel to Washington and extend the treaty's expiration period in the hope that the administration might yet build enough support to achieve annexation. On May 14, Fish signed an agreement extending the treaty's expiration date to July 1, 1870, and Grant tried to build support for annexation by rhetorically asking Congress, if the United States did not annex Santo Domingo, "with what grace can we prevent a foreign power from attempting to secure the prize?"[63] Unfortunately for the president, if anything, the additional time made annexation less likely. In June, the Senate held hearings into the case of Davis Hatch, a Connecticut businessman arrested in Santo Domingo for opposing annexation, which made public the nature of Báez's regime.

Stymied in his attempt to annex Santo Domingo, Grant decided to play hardball. He wanted his cabinet members to vocally support annexation, and he complained to Fish on June 13 that Attorney General Hoar, Interior Secretary Cox, and Treasury Secretary Boutwell were failing in this regard. At the Tuesday cabinet meeting, Grant reminded his cabinet members that he wanted them all to support annexation. The following day, Hoar resigned as attorney general. Shortly afterward, he complained to Fish that the resignation became public as the result of a leak from the White House. Meeting with Grant that evening, Fish noted that the president alluded to the cabinet meeting and obliquely asked if Hoar's resignation had anything to do with Santo Domingo. According to Fish, Grant's "reply was peculiar & guarded—after a momentary pause, he said 'If it was, no one knows it.' Another pause—& he proceeded—'I have great affection for Judge

Hoar . . . [but] I have said . . . that I mean to recognize my friends &
those who sustain my policy."[64] This was an understatement; not for
nothing would Grant boast, "If I should fail in my first choice, I shall
not at any time hesitate to make a second, or even a third trial."[65]

Yet all Grant's efforts amounted to little: on June 30, the Senate rejected the treaty 28 to 28 (ratification of treaties requires approval by
two-thirds of the senators); Schurz claimed that the treaty "would
have received [fewer votes] but for Executive pressure."[66] This was
Grant's first major legislative defeat, and it was one he never accepted.
Railing about it, Grant confided to Fish that he would not "consider
those who oppose his policy as entitled to influence in obtaining positions under him," later specifically referencing Sumner and Motley.[67]
The day after the Senate's defeat of the treaty, Grant removed Motley
as minister to Great Britain. Yet there was something self-defeating in
the president's actions: firing Motley created a minor scandal (particularly after Fish publicly rebuked the ex-minister). Worse, Grant's preferred choice to replace Motley, US senator Oliver P. Morton of
Indiana, initially accepted the nomination but, a month later, turned
it down out of fear he would be replaced in the Senate by a Democrat.
Grant nominated former US representative Robert C. Schenck of
Ohio, who was approved and sailed for London in July 1871. Unfortunately for Grant, despite an "excellent showing" as minister to Great
Britain, Schenck resigned in disgrace when a minor scandal involving
his connection to a mining scam became public.[68]

Meanwhile, in the House, Nathaniel P. Banks responded to the Senate's failure to ratify the treaty by trying to seize leadership of the issue.
Though Banks and Grant disliked each other, the two shared a desire
to annex Santo Domingo. On his own initiative, and without consulting the administration, Banks prepared a resolution *directing* the president to appoint a commission charged with negotiating a new treaty.
Grant made it clear that he opposed such a resolution as an infringe-
ment of the executive's prerogatives, but Banks persisted. It was only
when Grant made it clear to Banks's colleagues that the cost of supporting the resolution would be the loss of administration patronage
that the congressman backed down, contenting himself with a resolution favored by the White House that created a commission to investigate the possibility of annexing Santo Domingo.[69] In a slap at Banks,
the resolution was introduced in the Senate on December 12, where it

was approved 32 to 9, despite Sumner's strenuous efforts. On the Senate floor, Sumner lambasted Grant's request to dispatch to Santo Domingo a commission of inquiry. Grant and his supporters were understandably offended, though Schurz claimed (disingenuously) that Sumner "earnestly disclaimed any disrespect."[70] In January 1871, the House passed a similar resolution, but this one carried an amendment stating that the resolution did not commit the United States to annex Santo Domingo. Immediately, Grant signed the joint resolution and appointed the commissioners: former senator Wade of Ohio, Cornell University president Andrew D. White, and noted philanthropist Samuel G. Howe. In addition, Grant appointed noted abolitionist (and former slave) Frederick Douglass to accompany the commission and offer his perspective on annexation.

At this point, things seemed to have turned in Grant's favor: the committee members reported favorably on annexation, and the president successfully worked behind the scenes to deprive Sumner of his chairmanship of the Foreign Relations Committee. When the new Congress convened in March 1871, Pennsylvania's Simon Cameron (an administration ally) became the committee's chairman in a move that Schurz called "a bare-faced, wanton act of revenge."[71] Deposing Sumner was an unprecedented step; reflecting on these events more than thirty years later, Senator George F. Hoar noted that no such thing had happened in the Senate before or since "except the single and well-known case of Mr. Sumner."[72]

Yet despite the committee's recommendations and an administration ally chairing the Foreign Relations Committee, it soon became clear that the annexation treaty would not pass the Senate. Forced to concede defeat, on April 5, Grant merely submitted the commission's report to Congress and asked that it be printed to educate the public about the merits of annexation. However, the accompanying letter betrayed his anger and indignation. Grant asserted that while "the mere rejection by the Senate of a treaty negotiated by the President only indicates a difference of opinion among different departments of the Government . . . when such rejection takes place simultaneously with charges openly made of corruption on the part of the President, or those employed by him, the case is different."[73] Congress never took up the matter again, and the United States did not annex Santo Domingo. That fact haunted Grant for the rest of his term of office;

shortly before the presidential election of 1876, he confided to a friend that the United States "will have occasion to regret that [the question of annexation] was disposed of without adequate discussion," and in his eighth and final annual message, Grant lectured Congress, "If [Santo Domingo had been annexed], the country would be in a more prosperous condition to-day, both politically and financially."[74] However, deposing Sumner did have benefits for the administration because Cameron was easier to work with as head of the Foreign Relations Committee than his predecessor. In May 1871, Fish sent the Pennsylvanian a gushing letter thanking Cameron for "the generous & very efficient & effective aid & support you have rendered to the various subjects which have gone from the Department of State to the Senate."[75]

Despite Grant's commitment to the Monroe Doctrine and his desire to expand the United States, there were limits to his territorial acquisitiveness, as is illustrated by the administration's policy toward Cuba. Except for a brief period in the seventeenth century, Spain had ruled Cuba since the fifteenth century, but, beginning in the 1850s, the island's business and planter elite began pressing for reform. In spring 1865, the island's Creole elite issued four demands: that Cubans be represented in the Spanish parliament, that there be actual enforcement of the ban on importing African slaves, that there be legal equality between Spaniards and Cubans, and that the tariff be lowered. Meanwhile, the parliament was becoming more reactionary, ensuring that Cuban demands would receive a negative reception. Moreover, Madrid imposed a 6 percent tax on the island's businessmen and planters, exacerbating tension just as Cuba's economy went into recession in 1866. As a result, the following summer, Francisco Vicente Aguilera, Cuba's wealthiest plantation owner, founded the Revolutionary Committee of Bayamo, and resistance to colonial authority quickly spread across the island. In October 1868, resistance turned to uprising when sugar mill owner Carlos Manuel de Cespedes issued the 10th of October Manifesto, which called for Cuban independence, the abolition of slavery, and democratic reforms. Forces under Cespedes's control soon took the city of Bayamo, and other cities revolted against Spanish control. The following spring, a constitutional convention met with a goal of providing the revolution greater coordination and integration; on April 12, it elected Cespedes the first president of the Republic in Arms.

The Cuban Revolution presented a formidable challenge to US policymakers. On the one hand, it was democratic and promised the abolition of slavery on the island. On the other hand, overthrowing Spanish control on the island threatened key US economic interests. The cabinet was split at its first meeting over whether to support the Cuban revolutionaries. Rawlins was the strongest voice in Grant's cabinet advocating US intervention on the side of the Cubans (in part because he had a financial stake in the revolution's success), though Cox and Creswell also supported aiding the insurgents.[76] Other cabinet members were more ambivalent about supporting the revolutionaries. Fish recorded in his diary that Cox "referred to the delicacy & kindness due to Spain now that she is engaged in liberating her institutions," a position that Grant echoed in a comment about the distinctions he saw between "'old Spain' and & 'new Spain.'" Boutwell reminded the cabinet members that US trade with Cuba accounted for $30 million in import duties, which were the primary sources of federal revenue at the time.[77] Fish saw the Cuban Revolution as a distraction from what he considered the more pressing issue of relations with Great Britain. Moreover, the issues at stake were similar to those in the *Alabama* claims; how could the United States demand that the British indemnify American claims for damage caused by ships if, at the same time, it supported the revolutionaries in Cuba? He therefore worked to soften congressional calls for more aggressive action and to derail resolutions supporting US intervention.[78]

While the administration struggled to develop a coherent policy toward Cuba, events on the ground spun out of control. Fearing that the United States would be drawn into the conflict, Grant tried stemming the tide of American citizens traveling to Cuba to fight against the Spanish. This practice, known as filibustering, created tension between Spain and the United States and led the Spanish to begin seizing American vessels in Cuban waters. In March 1869, the Spanish seized two American ships—the *Mary Lowell* on the fifteenth and the *Lizzie Major* on the twenty-seventh—and in the process nearly precipitated a diplomatic crisis. Worse, at about the same time, Spain proclaimed that it would treat all vessels in Cuban waters, regardless of their nationality of port of origin, as "pirates." Though he opposed intervention in Cuba, Fish aggressively asserted American prerogatives, arguing that the Spanish proclamation was an assault on the United States' right of navigation, and Spain eventually revoked it. But that was not the end of the problem: in June, Spanish authorities in Cuba summarily executed two Americans, Charles Speakman and Albert Wyeth. The two had been aboard a schooner along with a detachment of Cuban rebels; despite promises that the ship would not enter Cuban waters, the rebels ran it aground off the island's coast and took Speakman and Wyeth with them when they disembarked. The Americans escaped and made for Spanish lines. Despite protesting that they had nothing to do with the insurgency, they were taken to Santiago and executed. The executions enraged Grant and inflamed American public opinion; in response, the president dispatched a number of ironclad warships to Cuban waters. He ordered the commander of US naval forces in the region to resist any Spanish attempt to capture American ships unless the ships in question were caught in the act of landing men or contraband on Cuba.

Yet despite the seeming inevitability of a war over Cuba, behind the scenes, conditions in Spain made it possible to strike a deal. On June 2, Grant and Fish reviewed a report prepared by Paul S. Forbes, a politically connected American businessman. Forbes had spoken to Spanish prime minster Juan Prim, who indicated that Spain, which was having economic problems, might be willing to sell Cuba to the United States for the right price. That was the carrot; the stick was that Prim planned on nearly tripling the number of Spanish soldiers in Cuba in order to break the rebellion once and for all. Prim suggested that Forbes ask Grant to send someone to Madrid to mediate between Spain and Cuba. After reading Forbes's report, Fish drafted a memorandum to guide the negotiations. According to Fish, the United States would be willing to mediate negotiations on the basis of Cuba paying Spain for its independence with funds raised from interest-bearing bonds issued by the Cubans but guaranteed by the United States. Furthermore, both sides would enter an armistice during the negotiations, and any agreement must include the emancipation of the island's slaves.[79] The revolutionaries' representatives in New York approved the terms Fish suggested and even agreed to a specific sum:

$100 million. On the basis of these developments, Grant approved the terms and sent them with his newly appointed minister to Spain, Daniel E. Sickles, who departed for Europe on July 1.

To call Sickles colorful is to understate the matter. Born in New York, Sickles apprenticed to a printer before attending the University of the City of New York (now New York University). He then studied law under Benjamin F. Butler and was soon elected to the New York State Assembly. Though only in the assembly briefly, Sickles became well known for his outrageous behavior and was censured for bringing his mistress, famed New York courtesan Fanny White, into the chamber. In 1852, he married Teresa Bagoli, who at 16 (or possibly 15) was less than half Sickles's age. The following year, President Franklin Pierce appointed Sickles secretary to the American legation in London, where he served under future president James Buchanan. Becoming a diplomat in no way moderated Sickles's behavior; he left his pregnant wife in the United States and was instead accompanied to London by White. In 1856, Sickles was elected to the New York State Senate. Though he took a decidedly relaxed view of his marital vows, he did not extend that privilege to his wife: when Sickles discovered she was having an affair with Phillip Barton Key II (son of "Star-Spangled Banner" author Francis Scott Key), he fatally shot the man. At the trial, Sickles managed to win acquittal by pleading temporary insanity, the first time that defense was used in the United States.

At the outbreak of the Civil War, Sickles organized volunteer units for the US Army, and he rose quickly through the ranks, in 1863 becoming the only corps commander who was not a West Point graduate. Disobeying orders at Gettysburg, Sickles was wounded in the leg (which was later amputated and can be seen to this day at the National Museum of Health and Medicine). After the war, he filled a number of important posts, including commanding various departments in the South during Reconstruction. In 1868, Sickles enthusiastically supported Grant's candidacy, and as a reward the president offered to appoint him minister to Mexico. Sickles considered the appointment insufficient reward for his services and turned it down, though he accepted Grant's offer of the mission to Madrid.[80] Naturally, Sickles was a controversial choice. Besides his checkered past, Sickles had supported the Ostend Manifesto, a circular drafted in 1854 that argued the United States should buy Cuba and declare war against Spain if it refused to sell the island. In that sense, Grant's decision to appoint Sickles could be read as a subtle threat to the Spanish, a fact that Attorney General Hoar mentioned to the cabinet after Grant announced the nomination. The president responded that he too had supported the Ostend Manifesto.[81]

While in Spain, Sickles acted in a predictably rakish manner that included a well-publicized affair with the former queen of Spain, Isabella II. There were also rumors that he had another mistress, a Cuban woman who (it was alleged) was trading sexual favors for Sickles's efforts to liberate Cuba.[82] In order to balance Sickles, Grant appointed Forbes as special agent to Madrid, subordinate to Sickles but reporting directly to the secretary of state. Forbes actually arrived in Madrid before Sickles and met with Prim. On July 16, Forbes reported to Fish that the prime minister's asking price for Cuba was $150 million, indicating that the countries could make a deal on Cuba. However, the acting Spanish secretary of state, Manuel Becerra, who adamantly opposed any concessions on Cuba, torpedoed the negotiations by leaking details to Spanish newspapers. The resulting backlash ensured that the Spanish could not accede to American demands, and negotiations ground to a halt.

Grant was annoyed by what he saw as Spain's intransigence, and in mid-August 1869, he expressed to Fish his concern about Spain's plan to introduce additional troops into Cuba. Specifically, Grant complained that "the rights of our citizens have been so wantonly invaded by Spanish troops, or volunteers, that such a course would arouse the sympathies of our citizens in favor of the Cubans to such a degree as to require all our vigilance to prevent them from giving material aid." In addition, Grant noted, "I am not clearly satisfied that we would not be justified in intimating to Spain that we look with some alarm upon her proposition to send 20,000 more troops to Cuba to put down, as Americans believe, the right of self government on this continent."[83]

Fortunately, even as Grant drafted these words, Sickles managed to persuade the Spanish to accept American mediation based on the following conditions: The rebels would lay down their arms in exchange for full amnesty from Spain. Then, on the basis of universal suffrage, Cubans would vote on the question of independence. If they voted in favor of independence, Cuba would compensate Spain, with the United States guaranteeing the payment. The agreement Sickles and Prim struck did not include a specific amount to be paid and made no mention of slavery. The latter issue was addressed in a June 1870 law promulgated by Spain that provided for gradual and incomplete emancipation, which Fish found unacceptable.

Crucially, these developments took place against the backdrop of the death of Grant's closest friend, Secretary of War John A. Rawlins. Jean Edward Smith described Rawlins as Grant's "confidant and alter ego," and he was so close to the Grants that Julia had invited him to live with the first family in the White House.[84] Interior Secretary Cox called Rawlins's death an "irreparable loss" to Grant and lamented that "no other man could be found who could be the successful intermediary between General Grant and his associates in public duty." Unhappily for Grant, he continued in office without his friend's advice and support, and at least one biographer has claimed that had Rawlins lived, he would have prevented the scandals that consumed Grant's administration in its last years. Grant's biographer describes William W. Belknap, who replaced Rawlins at the War Department, as "bluff, hypocritical, [and] unimaginative"; while this may be an unduly harsh assessment, it is nonetheless true that Belknap's actions ensnared the president on one of the biggest scandals of his administration.[85]

With the strongest advocate for intervention in Cuba dead, Grant was even less inclined toward supporting the insurgency. He noted in his first annual message to Congress in December 1869 that the insurrection did not seem to be making any tangible progress and that both sides had committed atrocities. He concluded that while future events might necessitate American intervention in the affair, no such necessity then existed "nor is its probability clearly to be seen."[86] Grant's statement did little to pacify pro-Cuban congressmen. The Cubans found a powerful ally in Banks, who consistently pressed resolutions supportive of the rebels and critical of the Spanish. Banks believed that the president sympathized with the insurgents but was deferring to Fish's more cautious instincts. In an attempt to gin up support for intervention, Banks issued a report in summer 1870 criticizing the Spanish and praising the Cubans. When Fish criticized the report, Banks lashed out on the House floor, claiming that "Congress has taught the President it was dangerous to hold an opinion" and that, as a result, the legislative branch should direct Grant what to do, a stark illustration of the ongoing conflict between the legislative and executive branches for control of policy.[87] Despite the hot rhetoric, the White House successfully pressured Republican congressmen to neuter Banks's resolution by amending it in such a way that it simply protested Spanish actions but did not recognize the rebels, thereby relieving the pressure on Grant to intervene in Cuba. For the time being, Cuba was eclipsed by other concerns, though the issue never completely disappeared, and the controversy flared again in Grant's second term.

Six

"Nations, Like Individuals, Are Punished for Their Transgressions"

B Y 1872, THE ADMINISTRATION had compiled a solid, if mixed, record of achievement, with its share of successes (the settlement of the *Alabama* claims and the effort to stem the New York Gold Conspiracy) and failures (the annexation of Santo Domingo and the lingering tension over Cuba). Grant's initial attempt to remain above the political fray had collided with reality, though by the end of his first term, the president had demonstrated an astute control over the levers of power. Yet Grant's election in 1868 had raised expectations—that the bickering between Republican factions would end, that the administration would find a way to peacefully adjust Southerners to the postwar reality while simultaneously protecting blacks' rights, and that it would dispense, once and for all, with the spoils system—to such an unreasonable level that disappointment was inevitable.[1] Grant's policies had earned the president more than his share of enemies (many in his own party). Called Liberal Republicanism, the movement quickly petered out, but it nonetheless demonstrated many Republicans' opposition to the president and waning interest in Reconstruction. Moreover, the administration had to contend with the Panic of 1873 and the resulting Long Depression, the longest-lasting contraction in US history. In its second term, the Grant administration found itself increasingly checkmated by political and economic realities.

When he took office in March 1869, Grant had high hopes for the country's ability to put the war behind it and was always looking for ways to facilitate reconciliation. Throughout 1869, the president, who prided himself on his political independence, did not believe he needed to work with, or placate with patronage, congressional Republicans in order to achieve his legislative goals. Certainly, this reflected Grant's belief that he was "above politics" and his "over simplified" perception that policymakers would "accept orders from the President, irrespective of political attachments."[2] However, by early 1870, Grant came to understand the need to work the system in order to achieve tangible goals, and he adjusted his tactics by assuming leadership of the party.[3] Grant, like many of his immediate predecessors, complained about the incessant demands of office seekers and the corruption inherent in the spoils system, asserting that "no duty so embarrasses the Executive and the heads of departments as that of appointments." Yet he also recognized that the judicious distribution of patronage was essential to achieving his larger political aims.[4]

The transformation in Grant's approach to the spoilsmen began about halfway through his first year in office. In mid-August 1869, Grant traveled to Kane, Pennsylvania, at the request of Thomas L. Kane, a former Union general and philanthropist. Unbeknownst to Grant, Kane had invited Senator Cameron of Pennsylvania to join them. Cameron controlled the state's Republican machine and had a reputation for corruption and spoilsmanship that repelled the new president. Nevertheless, Grant came away from the trip much impressed with Cameron, and he proved a useful ally in the Senate.[5] Grant increasingly came to rely on Cameron and other spoilsmen (like Senator Roscoe Conkling of New York) to move legislation through Congress. Grant's decision to ally with these spoilsmen helped achieve some of the administration's legislative priorities but alienated several other Republicans and fed a narrative about corruption that dogged the president in his second term. To his detractors, Grant lived down to Gideon Welles's caustic observation that the general had been "flattered, seduced, and led astray by bad men."[6] In 1871, future president Rutherford B. Hayes said, "I fear that such advisors as Chandler, Cameron, and Conkling are too influential with Grant. They are not safe counselors."[7]

Frustration with Grant coalesced in the Liberal Republican movement, an amalgam of civil service reformers, low tariff men, and opponents of the administration's Reconstruction policies.[8] Some Liberal Republicans criticized Grant for too aggressively pushing Reconstruction, seeing the administration's efforts as simply creating sinecures for Southern Republicans. Many Liberals opposed the Ku Klux Klan bill (Sumner was a notable exception), believing that the administration's vigorous efforts on behalf of blacks represented militarism. According to Carl Schurz, Grant "operated by a system of combinations, military, political, and even senatorial" that smacked of "unrepublican Caesarism."[9] According to Schurz, "We desire the questions connected with the Civil War to be disposed of forever, to make room as soon as possible for the new problems of the present and future."[10] This was naïve on Schurz's part; the bitterness of the war, and the decades of sectional tension that had caused it, could not be simply "wished away," but the senator's statement is an apt demonstration of the fact that seven years after Appomattox, many white Northerners were impatient with Reconstruction.

The Liberals also criticized Grant for failing to pursue civil service reform, a charge that was untrue, despite his reliance on Republican congressmen and senators whose political power derived from spoilsmanship (and despite his own effective and shrewd disposition of patronage). In 1871, Grant established a Civil Service Commission headed by *Harper's Weekly* publisher George W. Curtis and the *Chicago Tribune*'s Joseph Medill, both prominent Republicans and active social reformers. Their report, issued in December that year, became the basis of subsequent civil service reforms, and many of its recommendations were codified into federal law in 1883 with the passage of the landmark Pendleton Civil Service Reform Act. When Grant submitted Curtis and Medill's report to Congress, he requested "all the strength which Congress can give me to enable me to carry out the reforms in the civil service, recommended by the Commission[e]rs."[11] However, most Republicans had little interest in civil service reform— patronage was, after all, the basis of their political power—so the president gave up the cause, seeing "it was impossible to carry it out in the condition of public feeling at the time."[12] While Grant might have pushed harder for civil service reform, many people close to him suspected—correctly—that his critics were more interested in weakening him politically than in reforming government.[13] Moreover, the Liberals' diffuse criticisms demonstrate that it was not the administration's policies they opposed but Grant himself.[14]

Though far from totally united, the Republican Party was far more cohesive in 1872 than it had been in 1868. The identity crisis caused by the end of the war that contributed to Grant's nomination in 1868 had largely disappeared by 1872, in part because of the Liberals' defection. Thus, as the election year dawned, the Republican Party was "an entrenched institution which had developed a life and a purpose . . . of its own. Vested interests, patronage, and the preservation of power now were of prime importance."[15] In short, the very elements of politics that so enraged the Liberals made non-Liberal Republicans the stronger faction of the two. At the Republican National Convention in Philadelphia, the Liberal Republicans were simply overwhelmed by the more practiced party regulars who ensured that Liberals were dispersed throughout the convention hall to prevent them from coordinating their message or disrupting the proceedings. The platform adopted in Philadelphia repudiated many of the Liberals' critiques, committing the party to aggressive federal action on behalf of African Americans to "complete liberty and exact equality in the enjoyment of all civil, political, and public rights . . . throughout the Union, [maintained] by efficient and appropriate State and Federal legislation." In addition, the platform asserted that "Congress and the President have only fulfilled an imperative duty in their measures for the suppression of violent and treasonable organizations in certain lately rebellious regions, and for the protection of the ballot-box, and therefore they are entitled to the thanks of the nation." Moreover, observing the nation's "obligations to the loyal women of America for their noble devotion to the cause of freedom," Republicans promised "respectful consideration" of "the honest demand of any class of citizens for additional rights."[16]

At their own convention in Cincinnati, the Liberal Republicans nominated Horace Greeley. Described by historian William L. Richter as a "crackpot reformer" who was "lovable but idiotic [and] wise but full of buncombe," Greeley was a well-known abolitionist with a penchant for idiosyncratic actions (like contributing toward the bail bond that freed former Confederate president Jefferson Davis from imprisonment in Fort Monroe in spring 1867).[17] Interestingly, Grant seems to have respected Greeley, at least before 1872; in 1870, the president described Greeley as "an honest, firm, untiring supporter of the republican party" and claimed to "have long desired a free, full talk with Mr. Greeley because I have confidence in his intentions."[18] In summer 1870, Grant even briefly toyed with the idea of appointing Greeley minister to Great Britain, and in November, he invited Greeley to dine at the White House, noting "there will be no one but yourself and my family present." Greeley accepted. Julia Grant recalled that the men "conversed on many subjects, both gentlemen seeming pleasantly interested."[19]

The Democrats were in disarray following the collapse of the Tweed Ring in New York City the previous year. At their national convention, they also nominated Greeley for president and adopted a platform whose first principle recognized "the equality of all men before the law" and held that "it is the duty of the Government in its dealings with the people to mete out equal and exact justice to all, of whatever nativity, race, color or persuasion, religion or politics."[20] But state Democratic conventions, which selected nominees for state and local offices, frequently repudiated this plank, and even when they did not, Democrats' opposition to equal rights "still remained dominant, though often dormant, in the party."[21] The disconnect between the national party platform and the state conventions illustrates the disarray that plagued the party seven years after the war's end and led to a second Democratic convention, convened by a faction known as the Straight Out Democrats, held in Louisville in September 1872.

The election created such strange bedfellows that former Confederate lieutenant general Nathan Bedford Forrest (who would soon become the Ku Klux Klan's imperial grand wizard) supported Grant because, when compared to Greeley's prewar abolitionism and undisguised hatred of the South, the president seemed the lesser of two evils.[22] Meanwhile, Republican representative Banks denounced the "wickedness of the President" and of the "thieves and assassins" surrounding Grant, and predicted "trouble, high taxation, and a corrupt Government" if Grant won reelection.[23] Unlike Grant, who refused to campaign, Greeley actively pursued the presidency, delivering almost two hundred speeches in one twelve-day period in September 1872.[24] Unfortunately for Greeley, "almost every attack on the first Administration of President Grant was answered by the political speakers on his side by a quotation from Greeley or the *New York Tribune*."[25] Moreover, behind the scenes, Grant showed that he had learned much about the ways of power over the last four years. The president adroitly distributed patronage to shore up the support of influential politicians, demonstrating that he was "a resourceful and persistent politician intent upon being reelected."[26] On November 5, he decisively won reelection by more than 800,000 votes, 3.6 million to Greeley's 2.8 million. The tally in the Electoral College was even more one-sided, with the president winning 282 votes to Greeley's 62. Greeley was devastated by the result (and by the death of his wife in October) and died three weeks later. Despite the bitterness of the election, Grant attended Greeley's funeral. Seemingly vindicated by reelection, Grant remarked in his second inaugural address, "from my candidacy for my present office in 1868 to the close of the last Presidential campaign, I have been the subject of abuse and slander scarcely ever equaled in political history, which today I feel I can afford to disregard in view of your verdict, which I gratefully accept."[27]

The practical consequence of the Liberal Republican insurgency during the campaign was a tightening of Republican Party discipline. In the House, many of the leading Liberals lost their bids for reelection in 1872, while in the Senate a number of leading Republicans sought to punish the Liberals for their defection. For instance, Senator Conkling's allies got control of the Committee on Committees, which controlled committee assignments in the upper house, and deprived the Liberals of seats on the panels, thereby limiting their power and influence. This move had the added benefit of strengthening Conkling and his allies' control of federal patronage. As Senate historian David J. Rothman noted, "Any presidential appointment for a port or harbor post was first referred to the [Committee on Committees] for advice on the nominee's fitness," giving the committee's members *de facto* veto power over presidential appointments.[28] The increasing focus on party discipline was best demonstrated by Indiana senator Oliver P. Morton's exclamation in a speech on the Senate floor, "I hold the Republican party superior in importance to any man who is a member of it [and] I intend to stand honestly and in good faith by its organization."[29] Grant's victory, which was the most decisive popular vote margin in US history up to that point, shielded the fact that the president's political standing was actually weaker than in his first term. Despite Grant's commanding victory, Republicans lost four Senate seats, though the party won more than three dozen additional seats in the House. Moreover, many of the events and decisions that contribute to Grant's low ranking among American presidents emerged during his second term, when a cascade of scandals implicated several members of his cabinet and tarnished him by association.

Despite his commanding reelection victory, Inauguration Day was an inauspicious start to Grant's second term. March 4, 1873, was a bitterly cold day made worse by strong gusts of wind, and many of the cadets marching in the parade suffered frostbite; several even died of pneumonia. That night, at the inauguration ball (paid for by contributions from Republican officeholders who had been pressured to donate), which was held in a gigantic wooden building constructed for the purpose, the temperature dipped below zero. The building, which did not have heaters, was less than half full, the food froze, and, shockingly, a guest died on the dance floor because of the cold, which had exacerbated her bronchial problems. If that was not enough, the ball featured a conspicuous mixing of the races, outraging conservatives.[30]

Nor did the administration get a honeymoon from challenges. Just as in Grant's first term, an economic crisis developed, but unlike in 1869, the president did not avoid catastrophe through decisive executive action. The Panic of 1873, which inaugurated the longest depression in US history up to that point (known as the Long Depression), was caused by the collapse of Jay Cooke & Company. Cooke was a Philadelphia-based investment banker known as the "financier of the Civil War" for having sold federal government bonds during the war. A Radical Republican, Cooke knew Grant personally (the president had an account at Cooke's bank), though he had supported Salmon Chase for the 1868 Republican presidential nomination. This appears not to have troubled Grant, who stayed at Cooke's house on several occasions, contributing to widespread criticism that the president had ignored warning signs.

America's economy boomed after the war, making it possible for Republicans to pay down the federal debt and provide generous subsidies to railroads to expand their networks; as a consequence, the country's railroad companies laid thirty-five thousand new miles of railroad.[31] Fueling the expansion in railroad lines was the discovery of the Comstock Lode, a major deposit of silver ore in western Nevada in the 1850s. After the war, the goal was to get the silver from Nevada to the industrial East, where it could be minted into coins or exported to Europe. When Germany ceased minting silver coins in 1871, and the US Congress passed a bill that stopped backing currency with silver in February 1873, the price of the metal dropped precipitously. This depressed the market for silver, which was one of the most important commodities shipped by rail; consequently, it lowered the railroads' expected revenues and dampened enthusiasm for investing in them. Add to that the rising interest rates fueled by the Grant administration's tight money policies and what existed was the perfect recipe for a disastrous economic depression. All that was needed was the spark, and it came September 18, 1873. Cooke had invested heavily in railroads, but due to the slowing of the silver market, Jay Cooke and Company was unable to sell its latest bond issue and went into bankruptcy. Two days later, the New York Stock Exchange suspended trading. On September 20, Grant and Treasury Secretary William A. Richardson (who had only been on the job six months) traveled to New York to meet with the city's bankers. They gave the president conflicting advice: some advocated staying the course, or even increasing the pace, of tightening the money supply while others argued that the system needed an infusion of cash. Acting on his own initiative, Richardson tried to ameliorate the effects of the crisis by reissuing $26 million in greenbacks he had just retired, but this was too small an action to affect the quickly spreading financial catastrophe. Later that month, Grant urged bankers to increase their lending and thereby avert a financial catastrophe, but he did not take decisive action to inject liquidity into the economy, which might have blunted the panic's effects.

The results of the panic and ensuing depression were catastrophic: workers' wages dropped by one quarter, and three million workers lost their jobs. One in four railroads defaulted on their bonds, spooking investors and weakening railroads' access to capital, magnifying the job losses. This led to the outbreak of violence, often directed at railroads, including by the infamous Molly Maguires of northeastern Pennsylvania. Lawmakers grasped for ways to restore the economy's health, unleashing a flood of legislative proposals that Senator John Sherman denigrated as "the wildest schemes for relief."[32] Right before the end of its session in March 1875, the lame duck Congress passed a massive tariff increase, bucking the trend since the end of the war of lowering duties on imports. The goal was twofold: provide protection to American industries against foreign imports and raise badly needed revenue for the Treasury Department. Another response was the Inflation Bill, which would have retroactively approved Richardson's reissue of the $26 million in greenbacks and authorized the Treasury secretary to emit another $18 million of bills. Despite enormous political pressure—Julia Grant recalled people lobbying her to influence her husband's decision—the president ultimately vetoed the bill, a move many of his close allies in Congress could not believe.[33] Most of Grant's cabinet supported the Inflation Bill, and Senator Cameron prophesied that the veto would cost the Republicans in the midterm election.[34] In his veto message, Grant apologized for "not being able to give my assent to a measure which has received the sanction of . . . a majority of the legislators." However, Grant asserted that he could not sign the bill because he did not support any "method of making paper money equal to coin when the coin is not owed or held ready to redeem the promises to pay."[35] Such sentiments were a far cry from Grant's May 1868 promise to "have no policy of my own to interfere against the will of the people," a measure of how much he had evolved while in office.[36]

The Senate sustained Grant's veto, though only barely (a majority of senators voted to override, but the total did not reach the two-thirds required by the Constitution), and after catastrophic losses in the midterm elections, Congress (under enormous pressure from the White House) doubled down on Grant's contractionist policies by passing the Specie Resumption Act of 1875. That law committed the United States to redeem, on demand, greenbacks for specie beginning January 1, 1879. The bill passed the House despite united Democratic opposition and the defection of twenty Republicans.[37] Though Grant biographer Jean Edward Smith asserts that Grant "had the political wind at his back," his veto of the Inflation Bill spurred the emergence of the Greenback Party, which had officially formed in Indianapolis on November 25, 1874. Two years later, the party nominated a national ticket headed by Peter Cooper, an abolitionist and founder of the Cooper Union in Manhattan. He ran on a platform demanding repeal of the Specie Resumption Act and promised the free coinage of silver in an attempt to increase the money supply. Clearly, not everyone was pleased by the administration's tight money policies.[38]

Worse, the administration committed several unforced errors. Even as the economy collapsed, Congress passed—and the president signed—legislation that was guaranteed to cause a backlash. The so-called Salary Grab Act, passed by the Forty-Second Congress on its last day in session, doubled the president's salary and provided for hefty increases in the annual pay of the vice president, members of the cabinet, the chief justice of the United States, the associate justices of the Supreme Court, and (of course) members of Congress. Most shocking, it granted lame duck members of Congress a retroactive $5,000 bonus. The public outcry was swift, and Congress repealed most provisions of the act January 20, 1874, leaving only the provisions increasing the salaries of the president and the justices of the Supreme Court. The Salary Grab Act was such a politically tone-deaf and cynical move (particularly during an economic depression) that it contributed to the Republicans' defeat in the midterm elections of 1874 (giving Democrats control of the House for the first time since the war) and provided considerable fodder for Grant's opponents, who argued his administration was corrupt and out of touch.

Obviously, Grant should have known better than to sign the Salary Grab Act, but by 1873, his group of advisers had shrunk considerably and the character of the administration had changed. Many of Grant's clerks—the men who worked beside the president daily and ensured the smooth flow of paperwork through the White House—left the administration.[39] Moreover, Grant's cabinet had undergone significant changes during the preceding four years, and Grant's biographer has called the second term cabinet "weaker" than the first. At least some of the administration's missteps from 1873 to 1877 can be attributed to this and to the near constant turnover in executive offices during the second term.[40] Columbus Delano, who replaced Jacob D. Cox as interior secretary in November 1870, was easier to get along with but less insightful than his predecessor. Akerman's replacement as attorney general, George H. Williams, was less forceful in pursuing federal efforts to protect African Americans than his predecessor due to concerns about waning political support for Reconstruction.[41] Treasury Secretary George S. Boutwell left shortly after Grant's second inauguration in 1873; over the four years, no fewer than three men—William A. Richardson, Benjamin H. Bristow, and Lot M. Morrill—served as Treasury secretary, a shocking amount of upheaval given the unprecedented economic challenges facing the country. In August 1874, Grant appointed Marshall Jewell postmaster general but quickly regretted it. Jewell was obstinate and insubordinate, once boasting to a visitor, "Grant hasn't any influence in this department."[42] As a result, in July 1876, Grant demanded Jewell's resignation because he "could stand [his] annoyance no longer."[43] Writing decades after the fact, William H. Crook, who in 1870 Grant appointed to be executive clerk of the president, maintained that the frequent cabinet changes in the second term (particularly in its last two years) caused "the many difficulties . . . [that] brought discredit upon the administration."[44] These dynamics strengthened Fish's position in Grant's cabinet, and the president increasingly relied on the secretary of state for advice about domestic policy as well as foreign affairs.

In addition, the Grant administration was rocked by a series of scandals during the president's second term. During the presidential campaign, the *New York Sun* dropped a bombshell about political corruption. In 1864, Congress chartered the Union Pacific Railroad (UP) to build the eastern portion of the transcontinental railroad. The company's vice president, Thomas C. Durant, and George F. Train, who had helped organize the UP, created the Credit Mobilier of America corporation, whose role (at least on paper) was to construct the railroad (as opposed to operating it once it was built, which was the Union Pacific's raison d'être). Essentially, the UP signed contracts with Credit Mobilier to build the railroad at inflated prices, and the overages between the actual and reported costs were then kicked back to various members of the railroad's board of directors. The construction was such a boondoggle that of the nearly $95 million Congress paid to Credit Mobilier (through the Union Pacific), nearly $44 million was profit distributed to the UP's shareholders. In order to ensure Congress's continued friendliness to the railroad, in 1867, US representative Oakes Ames of Massachusetts became head of the Credit Mobilier and proceeded to offer various congressmen stock in the company at discounted prices. This was an outrageous conflict of interest, given that the company's profitability was dictated by Congress's continuing willingness to pay the invoices that the UP presented for reimbursement. After a falling out with Ames, Henry Simpson McComb, president of the Mississippi Central Railroad, leaked compromising letters to the *New York Sun*, which broke the story. At least partially, the *Sun* did so to embarrass Grant, whose reelection the newspaper's editors opposed, and though the president had no connection to the scandal, outgoing vice president Schuyler Colfax and Treasury Secretary George S. Boutwell were implicated. Ultimately, the House created two committees to investigate the matter: one to look into the UP and the other to investigate members of Congress and of the executive branch. That committee acquitted all but two individuals, creating the impression of a cover-up.

Nor was this the only scandal dogging the administration in the lead-up to the 1872 presidential election. Moses H. Grinnell and Thomas Murphy, Grant's appointees to the New York Customs House (the largest revenue-generating port in the United States), had charged importers enormous fees to store unclaimed freight in private warehouses. George K. Leet, one of the owners of these warehouses, shared the profits with members of Grant's administration, including Orville Babcock. Once the scheme became public, Treasury Secretary Boutwell instituted several reforms designed to curb these abuses, but as late as summer 1872, Congress continued investigating the matter, and Grant's opponents blasted the president for the company he kept. Again, there was no evidence that Grant had done anything wrong, but to embarrass him, the Senate ordered the printing of its report on the matter, which included damning testimony from several members of the administration, including Babcock. That November, Grant—under great political pressure—accepted Murphy's resignation (Grinnell had left office the year before). The president replaced Murphy with Chester A. Arthur, whose sole qualification was his closeness to New York political boss Roscoe Conkling. At the same time, Congress was investigating allegations that Postmaster General John Creswell had sold fictitious mail delivery routes. Allegations of bribery and influence peddling were rife, and despite the fact that Congress exonerated Creswell in 1872, the scandal did not die; in

1876, the Democratic-controlled House again looked into the matter and found evidence that the 1872 investigation had been influenced by a $40,000 bribe, though by then Creswell had left office.

Another scandal, dealing with the collection of federal revenue, contributed to what one contemporary called "the great epidemic of distrust that swept over the land in the second administration."[45] Beginning in 1872, the Bureau of Internal Revenue was empowered by Congress to hire private individuals to help collect money owed to the United States. Under the terms of this plan, collectors would be able to keep 50 percent of the funds they recovered. In 1873, Boutwell's successor at the Treasury Department, William A. Richardson, hired John D. Sanborn to collect $427,000 in unpaid taxes. Sanborn's success persuaded Congress to grant him the right to collect all unpaid taxes owed by railroad companies, but the continuous expansion of collections brought Sanborn into conflict with the revenue bureau's own efforts to collect taxes. In fact, in order to maximize his payment, Sanborn absorbed existing bureau tax cases, thereby getting paid for collection work done largely by federal employees. When the scandal broke in January 1874, it made corruption seem endemic. Worse, there were allegations—never proven—that Sanborn had shared his profits with Representative Butler and Treasury Secretary Richardson. These concerns were only exacerbated when Sanborn was acquitted of all charges. Though Richardson resigned as a result of the scandal and Grant signed a bill abolishing the contract system, the damage was done; the scandal fed an emerging narrative of corruption in the federal government that certainly helped Democratic candidates win election to Congress the following November.

Things went from bad to worse for Grant after the Democrats' win in the midterm elections of 1874, and in 1875, two scandals broke that reached directly into the cabinet. In October 1875, Interior Secretary Delano was forced to resign after it was discovered he had taken bribes for issuing fraudulent land grants. Subsequent revelations included the fact that Delano had granted cartographical contracts to his son and Grant's brother Orvil, despite the fact that neither man was qualified to carry out the work. Delano's successor, former US senator Zachariah Chandler of Michigan, discovered that there were several fictitious clerks on the Interior Department's payroll and that corruption was endemic throughout the department. Consequently,

Chandler dismissed nearly all the clerks in the Patent Office and, on Grant's orders, fired everyone working in the Department of Indian Affairs office. In spring 1875, Attorney General Williams had been forced to resign when evidence surfaced that he had taken bribes in exchange for dropping a case against merchants accused of failing to pay the full tariffs on imports.

In 1876, the Democratic-controlled House discovered that while serving as navy secretary, George M. Robeson had amassed a fortune of more than $300,000 on a government salary of $8,000 a year. During the investigation, it was discovered that one of the navy's grain and feed suppliers, A. G. Cattell & Company, had purchased for Robeson a vacation house in Long Branch, New Jersey. Despite the fact that the House investigators could not prove a direct quid pro quo, the appearance of wrongdoing was undeniable. Moreover, Robeson was accused of squandering more than $15 million in naval construction funds, largely because of shoddy bookkeeping practices. Because House investigators could find no proof that Robeson had broken any laws, he served as navy secretary until the end of Grant's administration. However, Grant's strident defense of Robeson—who certainly appeared guilty of something—added to the impression that the president surrounded himself with unsavory individuals.

This narrative was reinforced when an investigation in the House revealed that Secretary of War Belknap had taken money in exchange for lucrative trading post contracts. In 1870, Congress authorized the secretary of war to appoint private administrators of trading posts at army forts in the West. Native Americans came to the forts and traded for food, clothing, and other supplies, making these appointments incredibly lucrative. Belknap's wife, Carrie, arranged for a kickback scheme in which the incumbent trading post contractor at Oklahoma's Fort Sill, John S. Evans, paid $12,000 per year for the privilege of keeping his contract; Carrie Belknap split the money with her friend, Caleb P. Marsh. Within a year, Carrie died, but Belknap continued to receive payments that eventually totaled $20,000. At the end of February 1876, Marsh implicated Belknap in the scheme while testifying to a House committee investigating the matter. When Grant became aware of the matter March 2, he scheduled a meeting with the leading Republican on the committee, Lyman K. Bass. Hearing of the meeting, Belknap rushed to the White House with Interior Secretary Chandler and begged Grant to accept his resignation. Late for an appointment, Grant agreed; though the president could not have known it at the time, this had far-reaching consequences for the scandal: while the House impeached Belknap for the former secretary of war's actions, the Senate refused to convict him on the rationale that Belknap had left office and was now a private citizen. However, Grant's willingness to accept Belknap's resignation made it look like the president was complicit in, or at least tacitly condoned, the secretary's actions.

The most bizarre of the many scandals occurred in April 1876, when mercenaries posing as Secret Service agents burglarized the Washington district attorney's office safe and removed evidence to be used in an ongoing trial of corrupt building contractors. The contractors then tried to plant the stolen materials at the home of Columbus Alexander, one of the key witnesses in the contractors' trial; apparently, the goal was to discredit Alexander and thereby prevent the contractors from being convicted. The plan fell apart when the burglars knocked on Alexander's door but failed to rouse their victim (one newspaper claimed he was "sleeping the deep sleep of the just"); they were arrested by the very police officers they had alerted to witness Alexander receiving stolen goods. Several of the conspirators agreed to cooperate with authorities, and they implicated Grant's friend Orville Babcock, who was then superintendent of public works and was involved in the building contractors' peculations. Babcock was indicted in what came to be called the Safe Burglary Conspiracy but was not convicted, leading many contemporaries to argue that the "powerful politicians of the ring" had interfered with the jury.[46] Whatever the truth of that claim, the story was widely reported in the press and embarrassed the administration.

As alarming as these scandals were, they paled in comparison to the Whiskey Ring Scandal. Whiskey distillers in the Midwest had avoided paying the excise tax on whiskey by bribing local Treasury officials. Though this had gone on since the Lincoln administration, by the mid-1870s, it had coalesced into an efficient machine overseen by a ring of distillers who used a variety of unsavory tactics to keep Treasury officials in line. Acting on Grant's suggestion, in January 1875, Treasury Secretary Bristow ordered the Treasury officials rumored to be involved in the scandal transferred to different locations effective February 15 with an eye toward disrupting and exposing the

Whiskey Ring's operations. Fearing that advance notice would encourage the ring's leaders to destroy evidence, Grant rescinded the order; though his only goal was to ensure that "no guilty man escape," Grant's critics interpreted the reversal as proof that the president colluded in the ring's crimes.[47] Changing tactics, Bristow dispatched several spies to gather evidence, and on May 13, Attorney General Williams moved against the ring, seizing several distilleries and making hundreds of arrests. Alarmingly, John McDonald, supervisor of internal revenue, and Orville Babcock, Grant's personal secretary, were among the 350 individuals indicted for their roles in the scandal. It was later established that Babcock had sent McDonald coded letters directing the ring's operation in St. Louis.

Shrewdly, Grant appointed one of his strongest critics, former US senator John B. Henderson of Missouri, as special prosecutor in the case. This was the first time in US history that a federal special prosecutor was appointed. Henderson's appointment was designed to convince the American public that the investigation would be conducted scrupulously and honestly, but Grant came to regret the appointment almost immediately for two reasons: first, out of a misguided sense of loyalty to his friend, the president unsuccessfully sought to have Babcock tried in a military rather than a civilian court because he expected the former to show the defendant greater deference. Second, after several Whiskey Ring defendants were offered immunity in exchange for their testimony, Grant ordered Bristow not to make any more such deals because he wanted the guilty punished. Grant's actions were motivated by friendship on the one hand and a desire for justice on the other, but together they fueled concerns that he was trying to hamper the investigation. In response, Henderson publicly accused the president of interfering in the case and privately intimated that Grant was complicit in the scandal.[48] Grant responded to these charges by firing the special prosecutor and replacing him with former US representative James Broadhead of Missouri, which only encouraged speculation that the president had something to hide. To make matters worse, Grant wanted to testify on Babcock's behalf; his cabinet persuaded him not to do this. Instead, Grant submitted to a deposition that was read at Babcock's trial; in it, the president asserted that he had no knowledge of Babcock's involvement with the Whiskey Ring. This marked another, and troubling, first in US history: Grant had the dubious distinction of being the first sitting president to testify for a defendant in a criminal case. Partially as a result of Grant's deposition, the jury found Babcock not guilty. Though the investigation resulted in more than one hundred convictions and led to the recovery of $3 million in Treasury revenue, it diminished the president in the eyes of the public, particularly after Grant pardoned former Internal Revenue supervisor John McDonald in late January 1877.

There was, of course, an element of partisanship to these scandals. In the second term, most of the investigations that dogged the administration originated in the Democratic-controlled House and were driven as much by a desire to hobble the administration as they were by a desire to ferret out illegality and corruption. For instance, the majority report from the House investigating Robeson's actions as navy secretary was written entirely by Democrats; the minority report, written entirely by Republicans, exonerated Robeson and deplored the investigation as a partisan witch hunt designed to embarrass the administration. In addition, the Democrats on the committee that investigated the charges against Belknap were all too happy to promulgate stories (real and imagined) of the administration's corruption. However, the fact that these were partisan attacks on the administration does not change the fact that they discovered several credible instances of wrongdoing.

All told, the scandals damaged Grant's reputation, weakened him politically, and made pursuing his legislative agenda much more difficult. No evidence was ever presented, then or since, that Grant profited from or even knew about the corruption in his administration, and most historians concede that the most he was guilty of was being too trusting of questionable subordinates like Babcock. Nevertheless, the president's responses to these scandals tarnished his legacy, sapped his effectiveness by eroding public support for the administration, and, in 1874, helped to give Democrats control of the House. Grant seems to have believed that because he knew his decisions were not (explicitly) influenced by any gifts, the public should take his word for it. In the wake of the 1874 midterm elections, lawyer Everett P. Wheeler, a Democrat, summed up the prevailing wisdom when he said "the real cause of the defeat of the Republican party in the recent elections was because it had no principles and had become a mere party of plunder."[49]

There was more than a little truth to this assertion, and the consequences for the administration were dire: Grant faced an increasingly antagonistic Congress. During Grant's eight years as president, Congress overrode his vetoes four times; three of those four occurred in 1876, at a time when Republicans controlled the Senate. Worse, in April 1876, Congress passed a bill slashing the president's salary by 50 percent, which Grant vetoed. In addition, and despite the fact that Grant had all but ruled out seeking a third term the previous May, in December 1875, the House passed a resolution calling a third term "unwise, unpatriotic, and fraught with peril to our free institutions."[50] Perhaps most concerning was that several dozen Republican congressmen crossed the aisle to join Democrats in voting for the measure, a clear sign of Grant's declining popularity in the party. Executive Clerk William H. Crook recalled Grant's "decline in popularity was evident to himself as to those by whom he was surrounded. . . . But he took it all apparently as one of the fortunes of war."[51]

Seven

"The Northern Mind . . . Runs Away from the Past"

G RANT, AS A SECOND-TERM PRESIDENT with no love for the job, could afford to be philosophical about his political troubles, but they eroded his political power and made it much more difficult to effectively protect African Americans and Native Americans. By 1873, white Southern Democrats' attempts to "redeem" the South by rolling back rights for African Americans and end Republican rule of the South were making progress. The combination of Northern apathy toward Reconstruction, scandals, and economic depression contributed to the disastrous midterm elections of 1874, which in turn made it even more difficult for the administration to muster political support for Reconstruction.[1] Ominously, many of the Republicans' losses in the House occurred in Northern states, such as New York, New Jersey, Ohio, Pennsylvania, Michigan, and Wisconsin, which many in the party interpreted as waning support for Reconstruction. In 1871, Attorney General Amos Akerman noted the waning support for Reconstruction, saying "the northern mind . . . runs away from the past."[2] In February 1875, the lame-duck Forty-Third Congress passed the Civil Rights Act of 1875, which guaranteed to all citizens equal rights in public accommodations and conveyances (but not public schools); Grant signed it March 1. This law was the last gasp of legislative expansion of black rights; it was eight decades before Congress again passed civil rights legislation.

Though genuinely concerned about African Americans' rights, the administration was far less effective in protecting black rights after 1873 than it had been during Grant's first term. In several states of the former Confederacy, Republicans were voted out of office in elections frequently preceded by violence and bloodshed. In spring 1873, Attorney General Williams suspended the prosecutions of Klansmen in North Carolina and South Carolina, apparently in the belief that a carrot might be more effective than a stick in defeating the Klan. Yet even this could not satisfy Reconstruction's opponents; Williams was questioned by a congressional committee in 1874 about his allegedly "excessive" use of federal troops to protect black voters and Southern Republicans.[3] Moreover, the suspension of prosecutions failed to reduce violence, so Williams changed tactics in fall 1874 (not coincidentally a few weeks before Election Day), ordering federal law-enforcement officials to aggressively "detect, expose, arrest, and punish" Klansmen. After the elections, which were disastrous for the administration, Williams again changed course, advocating "proper care and economy" in pursuing criminal charges.[4]

Naturally, not all the failures of Reconstruction can be placed at the administration's feet. On the local level, Southern whites were often uncooperative with, if not outright hostile to, the federal government's attempts to enforce civil rights legislation. Federal prosecutors found it difficult to assemble juries willing to convict their friends and neighbors of violations of federal law, and witnesses were often too intimidated to testify. More often than not, state and local authorities impeded investigations and worked to frustrate prosecutions. As early as 1870, Akerman complained that Southerners took "all kindness on the part of the Government as evidence of timidity, and hence are emboldened to lawlessness by it."[5] Grant admitted as much, noting after he left the White House that the South consistently refused to accept the war's outcome. He complained "there has never been a moment since Lee surrendered that I would not have gone more than halfway to meet with the Southern people in a spirit of conciliation. But they have never responded to it. . . . I do not see what the North can do that has not been done, unless we surrender the results of the war."[6]

In April 1873, Louisiana witnessed the largest racial massacre in US history when, on Easter, white Southerners murdered approximately 150 blacks in Colfax, seat of Grant Parish. Massachusetts representative George F. Hoar recalled that the subsequent congressional investigation "disclosed a terrible story of murder, brutality, and crime."[7] Eventually, seventy-two whites were indicted for their roles in the massacre, but only nine were tried. Of those, only three were convicted (and those convictions were later vacated by the Supreme Court). In August 1874, members of the White League, a paramilitary organization affiliated with the Democratic Party, murdered six white Republican officeholders and five to twenty blacks in Coushatta. Things got so bad in the Bayou State that on September 5, 1874, some of Louisiana's blacks wrote to Grant and begged him to resettle them in a territory or even in Africa. Nine days later, fighting broke out between armed White Leaguers and local and state militias. The following day, Grant issued a proclamation instructing the armed bands to disperse. On the sixteenth, he dispatched troops to New Orleans, and the White Leaguers' rebellion was crushed, though only temporarily. On January 4, 1875, the Louisiana State Legislature convened, and Democrats seized control of it, seating five Democrats; US troops were required to expel them. The administration's efforts to control the violence in Louisiana were extremely controversial and split Grant's cabinet, with Secretary of State Fish and Treasury Secretary Bristow distancing themselves from the army's strong-arm tactics. Responding to a Senate inquiry into conditions in Louisiana, Grant complained, "To say that lawlessness, turbulence, and bloodshed have characterized the political affairs of that State since its reorganization under the reconstruction acts, is only to repeat what has become well known as a part of its unhappy history."[8] Ultimately, a congressional committee got both sides to compromise: Louisiana's Democrats got control of the state's House while Republicans controlled the Senate and GOP governor William P. Kellogg was allowed to serve out his term, quelling the violence for the moment.

Nor were these problems limited to Louisiana. In Arkansas, bloody fighting that eventually claimed the lives of two hundred people broke out in 1872 between two factions of the Republican Party, one supporting Elisha Baxter for governor, the other backing Joseph Brooks, who promised to reenfranchise former Confederates if elected. The state legislature, which was friendly to Baxter, decided the hotly contested election in his favor, but armed forces under Brooks ousted the would-be governor, and in 1874, a state judge swore Brooks in as governor. Grant tried to sidestep the issue, asking the state legislature to settle the matter, but Baxter refused to negotiate with people he viewed as usurpers. Grant eventually proclaimed Baxter the lawfully elected governor, but the writing was on the wall: in fall 1874, the state adopted a new constitution that enfranchised former Confederates. Grant condemned the constitution in February 1875, asking in a message to the US Senate, "What is there to prevent . . . each of the states, recently re-admitted to federal relations on certain conditions, changing their constitutions and violating their pledges if this . . . action in Ark is . . . acquiesced in? . . . I respectfully submit whether a precedent so dangerous to the stability of a state government, if not of the National Government also, should be recognized by Congress."[9]

Things were bad in Mississippi as well. In January 1874, Republican Adelbert Ames was inaugurated governor, but the following December, following the Democratic sweep in the midterm elections, race riots broke out in Vicksburg, unleashing a spree of white-on-black violence that cost the lives of nearly three hundred African Americans. Grant dispatched federal troops to Vicksburg in January 1875, but that was not the end of the matter. In early September 1875, White Leaguers rioted in Clinton and massacred blacks. Grant, under pressure from congressional Republicans who feared the political consequences of sending troops to prop up another Southern state government, decided against deploying federal resources, a decision that historian Eric Foner called "a milestone in the retreat from Reconstruction."[10] Seeing that no federal support was coming, Governor Ames and the Democrats reached a peace agreement in October; under its terms, Ames agreed to disarm the militia units loyal to him in exchange for Democrats' promises to hold fair elections. The Democrats violated their pledges, terrorizing blacks and white Republicans. As a consequence, Democrats won control of the legislature. In early March 1876, the Democratic-controlled legislature impeached Governor Ames, and because the outcome was never in doubt, he resigned rather than subject himself to trial and conviction in the state Senate.

In South Carolina in early July 1876, armed whites attacked a black militia company, executing five of the militiamen. In September, the state was racked by race riots designed to intimidate black voters. On October 17, his eye clearly on the upcoming presidential election, Grant described the conditions in South Carolina as nothing less than a state of "insurrection and domestic violence" and commanded "all persons engaged in said unlawful and insurrectionary proceedings to disperse and retire peaceably to their respective abodes."[11] On November 7, South Carolina narrowly elected former Confederate lieutenant general Wade Hampton III governor in a campaign generally considered the bloodiest in the state's history. Hampton's margin of victory was small—approximately one thousand one hundred votes— and because local whites had clearly intimidated black voters, the sitting Republican governor, Daniel H. Chamberlain, was kept in office by the power of federal troops; Hampton only became governor after Grant left office in March 1877 and President Hayes ordered US troops removed from South Carolina.

Reflecting on these events in 1878, Grant concluded ruefully, "the wisest thing would have been to have continued for some time the military rule [of the South]. That would have enabled the Southern people to pull themselves together and repair material losses. Military rule would have been just to all: the negro who wanted freedom, the white man who wanted protection, the Northern man who wanted union."[12] This was wishful thinking on Grant's part: prolonged military rule in the South would have been costly and controversial, running smack into the Republicans' other priorities (namely a quick Reconstruction and shrinking the federal government). Moreover, the man charged with implementing Reconstruction policy, Commanding General of the Army William T. Sherman, opposed a strong military presence in the South. In a January 1875 letter to his brother, Sherman confessed, "I have always thought it wrong to bolster up weak State governments by our troops. We should keep the peace always; but not act as bailiff constables and catch thieves. That should be beneath a soldier's vocation."[13]

In addition to vigorous military action on behalf of African Americans, Reconstruction also depended on enabling legislation, which Congress stopped passing in1875. However, it was not just Southern congressmen who hobbled Reconstruction; Northern Democrats and even some Republicans worked to weaken or eliminate protections for African Americans. Former Speaker of the House James G. Blaine recalled that beginning in 1872, Pennsylvania Democrat Samuel Randall offered a bill to fully restore the rights of everyone in the United States, including former Confederates. While this bill gained no traction before 1875, once the Democrats took control of the House, it moved forward, coming to a vote in January 1876. The Democrats were totally united behind the bill, but they could not muster the two-thirds supermajority required by the Constitution (despite being joined by several Republicans). While the Senate would not have passed such a bill and Grant would never have signed it, it nevertheless demonstrates that the era of strong federal protection for African Americans had come to an end.[14]

Worse, the Supreme Court rolled back existing legal protections for blacks during Grant's second term. In a series of 1873 decisions collectively known as the Slaughter-House Cases, the court ruled 5 to 4 that the Fourteenth Amendment affected only individuals' US citizenship, not their state citizenships. This decision "virtually emasculated" Section 1 of the Fourteenth Amendment—which provided "All persons born or naturalized in the United States . . . are citizens of the United States and of the State wherein they reside" and forbade states and the federal government from creating any law "which shall abridge the privileges or immunities of citizens of the United States"—and showed "a marked tendency to uphold the powers of the States," thereby seriously weakening the federal government's ability to protect blacks' rights.[15] In short, the Court rendered the Fourteenth Amendment powerless to redress racist state laws. On March 26, 1876, the Supreme Court announced two decisions that further dealt a blow to African Americans' rights. In *United States v. Cruikshank*, the court further narrowed the Fourteenth Amendment's scope, ruling 5 to 4 that it applied only to state actions, not individuals' actions, thereby depriving blacks of the right to sue whites for violations of their civil rights. In *United States v. Reese*, the Court ruled 7 to 2 that the Fifteenth Amendment did not confer on blacks the right to vote, it merely prohibited racially based limitations on suffrage rights. Practically, the effect was to weaken legal remedies for violations of blacks' rights, and here three of Grant's four court appointees ruled with the majority.

Indirectly, Grant played a role in these setbacks, given that by 1874, the court was largely his administration's creation. In May 1873, Chief Justice Salmon P. Chase died. Grant moved slowly in nominating a successor, waiting until November to offer the post to Senator Roscoe Conkling, who declined. Initially, Grant nominated Caleb Cushing to be chief justice. Cushing was a Unionist Democrat; after the war, he had negotiated a right-of-way treaty for a canal crossing the isthmus of Panama and then served as one of the US consuls at the Geneva Tribunal of Arbitration on the *Alabama* claims. However, political considerations forced Grant to withdraw Cushing's nomination on January 13, 1874. On January 19, Grant nominated Morrison R. Waite, largely at the behest of Interior Secretary Delano. Despite some nasty commentary—*The Nation* described Waite as "in the front-rank of second-rank lawyers"—he was unanimously confirmed January 21.[16]

It was not just Grant's Reconstruction policies that were under siege; his peace policy fell apart as well during the second term. In 1872, the US Army became embroiled in the short Modoc War, following an effort to relocate Modoc Indians from an area around the Lost River in northern California. Grant tried unsuccessfully to negotiate a peace with the Modocs, but the Indians killed the leader of the president's peace commission, Brigadier General Edward R. S. Canby. General Sherman responded by dispatching Colonel Alvan C. Gillem to the area with a mandate to kill or capture the Modocs' leader, Kintpuash (known to whites as Captain Jack). Sherman's chilling orders—"Any measure of severity to the savages will be sustained"—indicated that Grant's peace policy was in serious trouble, and in fact many historians date the beginning of the Indian Wars to this event.[17] Kintpuash and his followers were captured in June 1873, and after a cursory trial, they were hanged that October; Grant's peace policy suffered a "body blow" from which it never recovered.[18]

In 1874, fighting broke out between the army and Southern Plains tribes in what came to be called the Red River War. The proximate cause of the conflict was white overhunting of buffalo in Indian territory. Members of the Comanche, Cheyenne, and Kiowa nations retaliated by mounting raids on white settlements in Texas and Kansas. In response, General Sherman convinced the president to allow the army to pursue Native Americans onto reservations, leading to several engagements throughout the late summer and culminating in the defeat of the Indians at the Battle of Palo Duro Canyon. About two weeks after the battle, many of the Indians surrendered or simply returned to their reservations, ending the war. Around the same time, a reconnaissance mission commanded by Lieutenant Colonel George Custer reported the presence of gold in the Black Hills region of present-day South Dakota, an area sacred to local Native Americans. The rumors of gold in the Black Hills were sure to attract white miners, inviting conflict with the region's Indians. Red Cloud, leader of a subset of the Sioux known as the Lakota, resolved to see the president in order to enlist his help in halting white incursion in the Black Hills. Red Cloud had credibility with Grant: after commanding the Lakota Sioux in a two-year conflict against the US Army (known as Red Cloud's War, during which the army suffered its worst military defeat on the western plains up to that point), he led his people to a reservation. Grant met with Red Cloud's delegation several times in late May 1875, and offered the Indians $25,000 for the Black Hills. He also offered to resettle the Lakota Sioux in Indian territory, but the Native Americans refused both offers, and white intrusion in the Black Hills only increased. Consequently, in November 1875, Grant and several cabinet members met with Major General Philip Sheridan, commander of the Division of the Missouri, and Brigadier General George Crook, commander of the Department of the Platte. The administration decided to end the practice of evicting white miners from the reservation, thereby tacitly encouraging white infiltration of Native American lands and all but ensuring conflict.

Grant's decision came at the intersection of the administration's various competing priorities and concerns. On the one hand, the administration had committed itself to a tight-money policy; on the other hand, it faced pressure to inflate the money supply to inject badly needed liquidity into the depressed economy. A major gold strike in the Black Hills offered the tantalizing prospect of allowing the administration to do both. In addition, Grant had consistently advocated justice for Native Americans and the exploitation of natural resources; the discovery of gold in the Black Hills forced him to choose between these two priorities. As a result of Grant's decision to tacitly side with white miners, the army became embroiled in a series of battles called the Great Sioux War. On March 17, 1876, troops under Colonel

Joseph J. Reynolds's command attacked Crazy Horse's camp on the Little Powder River in the Montana Territory. The battle was a debacle: the US troops retreated under enemy fire, abandoning several soldiers, an action for which Reynolds was court-martialed. That spring, Sheridan's forces undertook a three-pronged offensive that resulted in the 7th Cavalry making contact with the Sioux on June 25, 1876. Commanded by Colonel Custer, the 7th Cavalry was decimated by the Sioux. Public reaction was swift and negative: overwhelmingly, Americans supported reprisals against the Sioux for what happened to Custer, bringing the "peace policy to the verge of collapse."[19] As a result, the United States simply took the Black Hills from the Sioux in a move that sparked more than a century of legal wrangling and led the Supreme Court to decide in 1980 that the Grant administration acted illegally.

No longer able to win elections by attacking the Democrats as secessionists (a technique known as "waving the bloody shirt"), Republicans in the mid-1870s began casting about for other domestic issues. In Grant's second term, he became embroiled in controversies over the limits of religious freedom and tolerance for religious minorities. The first of these controversies dealt with public funding of sectarian schools. Many public schools were avowedly anti-Catholic, which had led to several violent confrontations between Protestants and Catholics in the 1830s and 1840s. Consequently, Catholic parishes throughout the United States had established parochial schools, which now insisted they were entitled to public funding. In addition, urban Catholics, who were a growing force politically, successfully pressured their local school districts to soften or eliminate anti-Catholic practices such as daily readings from the King James Bible. Both of these developments alarmed Protestants, some of whom sought laws and constitutional amendments designed to enshrine Protestant Christianity in the nation's public schools.

Grant, who had dabbled with the anti-Catholic Know-Nothings during the 1850s, opposed the public funding of sectarian schools and attempts to codify discrimination into law. In a speech he delivered in late September 1875, Grant argued for public education and resolved "that not one dollar of money appropriated to their support no matter how raised, shall be appropriated to the support of any sectarian school." He further endorsed the idea "that either state of Nation, or both combined, shall support institutions of learning . . . sufficient to afford to every child growing up in the . . . land the opportunity of a good common school education, unmixed with sectarian, pagan or atheistical tenets."[20] In his annual message in December 1875, Grant called for a constitutional amendment to establish "and forever maintain free public schools adequate to the education of all the children in the rudimentary branches within their respective limits, irrespective of sex, color, birthplace, or religions; forbidding the teaching in said schools of religious, atheistic, or pagan tenets, and prohibiting the granting of any school-funds, or school-taxes . . . either by legislative, municipal, or other authority, for the benefit, or aid . . . of any religious sect or denomination." In addition, Grant suggested the taxation of church property to limit the wealth and influence of religious sects.[21] That being said, Grant was not opposed to religious schools per se. In June 1876, he conferred diplomas at the graduation ceremony of Baltimore's College of Notre Dame, and he advised Sunday school students, "Hold fast to the Bible as the sheet-anchor of your liberties."[22] Grant was not reflexively anti-Catholic or anti-Semitic; in May 1875, he greeted a papal delegation, though at the time the United States did not have official diplomatic relations with the Vatican, and in June the following year, Grant attended the consecration of a synagogue in Washington. A few weeks later, Grant wrote to congratulate the Independent Order of B'nai B'rith for contributing a statue celebrating religious liberty to the grounds of the Centennial Exposition then taking place in Philadelphia.[23]

For decades, US relations with members of the Church of Latter-day Saints—called Mormons—presented a vexing problem. The church emerged from the religious ferment of the Second Great Awakening that swept the United States at the end of the eighteenth and early decades of the nineteenth century. In 1823, Joseph Smith, a farmer in western New York, experienced a vision that he claimed led him to golden plates recording the history of an ancient people. Smith published what he claimed as a translation of the tablets in 1830, calling it *The Book of Mormon*, and he founded a church and began proselytizing. Smith eventually moved the church to Ohio and established congregations in Missouri and Illinois, though there was frequent conflict with local non-Mormons. In fact, Smith was killed in a confrontation between Mormons and non-Mormons in Carthage, Illinois, and leadership of the Latter-day Saints transitioned to Brigham Young, who led them first to Nebraska and then into the Utah Territory.

However, this was not the end of the conflict. The Mormons' practice of polygamy, as well as Young's theocratic rule of the Utah Territory, motivated President James Buchanan to dispatch federal troops in 1857 to reassert US control of the area. The short Utah War that followed led to Young's stepping down as governor of the territory—he was replaced by non-Mormon Alfred Cumming—but the Mormons continued to wield political power there. Moreover, conflict over plural marriage did not disappear with the cessation of hostilities in 1858; instead, Buchanan was weakened by the results of the 1858 midterm elections, and the Civil War forced a period of benign neglect between the US government and Mormons in Utah. Nevertheless, the underlying issues—what one correspondent, writing to Orville Babcock, called "the knotty Mormon question"—remained.[24]

In 1862, Lincoln signed into law the Morrill Anti-Bigamy Act (not to be confused with the Morrill Land Grant Act). Though it prohibited plural marriage in any US territories and placed limits on the amount of land churches and nonprofits could own, Lincoln specifically ordered local army commanders not to confront the Mormons about these issues. Construction of the transcontinental railroad, which reached Salt Lake City in 1869 and facilitated the Mormons' growth, reignited the controversy and ensured that the federal government would intrude on Mormons' affairs. During the 1868 presidential campaign, Grant promised to enforce the Morrill Act, which raised tensions between the territorial government and Washington. Moreover, once the railroad reached Salt Lake City, it encouraged a flood of non-Mormon immigrants to the area. Writing in 1871, Austrian diplomat Joseph Alexander, Graf Von Hübner, who visited Salt Lake City, noted that "influence of the railroad, of the discovery of the silver mines, and of the influx of miners in the last few months has already been felt in various ways."[25]

Tensions came to a boil in October 1871, when federal marshals arrested several Mormons in Utah for violations of the Morrill Act; at least one was convicted, receiving three years in prison at hard labor. However, the Morrill Act proved difficult to enforce, and Grant recommended that Congress enact a law "as will secure peace, the equality of all citizens before the law, and the ultimate extinguishment of polygamy." In 1874, Congress passed and Grant signed the Poland Act, which gave US district courts jurisdiction over the Utah Territory and tried to limit Mormon participation in juries. This too failed to completely eradicate the problem, and in 1875, Grant complained, "that polygamy should exist in a free, enlightened, and Christian country, without the power to punish so flagrant a crime against decency and morality, seems preposterous."[26] Julia Grant recalled that when she and the president met Brigham Young in Ogden, Utah, in October 1875, Young referred to the Mormons as "poor, despised, and hated." Julia corrected Young, claiming that the only objection to the Mormons was the practice of polygamy, and asserted, "I have heard more than one of our most distinguished and conservative statesmen predict that now the railroad was bringing [Mormons] into such close contact with all the country and the world, that this one and only trouble would die of itself."[27]

In 1873, Grant also signed what became a landmark piece of legislation, the Comstock Act. Named for its main proponent, moralist Anthony Comstock, the law aimed to suppress "Trade in, and Circulation of, Obscene Literature and Articles of Immoral Use" by making it illegal to mail pornography, contraception devices, and sex toys. Comstock, who was employed by the newly created New York Society for the Suppression of Vice, enjoyed enormous power under a federal commission that empowered him to destroy allegedly obscene material and to secure arrest warrants. This power made Comstock infamous and something of a joke, particularly after he prohibited the mailing of anatomy textbooks. Nevertheless, *comstockery*—the word coined to describe Comstock's censorship crusade—continued long after his death in 1915. The Comstock Act was enforced for nearly a century, until the Supreme Court began issuing decisions in the 1960s that eroded the law's reach.

Grant's last full year in office coincided with the one hundredth anniversary of the signing of the Declaration of Independence. As early as 1866, the country began planning for the centennial of independence. In December that year, a Wabash College professor named John L. Campbell suggested to Philadelphia's mayor, Morton McMichael, that the City of Brotherly Love should host an exposition to celebrate the momentous event. Of course, Philadelphia was far from the only candidate, so the city council and Pennsylvania's General Assembly lobbied Congress to select the city and provide funding. US representative Daniel J. Morrell of Pennsylvania introduced a bill to create the United States Centennial Commission, and it was passed March 3, 1871. The commission was to include one representative from each state and territory (appointed by the president of the United States); its duty was "to prepare and superintend the execution of a plan for holding the exhibition, and, after conference with the authorities of the city of Philadelphia, to fix upon a suitable site within the corporate limits of the said city, where the exhibition shall be held." Crucially, the bill also explicitly (and somewhat naively) asserted, "the United States shall not be liable for any expenses attending such an exhibition."[28]

Given that Grant was empowered to appoint the commissioners, he was naturally going to be heavily involved in the celebration, which suited him just fine: a strong proponent of technological innovation, the president saw the centennial exposition as an opportunity to not only reunite the country after the Civil War but also to announce the United States' arrival on the world stage. The 1876 exposition took place at a moment of profound optimism about US industrial might and deep anxiety about purported American cultural inferiority. These contradictory impulses are clearly reflected in the exhibitions of foreign cultures and in Grant's statements about the centennial. In July 1873, Grant proclaimed that the "International Exhibition of Arts, Manufactures and Products of the Soil and Mine" would open for six months from mid-April to mid-October 1876. In his proclamation, he commended the exposition "in the interest of peace, civilization and domestic and international friendship and intercourse."[29] Grant became the exposition's staunchest supporter; for instance, in February 1874, he pushed Congress to provide funds for the event, despite the language in the 1871 bill disclaiming any federal responsibility to support it.[30] A year later, Grant signed a bill appropriating more than $500,000 in federal funds to it, and in June 1875, he journeyed to Philadelphia for a tour of the exposition's buildings. He returned a week before Christmas, accompanied by a congressional delegation, and when the exposition needed an additional infusion of funds in February 1876, Grant signed the bill appropriating $1.5 million. Two months later, he was back in Philadelphia touring the exposition's grounds. Delays pushed the exposition's commencement back several

weeks, but when it opened to the public May 10, 1876, Grant attended, calling it an opportunity to "more thoroughly appreciate the
excellencies and deficiencies of our achievements, and also give em-
phatic expression to our earnest desire to cultivate the friendship of
our fellow members of the great family of nations."[31] Grant toured
the exposition grounds for three days in late September and was on
hand for the closing ceremonies November 10, 1876.

The Centennial Exhibition appealed to Grant in part because of his
lifelong enthusiasm for technological progress and commitment to
publicly sponsored infrastructure programs. Like the Whig he had
been as a young man, Grant remained committed to the model of an
activist federal government that funded internal improvements. In
April 1874, Grant signed legislation aimed at helping victims of flood-
ing along the Mississippi River; two months later, he approved legislation creating a committee to study flood protection on the river. The
following February, he supported legislation aimed at ameliorating the
effects of drought and grasshoppers on farmers in Kansas and Nebraska. Grant wanted to do even more to expand the country's infrastructure and frequently urged the House to pass such appropriations;
but because of the depression and the fact that the Democrats controlled the House after 1874, he was frequently frustrated.

Though the major foreign policy achievement of Grant's administration—settling the *Alabama* claims—was behind it, the administration acquitted itself competently in the international sphere during the
president's second term. Relations with Spain continued to trouble the
administration, in part because Madrid made little progress in ending
the Cuban insurgency. Grant and Secretary of State Fish continued
pursuing a two-pronged approach to Cuba, pressuring Spain to improve conditions on the island (or better yet grant it independence)
while at the same time trying to avoid being drawn into the conflict.
This was a delicate balancing act: on the one hand, in July 1872, Grant
ordered the *Pioneer*, a ship used to supply the Cuban insurgents, seized
while at anchor in Newport, Rhode Island.[32] On the other hand, in
late October 1872, Fish advised US minister to Spain Daniel Sickles
to convey to the Spanish that the Americans wanted Madrid to take
some positive steps to end slavery and deal with the problems in Cuba
or "Spain must not be surprised to find . . . a marked change in the
feeling and in the temper of the people and Government of the United

States."[33] Sickles reported that Spanish king Amadeo, recently raised to the throne, seemed inclined toward reform in Cuba, but he had little popular support and was forced to abdicate in February 1873. The new government deferred enacting any reforms in Cuba despite a State Department memorandum outlining America's complaints against the Spanish transmitted to Madrid in March 1873. When Spain failed to institute new policies on the island, in June 1873 Fish warned the Spanish that conditions in Cuba needed to be improved sooner rather than later. Even more audaciously, two months later, Fish intimated that American popular opinion greatly favored invading Cuba to restore order and ensure the protection of human rights. In short, relations were tense between the two nations, laying the groundwork for the most important foreign policy crisis of Grant's second term.

In August 1870, John F. Patterson purchased the former Confederate blockade-runner the *Virgin*. Built in Glasgow, Scotland, for the Confederacy, the *Virgin* was a side-wheel steamship; it was small and fast, making it the ideal blockade-runner. Captured in April 1865, it became the prize of the US Navy before being sold to Patterson, who was acting on behalf of Cuban insurgent Manuel Quesada and two Americans sympathetic to the revolutionaries, Marshall O. Roberts and J. K. Roberts. For three years, the *Virgin* (now renamed *Virginius*) transported men, weapons, and supplies to the Cuban rebels while the Spanish navy tried in vain to capture the outlaw ship. In October 1873, former Confederate commodore Joseph Fry was hired to captain the *Virginius*. He found a ship that was showing its age: moored in Jamaica, the *Virginius*'s boilers needed extensive repairs. Moreover, most of the crew had deserted, so Fry recruited several dozen Americans and Britons, most of whom were not experienced sailors and many of whom did not understand the ship's true mission. It was hardly an auspicious start to a dangerous mission.

In late October, the *Virginius* set sail for Cuba, but the Spanish navy had been alerted to the ship's departure. The Spanish dispatched the warship *Tornado*. The *Tornado* spotted the *Virginius* shortly after the latter entered open waters and immediately gave chase. The *Virginius*, laden with its heavy cargo and slowed by its aging boilers and inexperienced crew could not outrun the *Tornado*, and when the Spanish began firing on the *Virginius*, Captain Fry surrendered the ship. The Spanish boarded the ship and arrested the entire crew, sending them to Santiago de Cuba for trial as pirates. Ignoring the protests of the American vice-consul, Spanish authorities in Cuba convened a court-martial and found the *Virginius*'s entire crew guilty of piracy. On November 4, the Spanish executed four mercenaries who had accompanied the ship. Concerned that one of the mercenaries, George W. Ryan, claimed British citizenship, Britain's vice-consul wired the British navy to prevent any further executions. The British dispatched the HMS *Niobe* to Santiago, but before it arrived, the Spanish executed forty-nine *Virginius* crew members, including Captain Fry. Many of their bodies were decapitated and trampled by horses. The *Niobe*'s commander threatened to bombard Santiago if the Spanish executed anyone else.

When news of the executions reached the United States, many leading newspapers demanded war against Spain. While the cabinet thought it unwise to go to war, its members were nevertheless appalled by the executions; the normally temperate Fish denounced Cuban actions as "butchery and murder."[34] On November 13, he officially protested the executions to the Spanish minister to the United States, Don José Polo de Bernabé. Two days later, Fish cabled Sickles and demanded the Spanish return the *Virginius* and the remaining crew members to the United States, provide reparations for the executed men's families, punish the authorities who orchestrated the executions, and order Spanish forces in Santiago to salute the US flag. Believing war with Spain was imminent, former Confederate cavalry battalion commander John S. Mosby offered his military services. But by that time, the administration had nearly concluded negotiations with the Spanish, thereby avoiding a military confrontation. From November 27–29, Fish and Polo worked out the details, with Madrid agreeing to most US terms. Spain returned the surviving *Virginius* crew members on December 8 and eventually paid an indemnity of $80,000, though Fish did offer a fig leaf in the form of an admission to Polo that the ship should not have been flying the American flag since it had been purchased on behalf of Cuban revolutionaries. Shortly before Christmas 1873, Fish notified the Spanish minister that the US government was satisfied with Spain's actions in settling the matter, but overall relations between the two countries did not improve, and the situation in Cuba deteriorated.

In December 1874, a group of Spanish generals overthrew the existing government and installed Alfonso XII as the country's king. Following longstanding US practice of recognizing the *de facto* regime in power (which Fish called "the only true and wise principle and policy"), the secretary of state ordered the new US minister to Spain, Caleb Cushing (Sickles's replacement), to present his papers to the king. In November 1875, Fish sent Cushing a memo outlining the deleterious effect the Cuban Revolution was having on US interests and instructing him to push for Cuban independence. Fish included a not-so-subtle threat: if the Spanish refused to acquiesce to Cuban independence, it might become "the duty of other governments to intervene."[35] To make this threat credible, the United States made a very public show of building up naval forces in South Carolina and Florida. Moreover, Fish forwarded copies of the memo to the US ministers to France, Germany, Great Britain, Italy, and Russia with instructions to report back on those governments' reactions. Contrary to Fish's expectations, none of the European powers offered their support to an American adventure in Cuba, though several admitted that the situation there had gotten out of hand. Compounding the problem, word of Fish's gambit leaked to the American press, creating a minor scandal and prompting the Democratic-controlled House in January 1876 to demand the State Department turn over all communications related to the incident. Its object (embarrassing the administration) satisfied, the House did not press the matter further, and in March Fish again pushed the Spanish to make substantive progress toward ending the rebellion. In mid-April, the Spanish government promised Cushing it would take steps to do just that, though its policies amounted to an aggressive attempt to end the rebellion once and for all, which finally succeeded in 1878, more than a year after Grant left office.

The ongoing violence with Native Americans in the Southwest nearly turned into a foreign policy crisis for the administration in March 1875. In response to increased white incursions into American Indian territory, several groups of Apache Indians raided settlements before fleeing across the Mexican-American border. As early as January 1873, Fish had threatened Mexico that if it did not step up its efforts to stem the tide of cross-border raids, the US Army would pursue Indians into Mexican territory. This was no small threat given that the United States and Mexico had fought a war within living memory that had cost the Mexicans dearly. When raids continued, US soldiers crossed the border in May 1873, alarming Mexico's government. Beginning in 1875, the Mexican and American governments worked out a cooperation agreement designed to coordinate their responses to Apache raids, but so little was achieved that in mid-March, Fish sent the Mexican foreign minister a note essentially abjuring any responsibility for policing the border. But that was not a realistic response; two weeks after Fish sent his letter, Texas governor Richard Coke wrote to Grant, informing the president that "the depredations of organized bands of robbers from the Republic of Mexico have increased in frequency and atrocity to an extent which threatens the depopulation of the lower Rio Grande Country."[36] In response that June, Grant ordered the US Navy to patrol the Rio Grande, the river separating the United States and Mexico, in order to discourage Indian raids from Mexico. When even that failed to stem cross-border raids, Grant, on March 9, 1876, ordered the army to suppress Indian incursions from Mexico. Political instability in Mexico culminated in José de la Cruz Porfirio Díaz Mori's seizure of power in a coup in November 1876, just a few months before Grant left office.

With Grant still smarting from the Senate's rejection of the treaty annexing Santo Domingo and dogged by the depression caused by the Panic of 1873, the president's foreign policy in the second term was more focused on improving America's economy by expanding markets for US goods. Unfortunately, Congress was frequently uncooperative, and its members often tried to assert control over foreign policy, frustrating Grant and Fish.[37] For instance, the improved relations with Great Britain and Canada growing out of the *Alabama* settlement offered the administration a space to negotiate a treaty regulating trade with the United States' northern neighbor. In June 1874, Grant submitted to the Senate a treaty allowing US ships to navigate Canadian canals on the same terms as British ships in exchange for American acquiescence to Canada expanding those canals. In addition, the treaty contained a provision dispensing with arbitration regarding disputes between the two countries over fisheries, essentially voiding a clause in the Treaty of Washington.[38] Speaker of the House James G. Blaine, eyeing a presidential bid in 1876, opposed the treaty; fisheries were particularly important to his Maine constituents, and he used his influence to ensure the Senate made no moves on the treaty. The Senate's inaction on the treaty reflected, in part, the president's waning political strength as he entered the latter years of his administration. That being said, Grant still managed to bank some foreign policy achievements in his second term. In March 1875, the Senate ratified a treaty the administration had negotiated with the kingdom of Hawai'i providing for nearly free trade between the two nations for a period of seven years. However, the debate on the treaty was marred by denunciations of the administration's Reconstruction policies, including those made by former president Andrew Johnson, recently reelected to the Senate from Tennessee.

In relations with Asia, the administration's accomplishments were mixed. In 1871, the administration sought to open Korea to American trade, much as the United States had done in Japan in the lead-up to the Civil War. In late May, the US minister to China dispatched a squadron of navy ships to Seoul to pressure Koreans into signing a treaty with the United States. The Americans' mission was frustrated by a flotilla of Korean ships that blocked the entrance to the Han River and thereby prevented the navy from continuing to Seoul. In addition, the Koreans fired on the ships, causing little damage. The fleet's commander, Rear Admiral John Rodgers, gave the Korean government ten days to apologize and begin negotiating. When no apology came, on June 10 he destroyed several Korean forts. This conflict, known as the Battle of Ganghwa, led to the deaths of 250 Koreans and 3 Americans. Yet even this did not compel the Koreans to negotiate, and seeing no other option, Rodgers ordered the fleet to return to base.

On August 6, 1873, the Senate ratified a treaty between the United States and Japan committing the former to help organize a postal system. The truly important aspect of this treaty is that Japan had been granted full diplomatic equality with the United States, an equality that was reinforced by several American actions (ordering US citizens to conform to Japanese hunting and press laws and quarantine restrictions while in Japan). This helped cement Japan's "equal diplomatic status among world powers."[39]

But to his discredit, in March 1875, Grant signed into law the Page Act, which prohibited the immigration to the United States of those considered "undesirable." This was the first restrictive federal immigration law in US history, and it was designed to stem the flow of Chinese laborers. Grant supported such legislation; in his seventh annual message to Congress in December 1875, he called "the attention of Congress to . . . the importation of Chinese women . . . few of whom are brought to our shores to pursue honest or useful occupations."[40] In fact, Chinese women were the main targets of the legislation; racist propaganda of the day (coming from no less a source than the American Medical Association) asserted that Chinese women threatened the health of whites because they "carried distinct germs to which they were immune but from which whites would die if exposed."[41] Compounding this injustice, in mid-June 1876, Grant put off efforts to amend a treaty with China governing immigration, leaving it for his successor to handle. Building on the Page Act, over the coming decades Congress passed a number of racist immigration laws, including the infamous Chinese Exclusion Acts.

Grant's decision not to seek a third term created a scramble to succeed him; the contenders for the Republican nomination included Treasury Secretary Benjamin H. Bristow, Ohio governor Rutherford B. Hayes, Pennsylvania governor John F. Hartranft, and Senators Oliver P. Morton of Indiana, Roscoe Conkling of New York, and James G. Blaine of Maine. This was the first time since 1864 that the Republican nominating convention opened without the outcome being more or less a foregone conclusion. Blaine recalled, "This freedom of action imparted a personal interest to the preliminary canvass and a struggle in the Convention itself, which previous nominations had lacked."[42] Surveying the field of would-be nominees, one prominent Republican put it more succinctly: "The fight at Cincinnati will be like that of the Kilkenny cats, destroying each other."[43] Selections of delegates to the convention seemed to favor Blaine, who counted on nearly three hundred votes (of the 378 needed to secure the nomination), making him the prohibitive favorite when the convention was gaveled to order on June 14, 1876. Perhaps tempting fate, the Republicans chose to hold their convention in Cincinnati's Exposition Hall, the site where, four years earlier, the Liberal Republicans convened and nominated Horace Greeley for president. For five straight ballots, Blaine led the pack, cresting at 351 votes on the sixth ballot. By then, however, the anti-Blaine forces had settled on Hayes, and as the other candidates' supporters withdrew their names from consideration, the Ohioan's vote total surged, securing him the nomination on the seventh ballot.

The platform adopted at the convention reflected the political battles of Grant's presidency more than it provided a framework for moving the country forward. The Republicans called for the "permanent pacification of the Southern section of the Union and the complete protection of all its citizens in the free enjoyment of all their rights," and denounced the Democratic Party as "being the same in character and spirit as when it sympathized with treason." The platform lauded Grant for having signed the Public Credit Act in 1869. But the underlying tensions exposed by Grant's first-term cabinet nominations and the corruption scandals then consuming his presidency clearly led to the fifth plank, which asserted "the President and heads of departments are to make nominations for office, the senate is to advise and consent to appointments, and the house of representatives is to accuse and prosecute faithless officers. The best interest of the public service demands that these distinctions be respected; that senators and representatives who may be judges and accusers should not dictate appointments to office."

Perhaps the only truly progressive plank was the twelfth, which called for "the establishment of equal rights for women."[44] Grant had a long history supporting legal protections for women; as president, he signed a law allowing women to sue in Washington, DC's courts and another that guaranteed female federal clerks pay equal to their male counterparts. That being said, there was also an element of political calculation behind the Republicans' call for female suffrage: with Southerners working to disenfranchise blacks and Northerners ambivalent about Reconstruction, Republicans needed all the votes they could get. Ironically, it would take more than forty years and the grudging support of a Democratic president before all women achieved suffrage.

Meeting in St. Louis a few weeks later, the Democrats nominated New York governor Samuel J. Tilden. The sixty-year-old Tilden was a multimillionaire with a reputation for good government, giving him the bona fides to attack the current administration for the scandals that plagued Grant's second term. The Democratic platform adopted in St. Louis committed the party to hard money, cuts in government expenditure, and reform, making pointed references to the many scandals that had rocked Grant's administration. Despite the disastrous 1874 midterm elections and the ongoing depression, the results from the states that held their elections in October was inconclusive; as a result, Grant confided to Fish that he had "great confidence" that Hayes would be elected president.[45] There was some violence in the South in the weeks leading up to Election Day, and Grant feared that fraud, even if it did not change the election's outcome, would taint the next president's legitimacy. Writing to General Sherman from Philadelphia, Grant observed, "No man worthy of the office of President would be willing to hold it if 'counted in' or placed there by any fraud. Either party can afford to be disappointed in the result but the Country cannot afford to have the result tainted by the suspicion of . . . illegal or false returns."[46] In an effort to ensure the integrity of vote returns in New Orleans, and at the request of Louisiana governor William P. Kellogg, Grant asked several people, including Representative James A. Garfield of Ohio, Senator John A. Logan of Illinois, and Representative William D. Kelley of Pennsylvania to go to the Crescent City and observe voting returns.

On Election Day, November 7, the early returns favored Tilden, though the outcome was disputed in Florida, Louisiana, and South Carolina, where Republican-controlled election boards invalidated returns from counties plagued by violence or voting irregularities. In order to win the election, Hayes needed to sweep all these states. Shocked and exasperated by the outcome, Grant complained to his cabinet that the Fifteenth Amendment had been a mistake because, "It had done the Negro no good, and had been a hindrance to the South, and by no means a political advantage to the North."[47] When, on December 6, electors in the three disputed states met to officially record their votes, they presented Congress with two sets of vote totals; hanging in the balance were their nineteen electoral votes and, with those votes, the election. Prior to counting the electoral returns from the 1864 presidential election, both houses of Congress had adopted the rule that "no electoral vote objected to shall be counted except by a concurrent votes of the two houses." Though this rule expired with the end of the Thirty-Ninth Congress in 1867, congressional Democrats cited it as precedent and demanded that it be the basis for allotting electoral votes.[48] The problem was that Republican control of the Senate canceled Democratic control of the House, making it impossible to settle the dispute on a strictly partisan basis; neither house of Congress could force a solution on the other. On

January 25, 1877, Congress passed legislation establishing a fifteen-person commission charged with allocating the electoral votes; four days later, Grant signed the bill into law. The commission was composed of ten members of Congress—five Democrats and five Republicans—and five Supreme Court justices. Four of the justices were named in the bill—Democrats Nathan Clifford and Stephen Johnson Field and Republicans Samuel Freeman Miller and William Strong—and were empowered to choose the fifth member. Democrats accepted this proposal because they expected the last slot would go to Associate Justice David Davis, who, though a Republican appointed to the court by Abraham Lincoln, was considered fair and impartial by many Democrats.[49] Unfortunately for them, the state legislature in Illinois named Davis to the US Senate; upon his resigning from the commission, the Supreme Court delegates chose Republican Joseph P. Bradley.

In February, the commission, in a series of party-line, 8-to-7 votes, awarded all the disputed electoral votes to Hayes, thereby making the Ohioan president. Congressional Democrats, outraged by the defeat, threatened a filibuster to prevent Congress from accepting the commission's decision. To his credit, Tilden defused the potentially explosive situation by noting, "We have just emerged from one civil war and it will not do to engage in another."[50]

That being said, Democrats could rest easily, because Hayes had signaled during the campaign his administration would be less aggressive than Grant's in protecting African Americans' voting rights or assisting Southern Republican governments. There were even rumors that Hayes or his managers had privately promised congressional Democrats that in exchange for the presidency, he would end Reconstruction. Whether Hayes or his advisers made explicit promises, within weeks of taking office, Hayes removed federal troops from the South, officially ending Reconstruction on April 20, 1877. Eric Foner, who wrote the definitive history of Reconstruction, notes that this "marked a decisive retreat from the idea, born during the Civil War, of a powerful national state protecting the fundamental rights of American citizens."[51] It also inaugurated more than eight decades of legally codified efforts to deprive African Americans of their constitutional rights. In this sense, the South may have lost the Civil War, but for the time being, it had won the battle.

CONCLUSION

D ESPITE THE CIRCUMSTANCES of the 1876 presidential election
and subsequent end of Reconstruction, Grant was undeniably
happy to be free of the presidency. During his last year in the White
House, Grant confessed to a friend that he looked forward to the end
of his term "with the same longing which he had formerly had as a
cadet when looking forward to a furlough." Grant later called March
4, 1877—the day Hayes was inaugurated president—the happiest of
his life.[1] On leaving the White House, the Grants traveled to New
York and stayed for three weeks with Hamilton Fish, an indication of
how personally close the former president and secretary of state had
become. Over the next few months, the Grants visited friends and family all over the United States. On May 17, Julia and Ulysses Grant, accompanied by their son Jesse, sailed aboard the SS *Indiana* to begin a
two-and-a-half-year tour of Europe and Asia. When the Grants arrived in Liverpool, Julia recalled that her husband was greeted by a
crowd of fifty thousand and "given the freedom of the city," a testa-
ment to how thoroughly he and Fish had improved US-British relations during his two terms.[2] That summer, the Grants dined with the
Prince of Wales and Queen Victoria and then traveled to Belgium,
where they met King Leopold. After returning from their marathon
trip, the Grants settled in a town house in New York City where the
ex-president met a never-ending stream of callers. Should one of these

callers happen to remark on one of the hundreds of curios from Grant's military and political career or his travels, he would inevitably insist that the visitor take the item.[3]

Despite all the scandals, Grant remained one of the most popular men in the United States, and the passage of time gave his presidency the patina of the "good old days." Grant's reception during his world tour and Republicans' unhappiness with Hayes made party insiders consider running the former president for a third term. In 1880, a triumvirate of Republican Party leaders—Senators Roscoe Conkling of New York, J. Donald Cameron of Pennsylvania (son of former Secretary of War and Senator Simon Cameron), and John A. Logan of Illinois—led the charge to nominate Grant at the party's convention in Chicago. Despite his oft-expressed desire while president to be free of the White House, Grant was "extremely anxious to receive the nomination," for the same reason he ran for president in 1868: he saw the politicians as squandering the victory he and other veterans had won on the battlefield during the war.[4]

However, reentering political life served to dissipate some of the good will that had accrued to Grant since leaving the White House and again made him the target of partisan attack. In addition, Americans were instinctively opposed to any one individual serving more than two terms as president; though not illegal at the time (it only became so with ratification of the Twenty-Second Amendment in 1947), it nevertheless violated an unwritten rule established by George Washington. Sensing the shift in political winds, some of Grant's closest friends and supporters convinced him to withdraw his name from consideration, a move that the astonished Julia, who fantasized about a return to the White House, vehemently opposed.[5] Despite her opposition, Grant drafted a letter withdrawing his name, which his friend, journalist John Russell Young, delivered to Conkling, Cameron, and Logan on May 31, 1880. Despite Grant's letter, the three men decided to push ahead. Though Grant led on the first ballot on June 2, he failed to secure the 379 votes needed for the nomination. Through thirty-five ballots, the former president consistently received more votes than every other nominee but never enough to clinch the nomination. Finally, on the thirty-sixth ballot, the anti-Grant forces settled on Representative Garfield, who received 399 votes, 93 more than Grant, and more than enough to secure the Republican nomination.

Despite just barely missing the nomination, Grant campaigned for Garfield. The Democrats had nominated Winfield Scott Hancock, a former general from Pennsylvania who had served with distinction during the Civil War. Because of his background, the Republicans were reticent to attack him personally, and the campaign focused largely on issues like the tariff. In the end, Garfield won the popular vote by .02 percent, though he swept the Electoral College 214 to 155. Writing to his daughter, Grant said of the election's outcome, "the country, in my judgment, has escaped a great calamity."[6] When Garfield was assassinated less than a year into his presidency, Grant attended his funeral, where he was observed weeping inconsolably.

Over the next several years, the Grants traveled across the United States and to Mexico. Grant remained popular with the industrialist wing of the Republican Party and was frequently invited to join boards of directors or invest in companies. Unfortunately for Grant, the Senate rejected a treaty with Mexico establishing free trade between the two countries. Grant had invested in the Mexican Southern Railroad in 1881 in the belief that Mexico and the United States would ratify the treaty and the railroad would make a fortune carrying freight between them. When the treaty was rejected, the Mexican Southern fell into bankruptcy, seriously injuring the Grants' finances. Moreover, Grant's son Ulysses Jr. had partnered with a rising star on Wall Street named Ferdinand Ward to open a brokerage firm. Grant invested in his son's firm, but in 1883 it collapsed when it became clear that Ward had been cooking the books. Grant tried to buoy the firm with $150,000 he borrowed, but even that could not prevent the inevitable. Ward & Grant's failure left the former president essentially penniless and heavily in debt; as a result, he was reduced to selling many of his Civil War trophies and depending on the generosity of friends.

More devastating, in summer 1884, Grant was diagnosed with terminal throat cancer, an outgrowth of his decades of smoking several dozen cigars a day. One friend recalled, "I have known him to go to bed with a heavy Havana in his mouth, put out the lights, and continue smoking for a time in the dark. He would never finish this nightcap cigar, but when it was about half done he would put it somewhere where it might be reached easily in the morning. The first thing he did when he awakened was to get this stub and light it. Sometimes he would smoke another whole cigar before breakfast."[7] Grant's diagnosis became public in March 1885, and in an act of compassion, Congress reinstated his military rank and, with it, his retirement pay, but his debts still exceeded his income. In order to settle his debts and leave Julia with some money, Grant decided to write his memoirs. Again, he was saved by the compassion of a friend: Mark Twain, who had befriended the former president, offered Grant an unheard of 75 percent royalty rate to publish his memoirs. Working diligently through spring and early summer 1885, Grant completed the manuscript for the two-volume *The Personal Memoirs of Ulysses S. Grant*, which became an instant best seller, helped largely by an army of sales agents (many of whom were Union veterans) who traveled door to door selling the book, restoring the family's finances. Grant did not live to see this; he died a few days after completing the book, which does not discuss his presidency.

Though Grant's tragic last years caused his popularity to spike in the short term, as his presidential administration migrated from current events into the realm of history, public and scholarly opinion soured. In large measure, the negative assessment of Grant's presidency is a by-product of the fact that it overlapped, and was consumed by, Reconstruction. The urge to put the war behind the country, so evident at the fiftieth anniversary celebrations of the war in the 1910s, cast Reconstruction as an era of corruption driven by a vindictive and unscrupulous North inflicting unreasonable punishments on a genuinely penitent South. Historians have hardly been kinder. In 1917, one commentator compared his interest in Grant's presidency with that of "a physician [who] receives a new treatise on cancer."[8] Moreover, historians of the era claimed that black enfranchisement had been a mistake because newly freed slaves were simply incapable of self-government and were a threat to whites, necessitating segregation. This line of argument was called the Dunning School, named for its leading light, Columbia University historian William A. Dunning, and was popularized in director D. W. Griffith's 1915 blockbuster film *Birth of a Nation*. Even those historians who dissented from the Dunningite vision of Reconstruction nonetheless conceded, "the corruption was real, the failures obvious, the tragedy undeniable. Grant [was] not their idea of a model President. . . . In short . . . [t]hey recognize[d] that much of what Dunning's disciples have said about reconstruction is true."[9] Writing in 1935, William Hesseltine claimed that Grant was "peculiarly ignorant of the Constitution and inept at handling men."[10] Thirty-four years later, Avery Craven described President Grant as "a pathetic, bewildered, shuffling figure whom others used for ends he never understood."[11]

Beginning in the 1960s (a period sometimes called the Second Reconstruction), a younger generation of historians, aroused by the civil rights and liberation movements of the day, began questioning the Dunning School's racist assumptions. Writing an important synthesis in 1965, historian Kenneth M. Stampp called Radical Republicanism "the last great crusade of the nineteenth century romantic reformers . . . [who] supplied much of the idealism of the Union cause."[12] This was obviously a far cry from the Dunningites' condemnation of Reconstruction's architects, but it did little to improve Grant's reputation; he was now criticized for not doing enough for African Americans. By 1979, Yale historian C. Vann Woodward called Reconstruction "essentially nonrevolutionary and conservative."[13] Thus, in a generation, the historical consensus on Reconstruction shifted from seeing it as a top-down attempt to unnecessarily remake Southern society to a missed opportunity to fulfill the promise of equal rights. For the Dunning School, Reconstruction went too far; for historians of the 1960s, it did not go far enough—but in both cases, historians faulted Ulysses S. Grant's presidential administration. In 1948, Arthur M. Schlesinger Sr. asked fifty-five historians to rank presidents, and Grant came in second to last. In 1962, his son conducted a similar poll, and Grant remained second from the bottom. When Schlesinger Jr. conducted his poll again in 1996, Grant's star had risen somewhat—sixth from the bottom—but he remained squarely in the "failure" category. C. Van Woodward summed up the prevailing wisdom in 1982 when he claimed that Grant's presidency "stands for the all-time low point in statesmanship in our nation's history."[14]

In part, this negative conclusion reflected a shortage of sources depicting Grant's perspective. His contemporary critics were many and left long paper trails that provided sources for historians. By contrast, Grant's memoirs, published in 1885 and long considered the standard by which presidential memoirs are judged, ended in 1865 and include nothing about his presidency. Furthermore, a serious effort to gather and publish Grant's papers did not coalesce until the mid-1960s, and it is only since the mid-1990s that scholars have had access to the published and annotated version of his presidential papers, which has had a tonic effect: since that time, Grant's reputation as a president has begun improving. As a result, historian Sean Wilentz concluded in 2010, "No great American has suffered more cruelly and undeservedly at the hands of historians than Ulysses S. Grant."[15]

This book is an attempt to remedy that by depicting an administration that, for all its shortcomings and missteps, genuinely tried to reconstruct the United States on the basis of justice and political equality. Could the administration have done more to advance civil rights and protect African American citizens? Absolutely, and for the blacks who suffered as a result of this failure, that fact should not be minimized or overlooked. While it is true that Grant frequently missed opportunities because of political and economic considerations, to the detriment of blacks and Republican officeholders in the South, at the same time, his administration achieving some notable successes that created a legal and institutional framework for moving toward political equality for African Americans. Moreover, the administration's foreign policies improved relations with Great Britain and laid the groundwork for US emergence as a world power.[16] We should neither minimize Grant's failures nor ignore his successes; like all presidents, his administrations had a share of both, and in the last analysis, though mistakes were clearly made, they were "errors of judgment, not of intent."[17]

APPENDIX

Grant and His Cabinet Members, 1869–1877

PRESIDENT OF THE UNITED STATES

Ulysses S. Grant	March 4, 1869, to March 3, 1877

VICE PRESIDENT

Schuyler Colfax	March 4, 1869, to March 4, 1873
Henry Wilson	March 4, 1873, to Nov. 22, 1875
Vacant	Nov. 22, 1875, to March 3, 1877

SECRETARY OF STATE

Elihu Washburne	March 5, 1869, to March 16, 1869
Hamilton Fish	March 17, 1869, to March 12, 1877

SECRETARY OF THE TREASURY

George S. Boutwell	March 12, 1869, to March 16, 1873
William A. Richardson	March 17, 1873, to June 3, 1874
Benjamin H. Bristow	June 4, 1874, to June 20, 1876
Lot M. Morrill	June 20, 1876, to March 9, 1877

SECRETARY OF WAR

John A. Rawlins	March 13, 1869, to Sept. 6, 1869
William T. Sherman (interim)	Sept. 6, 1869, to Oct. 25, 1869
William W. Belknap	Oct. 25, 1869, to March 2, 1876
Alphonso Taft	March 8, 1876, to May 22, 1876
J. Donald Cameron	May 22, 1876, to March 4, 1877

ATTORNEY GENERAL

Ebenezer R. Hoar	March 5, 1869, to Nov. 22, 1870
Amos T. Akerman	Nov. 23, 1870, to Dec. 13, 1871
George H. Williams	Dec. 14, 1871, to April 25, 1875
Edwards Pierrepont	April 26, 1875, to May 21, 1876
Alphonso Taft	May 22, 1876, to March 4, 1877

SECRETARY OF THE NAVY

Adolph E. Borie	March 9, 1869, to June 25, 1869
George M. Robeson	June 25, 1869, to March 12, 1877

POSTMASTER GENERAL

John A. J. Cresswell	March 5, 1869, to June 22, 1874
James W. Marshall	July 3, 1874, to August 24, 1874
Marshall Jewell	August 24, 1874, to July 12, 1876
James N. Tyner	July 12, 1876, to March 3, 1877

SECRETARY OF THE INTERIOR

Jacob D. Cox	March 5, 1869, to Oct. 31, 1870
Columbus Delano	Nov. 1, 1870, to Sept. 30, 1875
Zachariah Chandler	Oct. 19, 1875, to March 11, 1877

NOTES

INTRODUCTION

1. Ulysses S. Grant, "Eighth Annual Message (December 5, 1876)," American Presidency Project, accessed August 30, 2017, http://www.presidency.ucsb.edu/ws/index.php?pid=29517.

2. John Russell Young, *Men and Memories: Personal Reminiscences*, vol. 2 (New York: F. T. Neely, 1901), 359.

3. James J. Broomall, "Ulysses S. Grant Goes to Washington: The Commanding General as Secretary of War," in *A Companion to the Reconstruction Presidents, 1865–1881,* ed. Edward O. Frantz (Malden, MA: Wiley-Blackwell, 2014), 226.

4. Robert L. Beisner, *From the Old Diplomacy to the New, 1865–1900* (Wheeling, IL: Harlan Davidson, 1986), 6, and Senator John Sherman, quoted in H. W. Brands, *The Man Who Saved the Union: Ulysses Grant in War and Peace* (New York: Doubleday, 2012), 449.

5. Quoted in William S. McFeely, *Grant: A Biography* (New York: W. W. Norton, 1982), 294.

6. Quoted in Brands, *Man Who Saved the Union*, 466, and Rutherford B. Hayes, *The Diary and Letters of Rutherford Birchard Hayes*, vol. 5, ed. Charles Richard Williams (Columbus: Ohio State Archeological and Historical Society, 1926), 111.

7. Grant to Cameron, November 3, 1873, *The Papers of Ulysses S. Grant,* vol. 24: 1873, ed. John Y. Simon (Carbondale: Southern Illinois University Press, 2000), 234; McFeely, *Grant,* 350.

8. Hamilton Fish Diary, June 17, 1870, Fish Papers, Manuscript Division, Library of Congress, Washington, DC.

9. John Sherman to W. T. Sherman, December 24, 1868, *The Sherman Letters: Correspondence between General and Senator Sherman from 1837 to 1891,* ed. Rachel Sherman Thorndike (New York: Charles Scribner's Sons, 1894), 325.

10. John Y. Simon, "Introduction," *The Papers of Ulysses S. Grant,* vol. 21: November 1, 1870–May 31, 1871, ed. John Y. Simon (Carbondale: Southern Illinois University Press, 1998), xi.

11. Quoted in Brands, *Man Who Saved the Union,* 3.

12. Brooks D. Simpson, *Let Us Have Peace: Ulysses S. Grant and the Politics of War and Reconstruction, 1861–1868* (Chapel Hill: University of North Carolina Press, 1991), xix.

13. Grant to Badeau, November 19, 1871, *The Papers of Ulysses S. Grant,* vol. 22: June 1, 1871—January 31, 1872, ed. John Y. Simon (Carbondale: Southern Illinois University Press, 1998), 239–240.

CHAPTER I

1. Geoffrey Perret, *Ulysses S. Grant: Soldier and President* (New York: Random House, 1997), 8.

2. Ulysses S. Grant, *Personal Memoirs* (New York: Modern Library, 1990), 13.

3. Ibid.

4. Simon, "Introduction," *Papers*, 21:xi.

5. Julia Dent Grant, *The Personal Memoirs of Julia Dent Grant (Mrs. Ulysses S. Grant)*, ed. John Y. Simon (New York: G. P. Putnam & Sons, 1975), 50.

6. Steven E. Woodworth, *Manifest Destinies: America's Westward Expansion and the Road to the Civil War* (New York: Vintage Books, 2010), 103.

7. Grant, *Personal Memoirs*, 58–59.

8. McFeely, *Grant*, 35.

9. Simpson, *Let Us Have Peace*, 3.

10. This and the following three quotations by Grant are from *Personal Memoirs*, 58, 47, 68, and 107.

11. "Visit with Mrs. Grant, 1899 Washington, DC," Ulysses S. Grant Homepage, accessed August 29, 2017, http://www.granthomepage.com /intjd-grant3.htm.

12. Quoted in Joan Waugh, *U.S. Grant: American Hero, American Myth* (Chapel Hill: University of North Carolina Press, 2009), 38.

13. A. J. Langguth, *After Lincoln: How the North Won the Civil War and Lost the Peace* (New York: Simon & Schuster, 2014), 241.

14. Quoted in Brands, *Man Who Saved the Union*, 73.

15. Ibid., 77.

16. Quoted in Waugh, *U.S. Grant*, 41.

17. Julia Grant, *Personal Memoirs*, 79.

18. Quoted in Waugh, *U.S. Grant*, 12.

19. Quoted in Simpson, *Let Us Have Peace*, 7.

20. Brands, *Man Who Saved the Union*, 86, 87.

21. Quoted in Brands, *Man Who Saved the Union*, 86, 94.

22. Perret, *Ulysses S. Grant*, 110.

23. Quoted in ibid., 111.

24. Julia Grant, *Personal Memoirs*, 83.

25. Quoted in Brands, *Man Who Saved the Union*, 95.

26. Grant, *Personal Memoirs*, 107.

27. Paul Kahan, *Amiable Scoundrel: Simon Cameron, Lincoln's Scandalous Secretary of War* (Lincoln: University of Nebraska Press/Potomac Books, 2016), 105–106.

28. Grant, *Personal Memoirs*, 107–108, 110.

29. Julia Grant, *Personal Memoirs*, 87, and quoted in McFeely, *Grant*, 68.

30. Quoted in Waugh, *U.S. Grant*, 45.

31. John Russell Young, *Around the World with General Grant: A Narrative of the Visit of General U.S. Grant, Ex-President of the United States, to Various Countries in Europe, Asia, and Africa, in 1877, 1878, 1879*, vol. 2 (New York: American News, 1879), 446.

32. Grant, *Personal Memoirs*, 108.

33. Ibid.

34. Quoted in Brands, *Man Who Saved the Union*, 111.

35. Grant, *Personal Memoirs*, 109.

36. "Republican Party Platform of 1860," American Presidency Project, accessed August 29, 2017, http://www.presidency.ucsb.edu/ws/?pid=29620.

37. Grant to Jesse Root Grant, April 21, 1861, *Ulysses S. Grant: Memoirs and Selected Letters* (New York: Modern Library, 1990), 956–957.

38. Langguth, *After Lincoln*, 244.

39. Ibid., 245–26.

40. Quoted in David Von Drehle, *Rise to Greatness: Abraham Lincoln and America's Most Perilous Year* (New York: Henry Holt, 2012), 140.

41. *The Papers of Ulysses S. Grant*, vol. 5: April 1–August 31, 1862, ed. John Y. Simon (Carbondale: Southern Illinois University Press, 1974), 114.

42. Grant, *Memoirs and Selected Letters*, 246.

43. Grant, *Personal Memoirs*, 305.

44. Brands, *Man Who Saved the Union*, 218.

45. Quoted in Jeffrey S. Gurock, ed., *American Jewish History*, vol. 6 (New York: Taylor & Francis, 1998), 14.

46. Langguth, *After Lincoln*, 245.

47. Quoted in H.W. Brands, *The Man Who Saved the Union: Ulysses Grant in War and Peace* (New York: Doubleday, 2012), 281.

48. Quoted in Simpson, *Let Us Have Peace*, 53.

49. Quoted in Waugh, *U.S. Grant*, 83.

50. Grant, *Personal Memoirs*, 378.

51. Quoted in Simpson, *Let Us Have Peace*, 59.

52. Quoted in Waugh, *U.S. Grant*, 86.

53. "1864 Democratic Party Platform," American Presidency Project, accessed August 29, 2017, http://www.presidency.ucsb.edu/ws/?pid=29578.

54. Quoted in Michael Burlingame, *Abraham Lincoln: A Life*, vol. 2 (Baltimore: Johns Hopkins University Press, 2008), 674.

55. *The Papers of Ulysses S. Grant*, vol. 11: June 1–August 15, 1864, ed. John Y. Simon (Carbondale: Southern Illinois University Press, 1984), 361.

56. Quoted in Waugh, *U.S. Grant*, 87.

57. Doris Kearns Goodwin, *Team of Rivals: The Political Genius of Abraham Lincoln* (New York: Simon & Schuster, 2006), 713.

58. Waugh, *U.S. Grant*, 3.

CHAPTER 2

1. Julia Grant, *Personal Memoirs*, 156.

2. "Proclamation of Amnesty and Reconstruction," Avalon Project: History of the Impeachment of Andrew Johnson, ch. 1, The Problem of Reconstruction, accessed August 29, 2017, http://avalon.law.yale.edu/19th_century/john_chap_01.asp.

3. Kenneth M. Stampp, *The Era of Reconstruction, 1865–1877* (New York: Vintage Books, 1965), 48.

4. Quoted in Hans L. Trefousse, *Andrew Jackson: A Biography* (New York: W. W. Norton, 1989), 71.

5. Quoted in Kahan, *Amiable Scoundrel*, 235.

6. Eric Foner, *Reconstruction: America's Unfinished Revolution, 1863–1877* (New York: Harper Perennial, 2002), 177.

7. Quoted in Brooks D. Simpson, *The Reconstruction Presidents* (Lawrence: University Press of Kansas, 1998), 69.

8. "Interview with Delegation of Blacks," February 7, 1866, in *The Papers of Andrew Johnson*, vol. 10: February–July, 1866, ed. Paul H. Bergeron (Knoxville: University of Tennessee Press, 1993), 44.

9. Foner, *Reconstruction*, 179.

10. Stampp, *Era of Reconstruction*, 83.

11. Foner, *Reconstruction*, 241.

12. Stampp, *Era of Reconstruction*, 84.

13. Langguth, *After Lincoln*, 119–120.

14. Foner, *Reconstruction*, 197.

15. Simpson, *Let Us Have Peace*, 101.

16. "April 18, 1865 Agreement between Johnston and Sherman," Civil War Trust, accessed June 16, 2016, http://www.civilwar.org/education/history/primarysources/april-18-1865-agreement.html.

17. Martin E. Mantell, *Johnson, Grant, and the Politics of Reconstruction* (New York: Columbia University Press, 1973), 9.

18. Stampp, *Era of Reconstruction*, 79, and Erik Mathisen, "Andrew Johnson and Reconstruction," in *A Companion to the Reconstruction Presidents, 1865–1881*, ed. Edward O. Frantz (Malden, MA: Wiley-Blackwell, 2014), 29.

19. Mantell, *Johnson, Grant*, 14–15.

20. Foner, *Reconstruction*, 200.

21. Stampp, *Era of Reconstruction*, 79

22. Simpson, *Reconstruction Presidents*, 83.

23. Quoted in Nicholas Barreyre, *Gold and Freedom: The Political Economy of Reconstruction*, translated by Arthur Goldhammer (Charlottesville: University Press of Virginia, 2015), 116.

24. Simpson, *Let Us Have Peace*, 208.

25. Foner, *Reconstruction*, 239.

26. Andrew Johnson, "First Annual Message (December 6, 1865)," Miller Center, accessed July 1, 2016, http://millercenter.org/president/johnson/speeches/speech-3555.

27. Stampp, *Era of Reconstruction*, 69.

28. Andrew Johnson, "Speech to the Citizens of Washington," February 22, 1866, TeachingAmericanHistory.org, accessed August 29, 2017, http://teachingamericanhistory.org/library/document/speech-to-the-citizens-of-washington/.

29. Langguth, *After Lincoln*, 134.

30. Johnson, "Speech to the Citizens of Washington."

31. "14th Amendment," Legal Information Institute, Cornell Law School, accessed August 29, 2017, https://www.law.cornell.edu/constitution/amendmentxiv.

32. Mantell, *Johnson, Grant*, 17.

33. Quoted in Simpson, *Let Us Have Peace*, 148.

34. Quoted in ibid., 137.

35. Quoted in Simpson, *Reconstruction Presidents*, 110.

36. "The Reconstruction Acts: 1867," Texas State Library and Archives Commission, accessed August 29, 2017, https://www.tsl.texas.gov/ref/abouttx/secession/reconstruction.html.

37. Broomall, "Ulysses S. Grant," 216.

38. Simpson, *Let Us Have Peace*, 113.

39. Quoted in ibid., 21, 194.

40. Beisner, *From the Old Diplomacy*, 43.

41. "Speech of Señor Don Matías Romero, . . . Read on the 65th Anniversary of the Birth of General Ulysses S. Grant" (New York: W. Lowey, Printer, 1887), 3.

42. Simpson, *Let Us Have Peace*, 112.

43. Quoted in ibid., 156.

44. Quoted in ibid., 157.

45. Mantell, *Johnson, Grant*, 35.

46. Julia Grant, *Personal Memoirs*, 165.

47. Broomall, "Ulysses S. Grant," 217.

48. Mantell, *Johnson, Grant*, 37.

49. Andrew Johnson, "Third Annual Message (December 3, 1867)." American Presidency Project, accessed August 29, 2017, http://www.presidency.ucsb.edu/ws/?pid=29508.

50. Mantell, *Johnson, Grant*, 82.

51. Luis Fuentes-Rohwer, "The Impeachment of Andrew Johnson," in *A Companion to the Reconstruction Presidents, 1865–1881*, ed. Edward O. Frantz (Malden, MA: Wiley-Blackwell, 2014), 78.

52. Langguth, *After Lincoln*, 237.

53. Ibid., 221.

54. Everette Swinney, "Enforcing the Fifteenth Amendment, 1870–1877," *Journal of Southern History* 28 no. 2 (May, 1962): 202.

55. *Sherman Letters*, 320–321.

56. Perret, *Ulysses S. Grant*, 379.

57. Quoted in Langguth, *After Lincoln*, 247.

58. Quoted in McFeely, *Grant*, 277.

59. Grant to Sherman, June 21, 1868, *The Papers of Ulysses S. Grant*, vol. 18: October 1, 1867–June 30, 1868, ed. John Y. Simon (Carbondale: Southern Illinois University Press, 1991), 292–293.

60. Quoted in Perret, *Ulysses S. Grant*, 379.

61. "Republican Party Platform of 1868," American Presidency Project, accessed August 29, 2017, http://www.presidency.ucsb.edu/ws/?pid=29622.

62. Grant to Sherman, June 21, 1868, *Papers of Ulysses S. Grant*, 18:293

63. Brooks D. Simpson, "The Reforging of the Republican Majority," in *The Birth of the Grand Old Party: The Republicans' First Generation*, ed. Robert Francis Engs and Randall M. Miller (Philadelphia: University of Pennsylvania Press, 2002), 150.

64. Quoted in Jonathan D. Sarna and Adam Mendelsohn, eds., *Jews and the Civil War: A Reader* (New York: New York University Press, 2010), 44.

65. Langguth, *After Lincoln*, 249.

66. Simpson, "Reforging," 150.

CHAPTER 3

1. George Frisbie Hoar, *Autobiography of Seventy Years*, vol. 1 (New York: Charles Scribner's Sons, 1903), 245–246.

2. James G. Blaine, *Twenty Years of Congress: From Lincoln to Garfield*, vol. 2 (Norwich, CT: Henry Bill, 1886), 422.

3. "Inaugural Address," March 4, 1869, *The Papers of Ulysses S. Grant*, vol. 19: July 1, 1868–October 31, 1869, ed. John Y. Simon (Carbondale: Southern Illinois University Press, 1995), 140, 142.

4. "How Gen. Grant Is Misrepresented by Inquisitive Politicians," *New York Times*, February 27, 1869.

5. Grant to Cramer, March 31, 1869, *Papers of Ulysses S. Grant*, 19:160.

6. William Best Hesseltine, *Ulysses S. Grant: Politician* (New York: Frederick Ungar, 1957), 145.

7. William H. Crook, *Through Five Administrations: Reminiscences of Colonel William H. Crook, . . .* comp. and ed. Margarita Spalding Gerry (New York: Harper & Bros., 1910), 165.

8. Hoar, *Autobiography*, 247–248.

9. John Sherman, *John Sherman's Recollections of Forty Years in the House, Senate, and Cabinet* (Chicago: Werner, 1895), 377.

10. Quoted in Frank J. Scaturro, *President Grant Reconsidered* (Lanham, MD: University Press of America, 1998), 58.

11. Henry Adams, *The Education of Henry Adams: An Autobiography* (New York: Houghton Mifflin, 1918), 262.

12. Sherman, *Recollections*, 398.

13. Louis Arthur Coolidge, *Ulysses S. Grant* (New York: Houghton Mifflin, 1922), 290.

14. Hoar, *Autobiography*, 210–211.

15. Though this is the generally accepted interpretation, Pulitzer Prize-winning Grant biographer William S. McFeely claimed that the president offered Washburne the State Department in a "snap decision" that he soon came to regret. McFeely, *Grant*, 295. His basis for this assertion is Grant's letter of March 11, 1869, to Washburne accepting the latter's resignation and an entry in former secretary of the Navy Gideon Welles's diary. Washburne's letter of resignation, dated March 10, 1869, mentions that when he accepted the State Department job, "I felt constrained to state to you that my health would prevent me from holding the position for any considerable length of time," seemingly indicating that the standard narrative is, in fact, true. Washburne to Grant, March 10, 1869, *Papers of Ulysses S. Grant*, 19:151.

16. Adam Badeau, *Grant in Peace: From Appomattox to Mount McGregor; a Personal Memoir* (Hartford, CT: S. S. Scranton, 1887), 153.

17. Sumner to the Duchess of Argyll, May 18, 1869, and Sumner to Lodge, May 20, 1869, in Charles Sumner, *The Selected Letters of Charles Sumner*,

vol. 2: 1859–1874, ed. Beverly Wilson Palmer (Boston: Northeastern University Press, 1990), 463–465.

18. William L. Richter, *The ABC-Clio Companion to American Reconstruction, 1862–1877* (Santa Barbara, CA: ABC-Clio, 1996), 166.

19. McFeely, *Grant*, 297.

20. Quoted in Hesseltine, *Ulysses S. Grant*, 148.

21. Hoar, *Autobiography*, 306.

22. Grant to Stewart, February 11, 1869, *Papers of Ulysses S. Grant*, 19:127.

23. "Act of Congress Establishing the Treasury Department," US Department of the Treasury, accessed August 29, 2017, https://www.treasury.gov/about/history/Pages/act-congress.aspx.

24. Quoted in Young, *Around the World*, 276.

25. Sumner to Wright, March 12, 1869, *Selected Letters of Charles Sumner*, 455.

26. Blaine, *Twenty Years of Congress*, 415.

27. McFeely, *Grant*, 298.

28. Hoar, *Autobiography*, 241.

29. Blaine, *Twenty Years of Congress*, 427.

30. Quoted in Hamlin Garland, *Ulysses S. Grant: His Life and Character* (New York: Doubleday & McClure, 1898), 427.

31. McFeely, *Grant*, 302.

32. Crook, *Through Five Administrations*, 153.

33. Henry Adams, "The Constitution and Civil Service Reform," in *The Annals of America*, ed. William Benton, vol. 10: 1866–1883, *Reconstruction and Industrialization* (Chicago: Encyclopaedia Britannica, 1968), 212.

34. Adams to Charles Francis Adams, Jr., March 11, 1869, in *The Letters of Henry Adams*, ed. J. C. Levenson et al., vol. 2: 1868–1885 (Cambridge, MA: Harvard University Press, 1982), 21.

35. Hesseltine, *Ulysses S. Grant*, 149.

36. Hesseltine, *Ulysses S. Grant*, 153.

37. George H. Mayer, *The Republican Party, 1854–1966*, 2nd ed. (New York: Oxford University Press, 1967), 177.

38. Perret, *Ulysses S. Grant*, 402.

39. Crook, *Through Five Administrations*, 177.

40. Grant to Washburne, January 28, 1870, *The Papers of Ulysses S. Grant*, vol. 20: November 1, 1869–October 31, 1870, ed. John Y. Simon (Carbondale: Southern Illinois University Press, 1995), 91.

41. McFeely, *Grant*, 42.

42. Quoted in Perret, *Ulysses S. Grant*, 444.

43. "To The House of Representatives," *The Papers of Ulysses S. Grant*, vol. 27: January 1, 1876–October 31, 1876, ed. John Y. Simon (Carbondale: Southern Illinois University Press, 2005), 103–106.

44. Thomas F. Pendel, *Thirty-Six Years in the White House: A Memoir of the White House Doorkeeper from Lincoln to Roosevelt* (Bedford, MA: Applewood Books, 2008), 169–176.

45. Crook, *Through Five Administrations*, 178.

46. Ronald C. White, *American Ulysses: A Life of Ulysses S. Grant* (New York: Random House, 2016), 477.

47. Julia Grant, *Personal Memoirs*, 174, and Pendel, *Thirty-Six Years*, 64.

48. Quoted in Waugh, *U.S. Grant*, 146.

49. Bernard Schwartz, *A History of the Supreme Court* (New York: Oxford University Press, 1995), 158.

50. Quoted in Barreyre, *Gold and Freedom*, 44.

51. Ibid., 49.

52. Perret, *Ulysses S. Grant*, 390.

53. Henry Adams, *The Great Secession Winter of 1860–1861 and Other Essays*, ed. George Hochfield (New York: Sagamore Press, 1958), 162–163.

54. Edwin Palmer Hoyt, *The Goulds: A Social History* (New York: Weybright and Talley, 1969), 49.

55. *Investigation into the Causes of the Gold Panic: Report of the Majority of the Committee on Banking and Currency, March 1, 1870* (Washington, DC: Government Printing Office, 1870), 1-2.

56. Perret, *Ulysses S. Grant*, 391.

57. Ulysses S. Grant, "Proclamation," May 19, 1869, in *Papers of Ulysses S. Grant*, 19:189.

58. *Papers of Ulysses S. Grant*, 19:244n.

59. Julia Grant, *Personal Memoirs*, 182.

60. Quoted in Hoyt, *Goulds*, 50.

61. Perret, *Ulysses S. Grant*, 391, and Brands, *Man Who Saved the Union*, 439.

62. *Investigation into the Causes of the Gold Panic*, 9.

63. Grant to Boutwell, September 12, 1869, *Papers of Ulysses S. Grant*, 19: 243–244.

64. Quoted in McFeely, *Grant*, 325.

65. Quoted in Brands, *Man Who Saved the Union*, 443.

66. Quoted in McFeely, 326.

67. Whether Gould actually read it was a matter of dispute; Gould claimed he did, while Corbin claimed he did not. McFeely, *Grant*, 327.

68. McFeely, *Grant*, 328.

69. *Investigation into the Causes of the Gold Panic*, 17.

70. Jean Edward Smith, *Grant* (New York: Simon & Schuster, 2002), 490.

71. Ibid.

72. *Investigation into the Causes of the Gold Panic*, 20.

73. Grant to Conner, October 13, 1869, *Papers of Ulysses S. Grant*, 19:255.

74. Perret, *Ulysses S. Grant*, 393.

75. Waugh, *U.S. Grant*, 131.

CHAPTER 4

1. Speech, October 13, 1869, *Papers of Ulysses S. Grant*, 19:107.

2. "Speech," December 11, 1869, *Papers of Ulysses S. Grant*, 20:50.

3. William Gillette, *Retreat from Reconstruction, 1869–1879* (Baton Rouge: Louisiana State University Press, 1979), 21.

4. Thomas R. Pegram, "Reconstruction during the Grant Years: The Conun-

drum of Policy," in *A Companion to the Reconstruction Presidents, 1865–1881*, ed. Edward O. Frantz (Malden, MA: Wiley-Blackwell, 2014), 280.

5. Gillette, *Retreat*, x.
6. "Fifteenth Amendment to the Constitution of the United States," accessed August 29, 2017, https://memory.loc.gov/cgi-bin/ampage?collId=llsl&fileName=015%2Fllsl015.db&recNum=379.
7. Quoted in Gillette, *Retreat*, 22.
8. Quoted in Brands, *Man Who Saved the Union*, 466.
9. Perret, *Ulysses S. Grant*, 412.
10. Gillette, *Retreat*, 13.
11. Quoted in Gillette, *Retreat*, 19.
12. Quoted in Brands, *Man Who Saved the Union*, 466, and Michael Perman, "The Politics of Reconstruction," in *A Companion to the Civil War and Reconstruction*, ed. Lacy K. Ford (Malden, MA: Wiley-Blackwell, 2011), 335.
13. Foner, *Reconstruction*, 346.
14. Wyn Craig Wade, *The Fiery Cross: The Ku Klux Klan in America* (New York: Oxford University Press, 1998), 46–47.
15. Quoted in ibid., 50.
16. Foner, *Reconstruction*, 425.
17. "Enforcement Act of 1870," accessed August 29, 2017, https://www.senate.gov/artandhistory/history/resources/pdf/EnforcementAct_1870.pdf.
18. James E. Sefton, *The United States Army and Reconstruction, 1865–1877* (Baton Rouge: Louisiana State University Press, 1967), 221.
19. Wade, *Fiery Cross*, 83.
20. Sefton, *United States Army*, 224–225.
21. Richter, *ABC-CLIO Companion*, 155.
22. Wade, *Fiery Cross*, 85.
23. "Third Enforcement Act," accessed August 29, 2017, https://www.senate.gov/artandhistory/history/common/image/EnforcementAct_Apr1871_Page_1.htm.
24. Swinney, "Enforcing the Fifteenth Amendment," 205.
25. Smith, *Grant*, 542–547.
26. Foner, *Reconstruction*, 458–459.
27. Quoted in ibid., 454, 458.
28. Philip Leigh, *Southern Reconstruction* (Yardley, PA: Westholme, 2017), x.
29. Swinney, "Enforcing the Fifteenth Amendment," 205.
30. Foner, *Reconstruction*, 455.
31. Sefton, *United States Army*, 223.
32. Perret, *Ulysses S. Grant*, 413. There was also an element of competition between the secretary of war and the commanding general that poisoned relations between the administration and Sherman. For more on this, see White, *American Ulysses*, 475.
33. W. T. Sherman to John Sherman, October 23, 1874, *Sherman Letters*, 341.
34. Grant to Smith, July 28, 1872, *The Papers of Ulysses S. Grant*, vol. 23: February 1–December 31, 1872, ed. John Y. Simon (Carbondale: Southern Illinois University Press, 2000), 210–211.

35. Gillette, *Retreat*, 38–39.
36. Foner, *Reconstruction*, 447.
37. Gillette, *Retreat*, 48–49.
38. Foner, *Reconstruction*, 376–378.
39. Quoted in Gillette, *Retreat*, 37.
40. Foner, *Reconstruction*, 390, 385, 415.
41. Gillette, *Retreat*, 53.
42. Foner, *Reconstruction*, 349.
43. Pegram, "Reconstruction," 284.
44. Foner, *Reconstruction*, 412.
45. W. T. Sherman to John Sherman, April 26, 1868, *Sherman Letters*, 317.
46. "Authorization of the Board of Indian Commissioners, April 10, 1869," in *Documents of United States Indian Policy*, 3rd ed., ed. Francis P. Prucha (Lincoln: University of Nebraska Press, 2000), 125.
47. Arthur Caswell Parker, *The Life of General Ely S. Parker: Last Grand Sachem of the Iroquois and General Grant's Military Secretary* (Buffalo, NY: Buffalo Historical Society, 1919), 133.
48. McFeely, *Grant*, 312–313.
49. Quoted in *The Annals of America*, ed. William Benton, vol. 10: 1866–1883, *Reconstruction and Industrialization* (Chicago: Encyclopaedia Britannica, 1968), 244.
50. Perret, *Ulysses S. Grant*, 425.
51. "Draft Annual Message," *Papers of Ulysses S. Grant*, 21:41.
52. Brands, *Man Who Saved the Union*, 501, 505.
53. Quoted in *Papers of Ulysses S. Grant*, 22:78.
54. "To Congress," *Papers of Ulysses S. Grant*, 21:152.
55. Smith, *Grant*, 532.
56. Cox to Grant, May 21, 1870, *Papers of Ulysses S. Grant*, 20:204–205.

CHAPTER 5

1. "The Ten Best Secretaries of State," *American Heritage*, vol. 33, no. 1 (December 1981), accessed January 10, 2017, http://www.americanheritage.com/content/ten-best-secretaries-state%E2%80%A6.
2. Beisner, *From the Old Diplomacy*, 48.
3. Fred Harvey Harrington, *Fighting Politician: Major General N. P. Banks* (Philadelphia: University of Pennsylvania Press, 1948), 186.
4. Grant, *Personal Memoirs*, 612.
5. Brands, *Man Who Saved the Union*, 449.
6. Simon Wolf, *The Presidents I Have Known from 1860–1918* (Washington, DC: Byron S. Adams, 1918), 74–75.
7. Young, *Men and Memories*, 2:355.
8. Allan Nevins, *Hamilton Fish: The Inner History of the Grant Administration* (New York: Dodd, Mead, 1936), 116.
9. Beisner, *From the Old Diplomacy*, 40.
10. Ibid., 22.
11. Nicole M. Phelps, "The Gilded Age," in *Guide to U.S. Foreign Policy: A Diplomatic History* (Thousand Oaks, CA: Sage Publications, 2012), 56.

12. Graham H. Stuart, *The Department of State: A History of Its Organization, Procedure, and Personnel* (New York: Macmillan, 1949), 150.

13. Grant, *Personal Memoirs*, 614.

14. Schwartz, *History of the Supreme Court*, 142.

15. Beisner, *From the Old Diplomacy*, 13.

16. Quoted in Simpson, *Let Us Have Peace*, 124–125.

17. Scaturro, *President Grant*, 52.

18. Quoted in *The Dial*, vol. 35, July 1 to December 16, 1903 (Chicago: Dial Co., 1903), 413.

19. Nevins, *Hamilton Fish*, 122.

20. Charles Sumner, *Our Claims on England: Speech of Hon. Charles Sumner, of Massachusetts, Delivered in Executive Session of the Senate, April 13, 1869, on the Johnson-Clarendon Treaty for the Settlement of Claims* (Washington, DC: F. & J. Rives & Geo. A. Bailey, Reporters and Printers of the Debates of Congress, 1869), 3.

21. Blaine, *Twenty Years of Congress*, 491.

22. Nevins, *Hamilton Fish*, 148–149.

23. Carl Schurz, *Charles Sumner, an Essay*, ed. Arthur Reed Hogue (Urbana: University of Illinois Press, 1951), 122.

24. Beisner, *From the Old Diplomacy*, 6.

25. Nevins, *Hamilton Fish*, 130.

26. Ulysses S. Grant, "First Annual Message (December 6, 1869)," American Presidency Project, accessed August 30, 2017, http://www.presidency.ucsb.edu/ws/?pid=29510.

27. Nevins, *Hamilton Fish*, 159.

28. Adrian Cook, *The Alabama Claims: American Politics and Anglo-American Relations, 1865–1872* (Ithaca, NY: Cornell University Press, 1975), 107.

29. Cook, *Alabama Claims*, 115.

30. Beisner, *From the Old Diplomacy*, 41.

31. Joseph V. Fuller, "Hamilton Fish," in *The American Secretaries of State and Their Diplomacy*, vol. 7, ed. Samuel F. Bemis (New York: Cooper Square Publishers, 1963), 135.

32. McFeely, *Grant*, 352–353.

33. Cook, *Alabama Claims*, 114.

34. Savage to Grant, February 6, 1870, and Bingham to Grant, July 1870, in *Papers of Ulysses S. Grant*, 20:115–118.

35. "Proclamation," in *Papers of Ulysses S. Grant*, 20:151.

36. Grant to Badeau, October 23, 1870, in ibid., 20:318.

37. Brands, *Man Who Saved the Union*, 485.

38. John B. Brebner and Allan Nevins, *The Making of Modern Britain: A Short History* (New York: George Allen & Unwin, 1943), 184.

39. *The Papers of Ulysses S. Grant*, vol. 28: November 1, 1876–September 30, 1878, ed. John Y. Simon (Carbondale: Southern Illinois University Press, 2005), 245n3.

40. Grant, *Personal Memoirs*, 614–615.

41. Ibid., 613–614.

42. "Speech," March 10, 1871, *Papers of Ulysses S. Grant*, 21:218.

43. Grant, *Personal Memoirs*, 614.

44. "Proclamation," August 22, 1870, in *Papers of Ulysses S. Grant*, 20:235–240, and "To Congress," July 15, 1870, in ibid, 20:195.

45. Crook, *Through Five Administrations*, 170–172.

46. Brands, *Man Who Saved the Union*, 484.

47. "Annual Message," *Papers of Ulysses S. Grant*, 22:270–271.

48. Phelps, "The Gilded Age," 59.

49. Fish Diary, January 4, 1870, Fish Papers, Manuscript Division, Library of Congress, Washington, DC.

50. "Speech," September 9, 1870, in *Papers of Ulysses S. Grant*, 20:264–265.

51. Ulysses S. Grant, *Personal Memoirs*, 615.

52. Quoted in Brands, *Man Who Saved the Union*, 455.

53. Nevins, *Hamilton Fish*, 255–256.

54. William Javier Nelson, *Almost a Territory: America's Attempt to Annex the Dominican Republic* (Newark: University of Delaware Press, 1990), 61, 64–65.

55. Fish Diary, April 6, 1869, Fish Papers, Manuscript Division, Library of Congress, Washington, DC.

56. Nevins, *Hamilton Fish*, 265.

57. Quoted in Brands, *Man Who Saved the Union*, 453.

58. Quoted in Richter, *ABC-CLIO Companion*, 202.

59. Schurz, *Charles Sumner*, 119.

60. Allan Nevins asserts "Not concealing from Sumner and others his dislike of annexation, [Fish] completed his draft," though the historian provides neither direct evidence nor citation for this. Nevins, *Hamilton Fish*, 271.

61. McFeely, *Grant*, 344.

62. Nelson, *Almost a Territory*, 84, 96–97.

63. "Concerning the Annexation of the Dominican Republic," in *The Annals of America*, vol. 10: 1866–1883, *Reconstruction and Industrialization*, ed. William Benton (Chicago: Encyclopaedia Britannica, 1968), 232.

64. Fish Diary, June 17, 1870, Fish Papers, Manuscript Division, Library of Congress, Washington, DC.

65. Quoted in Hesseltine, *Ulysses S. Grant*, 139.

66. Schurz, *Charles Sumner*, 119.

67. Fish Diary, June 14, 1870, Fish Papers, Manuscript Division, Library of Congress, Washington, DC.

68. Schwartz, *History of the Supreme Court*, 149–150.

69. Harrington, *Fighting Politician*, 190–191.

70. Schurz, *Charles Sumner*, 120.

71. Ibid., 121, and Grant to Jones, February, 8, 1871, *Papers of Ulysses S. Grant*, 21:179.

72. Hoar, *Autobiography*, 262.

73. *Papers of Ulysses S. Grant*, 21:293.

74. Andrew Dickson White, *Autobiography of Andrew Dickson White*, vol. 1 (New York: Century Group, 1905), 154, and Grant, "Eighth Annual Message."

75. Fish to Cameron, May 30, 1871, *Papers of Ulysses S. Grant*, 21:362–363.

76. McFeely, *Grant*, 299.
77. White, *Autobiography*, 179.
78. Beisner, *From the Old Diplomacy*, 52.
79. Nevins, *Hamilton Fish*, 193.
80. Thomas Keneally, *American Scoundrel: The Life of the Notorious Civil War General Dan Sickles* (New York: Anchor Books, 2003), 334.
81. Nevins, *Hamilton Fish*, 190.
82. Keneally, *American Scoundrel*, 335–336.
83. Grant to Fish, August 14, 1870, *Papers of Ulysses S. Grant*, 19:234–235.
84. Smith, *Grant*, 478.
85. McFeely, *Grant*, 298–299, 385.
86. Quoted in Brands, *Man Who Saved the Union*, 460.
87. Quoted in Harrington, *Fighting Politician*, 192.

CHAPTER 6

1. Nevins, *Hamilton Fish*, 107.
2. Mayer, *Republican Party*, 174.
3. Simpson, "Reforging," 152. On Grant's assumption of party leadership, see White, *American Ulysses*, 524.
4. Quoted in Simon, "Introduction," *Papers of Ulysses S. Grant*, 21:xii.
5. Kahan, *Amiable Scoundrel*, 251.
6. Quoted in Simpson, *Let Us Have Peace*, 205.
7. Quoted in Kahan, *Amiable Scoundrel*, 258.
8. Mayer, *Republican Party*, 179.
9. Quoted in Brands, *Man Who Saved the Union*, 495.
10. Quoted in ibid., 477.
11. "To Congress," *Papers of Ulysses S. Grant*, 22:297–298.
12. Crook, *Through Five Administrations*, 173.
13. Norton to Grant, December 27, 1871, *Papers of Ulysses S. Grant*, 21:6–7.
14. In his memoirs, former House Speaker James G. Blaine asserted that Liberal Republicans' revolt against Grant was "in some degree a difference of policy, but more largely a clashing of personal interests and ambitions." Blaine, *Twenty Years of Congress*, 517.
15. Gillette, *Retreat*, 56–57.
16. "Republican Party Platform of 1872." American Presidency Project, accessed August 30, 2017, http://www.presidency.ucsb.edu/ws/?pid=29623.
17. Richter, *ABC-CLIO Companion*, 144.
18. Grant to Young, November 15, 1870, *Papers of Ulysses S. Grant*, 21:8.
19. Grant to Fish, August 21, 1870, *Papers of Ulysses S. Grant*, 20:232–233, and Grant to Greeley, December 10, 1870, *Papers of Ulysses S. Grant*, 21:84, and Julia Grant, *Personal Memoirs*, 180.
20. "1872 Democratic Party Platform," American Presidency Project, accessed August 30, 2017, http://www.presidency.ucsb.edu/ws/?pid=29580.
21. Gillette, *Retreat*, 59.
22. Richter, *ABC-CLIO Companion*, 145.
23. Quoted in Harrington, *Fighting Politician*, 202.

24. Gillette, *Retreat*, 66.

25. Hoar, *Autobiography*, 284.

26. Gillette, *Retreat*, 65.

27. "Second Inaugural Address of Ulysses S. Grant," Avalon Project, accessed August 30, 2017, http://avalon.law.yale.edu/19th_century/grant2.asp.

28. David J. Rothman, *Politics and Power: The United States Senate, 1869–1901* (New York: Atheneum, 1969), 28.

29. William Dudley Foulke, *Life of Oliver P. Morton, Including His Important Speeches*, vol. 2 (New York: AMS Press, 1974), 172.

30. Gillette, *Retreat*, 73–74.

31. Foner, *Reconstruction*, 461.

32. Sherman, *Recollections*, 418.

33. Julia Grant, *Personal Memoirs*, 183.

34. Kahan, *Amiable Scoundrel*, 266.

35. "Veto," *The Papers of Ulysses S. Grant*, vol. 25: 1874, ed. John Y. Simon (Carbondale: Southern Illinois University Press, 2003), 73–75.

36. *Papers of Ulysses S. Grant*, 18:265.

37. Blaine, *Twenty Years of Congress*, 563.

38. Smith, *Grant*, 581.

39. Crook, *Through Five Administrations*, 176.

40. Smith, *Grant*, 553.

41. Swinney, "Enforcing the Fifteenth Amendment," 206.

42. Quoted in Crook, *Through Five Administrations*, 195.

43. *Papers of Ulysses S. Grant*, 27:xxvii.

44. Crook, *Through Five Administrations*, 165.

45. Crook, *Through Five Administrations*, 191.

46. Frank M. O'Brien, "The Story of the *Sun*," *Munsey's Magazine*, vol. 62 (October 1917 to January 1918), 663.

47. *Papers of Ulysses S. Grant*, 27:224.

48. Crook, *Through Five Administrations*, 198.

49. Everett Pepperell Wheeler, *Sixty Years of American Life: Taylor to Roosevelt, 1850 to 1900* (New York: E. P. Dutton, 1917), 98.

50. Stephen W. Stathis, *Landmark Legislation: Major U.S. Acts and Treaties, 1774–2002* (Washington, DC: CQ Press, 2003), 113.

51. Crook, *Through Five Administrations*, 214.

CHAPTER 7

1. Pegram, "Reconstruction," 277.

2. Quoted in McFeely, *Grant*, 373.

3. Swinney, "Enforcing the Fifteenth Amendment," 206.

4. Quoted in Gillette, *Retreat*, 36.

5. Akerman to E. P. Jacobson, August 18, 1870, quoted in Brooks D. Simpson, "Ulysses S. Grant and the Failure of Reconstruction," *Illinois Historical Journal* 81, no. 4 (Winter 1988), 282n33.

6. Quoted in ibid., 283.

7. Hoar, *Autobiography*, 275.

8. "To Senate," *The Papers of Ulysses S. Grant*, vol. 26: 1875, ed. John Y. Simon (Carbondale: Southern Illinois University Press, 2003) 3.

9. Ibid., 52–53.

10. Foner, *Reconstruction*, 558, 563.

11. "Proclamation," *Papers of Ulysses S. Grant*, 27:329–330.

12. Smith, *Grant*, 571.

13. W. T. Sherman to John Sherman, January 7, 1875, *Sherman Letters*, 342.

14. Blaine, *Twenty Years of Congress*, 554.

15. Schwartz, *History of the Supreme Court*, 159, and Charles Warren, *The Supreme Court in United States History*, vol. 3: 1856–1918 (Boston: Little, Brown, 1922), 285.

16. David J. Rothkopf, *Power, Inc.: The Epic Rivalry between Big Business and Government—and the Reckoning that Lies Ahead* (New York: Farrar, Straus and Giroux, 2012), 182.

17. Alan Axelrod, *Political History of America's Wars* (Washington, DC: CQ Press, 2007), 257.

18. Smith, *Grant*, 535.

19. Ibid., 539.

20. "Speech," *Papers of Ulysses S. Grant*, 26:342–344.

21. "Annual Message," ibid., 26:388–389.

22. Grant to the Editor, *Sunday School Times*, June 6, 1876, *Papers of Ulysses S. Grant*, 27:124.

23. Grant to Wolf, June 28, 1876, ibid., 27:160.

24. Bross to Babcock, March 17, 1870, *Papers of Ulysses S. Grant*, 21:105.

25. Count Joseph Alexander Von Hübner, "Observations of an Austrian Diplomat," in *The Annals of America*, vol. 10: 1866–1883, *Reconstruction and Industrialization*, ed. William Benton (Chicago: Encyclopaedia Britannica, 1968), 286.

26. Ulysses S. Grant, "Fourth Annual Message (December 2, 1872)." American Presidency Project, accessed August 30, 2017, http://www.presidency.ucsb.edu/ws/?pid=29513, and "Annual Message," *Papers of Ulysses S. Grant*, 26:415.

27. Julia Grant, *Personal Memoirs*, 184–185.

28. Congressional Record: Containing the Proceedings and Debates of the Forty-Third Congress, 1st sess., vol. 2 (Washington, DC: Government Printing Office, 1874), 2026.

29. "Proclamation," *Papers of Ulysses S. Grant*, 24:158–159.

30. "To Congress," *Papers of Ulysses S. Grant*, 25:34–35.

31. "Address," *Papers of Ulysses S. Grant*, 27:107.

32. Grant to Coggeshall, July 24, 1872, *Papers of Ulysses S. Grant*, 23:209–210.

33. Quoted in Fuller, "Hamilton Fish," 178.

34. Ibid., 183.

35. Lester Brune, *Chronological History of United States Foreign Relations, 1776 to January 20, 1981*, vol. 1 (New York: Garland, 1985), 331, 333–334.

36. Coke to Grant, March 30, 1875, *Papers of Ulysses S. Grant*, 26:150–151.

37. Phil Roberts, "'All Americans Are Hero-Worshippers': American Observations on the First U.S. Visit by a Reigning Monarch," *Journal of the Gilded Age and Progressive Era* 7, no. 4 (October 2008): 465, and Peter Cozzens, "The Death and Resurrection of FRUS, 1868–1876," ch. 3 in Foreign Relations of the United States Series, Office of the Historian, Bureau of Public Affairs, US State Department, accessed August 28, 2017, https://history.state.gov/historicaldocuments/frus-history/chapter-3.

38. "To Senate," *Papers of Ulysses S. Grant*, 25:128–130.

39. Brune, *Chronological History*, 328.

40. "Annual Message," *Papers of Ulysses S. Grant*, 26:415.

41. Eithne Luibhéid, *Entry Denied: Controlling Sexuality at the Border* (Minneapolis: University of Minnesota Press, 2002), 37.

42. Blaine, *Twenty Years of Congress*, 567.

43. Quoted in Ross A. Webb, "The Presidential Boom of 1876," *Hayes Historical Journal: A Journal of the Gilded Age* 1, no. 2 (Fall 1976), 79.

44. "Republican Party Platform of 1860."

45. Fish Diary, October 10, 1876, Fish Papers, Manuscript Division, Library of Congress, Washington, DC.

46. Grant to Sherman, November 10, 1876, *Papers of Ulysses S. Grant*, 28:19–20.

47. Quoted in Foner, *Reconstruction*, 577.

48. Blaine, *Twenty Years of Congress*, 582.

49. Wheeler, *Sixty Years*, 107.

50. Quoted in Smith, *Grant*, 603.

51. Foner, *Reconstruction*, 582.

CONCLUSION

1. White, *Autobiography*, 179–180, and Simon, "Introduction," *Papers of Ulysses S. Grant*, 21:xi.

2. "Visit With Mrs. Grant."

3. Ferdinand Ward, "General Grant as I Knew Him," *New York Herald Magazine*, December 19, 1909, 1–2.

4. Badeau, *Grant in Peace*, 319.

5. Julia Grant, *Personal Memoirs*, 321.

6. Grant to Sartoris, November 4, 1880, *The Papers of Ulysses S. Grant*, vol. 30: October 1, 1880–December 31, 1882, ed. John Y. Simon (Carbondale: Southern Illinois University Press, 2008), 63.

7. Ward, "General Grant," 1–2.

8. Quoted in Scaturro, *President Grant*, i.

9. Stampp, *Era of Reconstruction*, 9.

10. Quoted in Edward O. Frantz, "Introduction," in *A Companion to the Reconstruction Presidents, 1865–1881*, ed. Edward O. Frantz (Malden, MA: Wiley-Blackwell, 2014), 2.

11. Avery Craven, *Reconstruction: The Ending of the Civil War* (New York: Henry Holt, 1969), 275.

12. Stampp, *Era of Reconstruction*, 101.

13. Quoted in Foner, *Reconstruction*, xvii.

14. Quoted in Scaturro, *President Grant*, 1.
15. Quoted in Frantz, "Introduction," 2.
16. Swinney, "Enforcing the Fifteenth Amendment," 209–210.
17. Grant, "Eighth Annual Message."

BIBLIOGRAPHY

PRIMARY SOURCES

"Act of Congress Establishing the Treasury Department." US Department of the Treasury. Accessed August 29, 2017, https://www.treasury.gov/about/history/Pages/act-congress.aspx.

Adams, Henry. "The Constitution and Civil Service Reform." In *The Annals of America*, edited by William Benton. Vol. 10: 1866–1883, *Reconstruction and Industrialization*. Chicago: Encyclopaedia Britannica, 1968.

———. *The Education of Henry Adams: An Autobiography*. New York: Houghton Mifflin, 1918.

———. *The Great Secession Winter of 1860–61 and Other Essays*. Edited by George Hochfield. New York: Sagamore Press, 1958.

———. *The Letters of Henry Adams*. Edited by J. C. Levenson, Ernest Samuels, Charles Vandersee, and Viola H. Winner. Vol. 2: 1868–1885. Cambridge, MA: Harvard University Press, 1982.

Babcock, Orville E. *Diary of Orville E. Babcock*. MSS, Ulysses S. Grant Collection, Mississippi State University Libraries.

Badeau, Adam. *Grant in Peace: From Appomattox to Mount McGregor; a Personal Memoir*. Hartford, CT: S. S. Scranton, 1887.

Blaine, James Gillespie. *Twenty Years of Congress: From Lincoln to Garfield*. Vol. 2. Norwich, CT: Henry Bill, 1886.

"Concerning the Annexation of the Dominican Republic." In *The Annals of America*, edited by William Benton. Vol. 10: 1866–1883, *Reconstruction and Industrialization*. Chicago: Encyclopaedia Britannica, 1968.

Congressional Record: Containing the Proceedings and Debates of the Forty-Third Congress, 1st sess. Vol. 2. Washington, DC: Government Printing Office, 1874.

Crook, William H. *Through Five Administrations: Reminiscences of Colonel William H. Crook, . . .* Compiled and edited by Margarita Spalding Gerry. New York: Harper & Bros., 1910.

The Dial. Vol. 35: July 1 to December 16, 1903. Chicago: Dial Co., 1903.

"1864 Democratic Party Platform." American Presidency Project. Accessed August 29, 2017, http://www.presidency.ucsb.edu/ws/?pid=29578.

"1872 Democratic Party Platform." American Presidency Project. Accessed August 30, 2017, http://www.presidency.ucsb.edu/ws/?pid=29580.

"Enforcement Act of 1870." Accessed August 29, 2017, https://www.senate.gov/artandhistory/history/resources/pdf/EnforcementAct_1870.pdf._

"Fifteenth Amendment to the Constitution of the United States." Accessed August 29, 2017, https://memory.loc.gov/cgi-bin/ampage?collId=llsl&fileName=015%2Fllsl015.db&recNum=379.

Fish, Hamilton. Hamilton Fish Papers, 1732–1914. MSS20602. Library of Congress, Washington, DC.

Foulke, William Dudley. *Life of Oliver P. Morton, Including His Important Speeches.* Vol. 2. New York: AMS Press, 1974.

"14th Amendment." Legal Information Institute, Cornell Law School. Accessed August 29, 2017, https://www.law.cornell.edu/constitution/amendmentxiv.

Grant, Julia Dent. *The Personal Memoirs of Julia Dent Grant.* Edited by John Y. Simon. New York: G. P. Putnam & Sons, 1975.

Grant, Ulysses S. "Eighth Annual Message (December 5, 1876)." American Presidency Project. Accessed August 30, 2017, http://www.presidency.ucsb.edu/ws/index.php?pid=29517.

———. "First Annual Message (December 6, 1869)." American Presidency Project. Accessed August 30, 2017, http://www.presidency.ucsb.edu/ws/?pid=29510.

———. "Fourth Annual Message (December 2, 1872)." American Presidency Project. Accessed August 30, 2017, http://www.presidency.ucsb.edu/ws/?pid=29513.

———. *The Papers of Ulysses S. Grant.* Edited by John Y. Simon. Vols. 5, 11, 18–28, 30. Carbondale: Southern Illinois University Press, 1974–2008.

———. "Second Inaugural Address of Ulysses S. Grant." Avalon Project. Accessed August 30, 2017, http://avalon.law.yale.edu/19th_century/grant2.asp.

————. *Ulysses S. Grant: Memoirs and Selected Letters*. New York: Modern Library, 1990.

Hayes, Rutherford B. *The Diary and Letters of Rutherford Birchard Hayes*. Vol. 5. Edited by Charles Richard Williams. Columbus: Ohio State Archaeological and Historical Society, 1926.

Hoar, George Frisbie. *Autobiography of Seventy Years*. Vol. 1. New York: Charles Scribner's Sons, 1903.

"How Gen. Grant Is Misrepresented by Inquisitive Politicians." *New York Times*, February 27, 1869.

Hübner, Joseph Alexander von. "Observations of an Austrian Diplomat." In *The Annals of America,* edited by William Benton. Vol. 10: 1866–1883, *Reconstruction and Industrialization*. Chicago: Encyclopaedia Britannica, 1968.

Investigation into the Causes of the Gold Panic: Report of the Majority of the Committee on Banking and Currency, March 1, 1870. Washington, DC: Government Printing Office, 1870.

Johnson, Andrew. "First Annual Message (December 6, 1865)." Miller Center. Accessed July 1, 2016, http://millercenter.org/president/johnson/speeches/speech-3555.

————. *The Papers of Andrew Johnson*. Edited by Paul H. Bergeron. Vol. 10: February–July, 1866. Knoxville: University of Tennessee Press, 1993.

————. "Speech to the Citizens of Washington," February 22, 1866. TeachingAmericanHistory.org. Accessed August 29, 2017, http://teachingamericanhistory.org/library/document/speech-to-the-citizens-of-washington/.

————. "Third Annual Message (December 3, 1867)." American Presidency Project. Accessed August 29, 2017, http://www.presidency.ucsb.edu/ws/?pid=29508.

Johnston, Joseph E., and William T. Sherman. "April 18, 1865 Agreement between Johnston and Sherman." Civil War Trust. Accessed June 16, 2016, http://www.civilwar.org/education/history/primarysources/april-18-1865-agreement.html.

Lincoln, Abraham. "Proclamation of Amnesty and Reconstruction." Avalon Project: History of the Impeachment of Andrew Johnson. Chapter 1. The Problem of Reconstruction. Accessed August 29, 2017, http://avalon.law.yale.edu/19th_century/john_chap_01.asp.

Pendel, Thomas F. *Thirty-Six Years in the White House: A Memoir of the White House Doorkeeper from Lincoln to Roosevelt*. Bedford, MA: Applewood Books, 2008.

Prucha, Francis Paul, ed. *Documents of United States Indian Policy*. 3rd ed. Lincoln: University of Nebraska Press, 2000.

"The Reconstruction Acts: 1867." Texas State Library and Archives Commission. Accessed August 29, 2017, https://www.tsl.texas.gov/ref/abouttx/secession/reconstruction.html.

"Republican Party Platform of 1860." American Presidency Project. Accessed August 29, 2017, http://www.presidency.ucsb.edu/ws/?pid=29620.

"Republican Party Platform of 1868." American Presidency Project. Accessed August 29, 2017, http://www.presidency.ucsb.edu/ws/?pid=29622.

"Republican Party Platform of 1872." American Presidency Project. Accessed August 30, 2017, http://www.presidency.ucsb.edu/ws/?pid=29623.

Romero, Matías. *Speech of Señor Don Matías Romero . . . Read on the 65th Anniversary of the Birth of General Ulysses S. Grant, Celebrated at the Metropolitan Methodist Episcopal Church, of the City of Washington, on the 25th of April, 1887*. New York: W. Lowey, Printer, 1887.

Sarna, Jonathan D., and Adam Mendelsohn, eds. *Jews and the Civil War: A Reader*. New York: New York University Press, 2010.

Schurz, Carl. *Charles Sumner, an Essay*. Edited by Arthur Reed Hogue. Urbana: University of Illinois Press, 1951.

Sherman, John. *John Sherman's Recollections of Forty Years in the House, Senate and Cabinet: An Autobiography*. Chicago: Werner, 1895.

Sherman, William Tecumseh, and John Sherman. *The Sherman Letters: Correspondence between General and Senator Sherman from 1837 to 1891*. Edited by Rachel Sherman Thorndike. New York: Charles Scribner's Sons, 1894.

Sumner, Charles. *Our Claims on England: Speech of Hon. Charles Sumner, of Massachusetts, Delivered in Executive Session of the Senate, April 13, 1869, on the Johnson-Clarendon Treaty for the Settlement of Claims. Injunction of Secrecy Removed by Order of the Senate*. Washington, DC: F. & J. Rives & Geo. A. Bailey, Reporters and Printers of the Debates of Congress, 1869.

————. *The Selected Letters of Charles Sumner*. Edited by Beverly Wilson Palmer. Vol. 2: 1859–1874. Boston: Northeastern University Press, 1990.

"Third Enforcement Act." Accessed August 29, 2017, https://www.senate.gov/artandhistory/history/common/image/EnforcementAct_Apr1871_Page_1.htm.

"Visit with Mrs. Grant, 1899 Washington, DC." Ulysses S. Grant Homepage. Accessed August 29, 2017, http://www.granthomepage.com/intjdgrant3.htm.

Ward, Ferdinand. "General Grant as I Knew Him." *New York Herald Magazine*, December 19, 1909, 1–2.

Wheeler, Everett Pepperell. *Sixty Years of American Life: Taylor to Roosevelt, 1850 to 1900*. New York: E. P. Dutton, 1917.

White, Andrew Dickson. *Autobiography of Andrew Dickson White*. Vol. 1. New York: Century Group, 1905.

Wolf, Simon. *The Presidents I Have Known from 1860–1918*. Washington, DC: Byron S. Adams, 1918.

Young, John Russell. *Around the World with General Grant: A Narrative of the Visit of General U.S. Grant, Ex-President of the United States, to Various Countries in Europe, Asia, and Africa, in 1877, 1878, 1879*. Vol. 2. New York: American News, 1879.

————. *Men and Memories; Personal Reminiscences*. New York: F. T. Neeley, 1901.

SECONDARY SOURCES

Axelrod, Alan. *Political History of America's Wars*. Washington, DC: CQ Press, 2007.

Barreyre, Nicolas. *Gold and Freedom: The Political Economy of Reconstruction*. Translated by Arthur Goldhammer. Charlottesville: University Press of Virginia, 2015.

Beisner, Robert L. *From the Old Diplomacy to the New: 1865–1900*. Wheeling, IL: Harlan Davidson, 1986.

Brands, H. W. *The Man Who Saved the Union: Ulysses Grant in War and Peace*. New York: Doubleday, 2012.

Brebner, John Bartlet, and Allan Nevins. *The Making of Modern Britain: A Short History*. New York: George Allen & Unwin, 1943.

Broomall, James J. "Ulysses S. Grant Goes to Washington: The Commanding General as Secretary of War." In *A Companion to the Reconstruction Presidents*, edited by Edward O. Frantz. Malden, MA: Wiley-Blackwell, 2014.

Brune, Lester H. *Chronological History of United States Foreign Relations, 1776 to January 20, 1981*. Vol. 1. New York: Garland, 1985.

Burlingame, Michael. *Abraham Lincoln: A Life*. Vol. 2. Baltimore: Johns Hopkins University Press, 2008.

Cook, Adrian. *The Alabama Claims: American Politics and Anglo-American Relations, 1865–1872*. Ithaca, NY: Cornell University Press, 1975.

Coolidge, Louis Arthur. *Ulysses S. Grant*. New York: Houghton Mifflin, 1922.

Cozzens, Peter. "The Death and Resurrection of FRUS, 1868–1876." Ch. 3 in Foreign Relations of the United States Series. Office of the Historian, Bureau of Public Affairs, US State Department. Accessed August 28, 2017, https://history.state.gov/historicaldocuments/frus-history/chapter-3.

Craven, Avery. *Reconstruction: The Ending of the Civil War*. New York: Henry Holt, 1969.

Drehle, David Von. *Rise to Greatness: Abraham Lincoln and America's Most Perilous Year*. New York: Henry Holt, 2012.

Engs, Robert Francis, and Randall M. Miller, eds. *The Birth of the Grand Old Party: The Republicans' First Generation*. Philadelphia: University of Pennsylvania Press, 2002.

Foner, Eric. *Reconstruction: America's Unfinished Revolution, 1863–1877*. New York: Harper Perennial, 2002.

Ford, Lacy K., ed. *A Companion to the Civil War and Reconstruction*. Malden, MA: Wiley-Blackwell, 2011.

Frantz, Edward O., ed. *A Companion to the Reconstruction Presidents, 1865–1881*. Malden, MA: Wiley-Blackwell, 2014.

Fuentes-Rohwer, Luis. "The Impeachment of Andrew Johnson." In *A Companion to the Reconstruction Presidents, 1865–1881*, edited by Edward O. Frantz. Malden, MA: Wiley-Blackwell, 2014.

Fuller, Joseph V. "Hamilton Fish." In *The American Secretaries of State and Their Diplomacy*, edited by Samuel Flagg Bemis. Vol. 7. New York: Cooper Square Publishers, 1963.

Garland, Hamlin. *Ulysses S. Grant: His Life and Character.* New York: Doubleday & McClure, 1898.

Gillette, William. *Retreat from Reconstruction: 1869–1879.* Baton Rouge: Louisiana State University Press, 1979.

Goodwin, Doris Kearns. *Team of Rivals: The Political Genius of Abraham Lincoln.* New York: Simon & Schuster, 2006.

Grant, Ulysses S., III. *Ulysses S. Grant: Warrior and Statesman.* New York: William Morrow, 1969.

Gurock, Jeffrey S., ed. *American Jewish History.* Vol. 6. New York: Taylor & Francis, 1998.

Harrington, Fred Harvey. *Fighting Politician: Major General N. P. Banks.* Philadelphia: University of Pennsylvania Press, 1948.

Hesseltine, William Best. *Ulysses S. Grant: Politician.* New York: Frederick Ungar, 1957.

Hoyt, Edwin Palmer. *The Goulds: A Social History.* New York: Weybright and Talley, 1969.

Kahan, Paul. *Amiable Scoundrel: Simon Cameron, Lincoln's Scandalous Secretary of War.* Lincoln: University of Nebraska Press/Potomac Books, 2016.

Keneally, Thomas. *American Scoundrel: The Life of the Notorious Civil War General Dan Sickles.* New York: Anchor Books, 2003.

Langguth, A. J. *After Lincoln: How the North Won the Civil War and Lost the Peace.* New York: Simon & Schuster, 2014.

Leigh, Philip. *Southern Reconstruction.* Yardley, PA: Westholme, 2017.

Luibhéid, Eithne. *Entry Denied: Controlling Sexuality at the Border.* Minneapolis: University of Minnesota Press, 2002.

Mantell, Martin E. *Johnson, Grant and the Politics of Reconstruction.* New York: Columbia University Press, 1973.

Mathisen, Erik. "Andrew Johnson and Reconstruction." In *A Companion to the Reconstruction Presidents, 1865–1881,* edited by Edward O. Frantz. Malden, MA: Wiley-Blackwell, 2014.

Mayer, George Hillman. *The Republican Party, 1854–1966.* 2nd ed. New York: Oxford University Press, 1967.

McFeely, William S. *Grant: A Biography.* New York: W. W. Norton, 1982.

Nelson, William Javier. *Almost a Territory: America's Attempt to Annex the Dominican Republic*. Newark: University of Delaware Press, 1990.

Nevins, Allan. *Hamilton Fish: The Inner History of the Grant Administration*. Introduction by John Bassett Moore. New York: Dodd, Mead, 1936.

O'Brien, Frank M. "The Story of the *Sun*." *Munsey's Magazine*, vol. 62 (October 1917 to January 1918), 657–670.

Parker, Arthur Caswell. *The Life of General Ely S. Parker: Last Grand Sachem of the Iroquois and General Grant's Military Secretary*. Buffalo, NY: Buffalo Historical Society, 1919.

Pegram, Thomas R. "Reconstruction during the Grant Years: The Conundrum of Policy." In *A Companion to the Reconstruction Presidents, 1865–1881*, edited by Edward O. Frantz. Malden, MA: Wiley-Blackwell, 2014.

Perman, Michael. "The Politics of Reconstruction." In *A Companion to the Civil War and Reconstruction*, edited by Lacy K. Ford. Malden, MA: Wiley-Blackwell, 2011.

Perret, Geoffrey. *Ulysses S. Grant: Soldier and President*. New York: Random House, 1997.

Phelps, Nicole M. "The Gilded Age." In *Guide to U.S. Foreign Policy: A Diplomatic History*, edited by Robert J. McMahon and Thomas W. Zeiler. Thousand Oaks, CA: Sage Publications, 2012.

Richter, William L. *The ABC-CLIO Companion to American Reconstruction, 1862–1877*. Santa Barbara, CA: ABC-CLIO, 1996.

Roberts, Phil. "'All Americans Are Hero-Worshippers': American Observations on the First U.S. Visit by a Reigning Monarch, 1876." *Journal of the Gilded Age and Progressive Era* 7, no. 4 (October 2008): 453–477. doi:10.1017/s1537781400000864.

Rothkopf, David J. *Power, Inc.: The Epic Rivalry between Big Business and Government—and the Reckoning That Lies Ahead*. New York: Farrar, Straus and Giroux, 2012.

Rothman, David J. *Politics and Power: The United States Senate, 1869–1901*. New York: Atheneum, 1969.

Scaturro, Frank J. *President Grant Reconsidered*. Lanham, MD: University Press of America, 1998.

Schwartz, Bernard. *A History of the Supreme Court*. New York: Oxford University Press, 1995.

Sefton, James E. *The United States Army and Reconstruction, 1865–1877*. Baton Rouge: Louisiana State University Press, 1967.

Simpson, Brooks D. *Let Us Have Peace: Ulysses S. Grant and the Politics of War and Reconstruction, 1861–1868*. Chapel Hill: University of North Carolina Press, 1991.

———. *The Reconstruction Presidents*. Lawrence: University Press of Kansas, 1998.

———. "The Reforging of the Republican Majority." In *The Birth of the Grand Old Party: The Republicans' First Generation*, edited by Robert Francis Engs and Randall M. Miller. Philadelphia: University of Pennsylvania Press, 2002.

———. "Ulysses S. Grant and the Failure of Reconstruction." *Illinois Historical Journal* 81, no. 4 (Winter 1988): 269–282.

Skidmore, M. *Maligned Presidents: The Late 19th Century*. New York: Palgrave Pivot, 2014.

Smith, Jean Edward. *Grant*. New York: Simon & Schuster, 2002.

Stampp, Kenneth M. *The Era of Reconstruction, 1865–1877*. New York: Vintage Books, 1965.

Stathis, Stephen W. *Landmark Legislation, 1774–2002: Major U.S. Acts and Treaties*. Washington, DC: CQ Press, 2003.

Stuart, Graham H. *The Department of State: A History of Its Organization, Procedure, and Personnel*. New York: Macmillan, 1949.

Swinney, Everette. "Enforcing the Fifteenth Amendment, 1870–1877." *Journal of Southern History* 28, no. 2 (1962): 202–218. doi:10.2307/2205188.

"The Ten Best Secretaries of State." *American Heritage*, vol. 33, no. 1 (December 1981). Accessed January 10, 2017, http://www.americanheritage.com/content/ten-best-secretaries-state%E2%80%A6.

Trefousse, Hans. *Andrew Jackson: A Biography*. New York: W. W. Norton, 1989.

Wade, Wyn Craig. *The Fiery Cross: The Ku Klux Klan in America*. New York: Oxford University Press, 1998.

Warren, Charles. *The Supreme Court in United States History*. Vol. 3: 1856–1918. Boston: Little, Brown, 1992.

Waugh, Joan. *U.S. Grant: American Hero, American Myth*. Civil War America. Chapel Hill: University of North Carolina Press, 2009.

Webb, Ross A. "The Presidential Boom of 1876." *Hayes Historical Journal: A Journal of the Gilded Age* 1, no. 2 (Fall 1976): 78–87.

White, Ronald C. *American Ulysses: A Life of Ulysses S. Grant.* New York: Random House, 2016.

Woodworth, Steven E. *Manifest Destinies: America's Westward Expansion and the Road to the Civil War.* New York: Vintage Books, 2010.

ACKNOWLEDGMENTS

Projects like *The Presidency of Ulysses S. Grant: Preserving the Civil War's Legacy* reflect the assistance (and forbearance) of people whose names do not appear on the book's cover. In particular, I want to thank my mother, Marian Kahan, who generously agreed to babysit so I could complete the manuscript. In addition, I would like to thank Tara Snyder Murphy, who read the galleys and made sure I crossed every "t" and dotted every "i." Finally, I want to thank my wife, Jennifer, and our children, Alec, Zoe, and Lucy, all of whom "picked up the slack" around the house so I could have the time to write.

INDEX